# LEFT OUT

# Left Out

*The forgotten tradition of radical
publishing for children
in Britain 1910–1949*

KIMBERLEY REYNOLDS

OXFORD
UNIVERSITY PRESS

# OXFORD

## UNIVERSITY PRESS

Great Clarendon Street, Oxford, OX2 6DP,
United Kingdom

Oxford University Press is a department of the University of Oxford.
It furthers the University's objective of excellence in research, scholarship,
and education by publishing worldwide. Oxford is a registered trade mark of
Oxford University Press in the UK and in certain other countries

© Kimberley Reynolds 2016

Published in the United States of America by Oxford University Press
198 Madison Avenue, New York, NY 10016, United States of America

British Library Cataloguing in Publication Data
Data available

Library of Congress Control Number: 2016930900

ISBN 978–0–19–875559–3

Printed in Great Britain by
Clays Ltd, St Ives plc

For Peter and Lynne—and
Nick, who should have written it!

# Acknowledgements

A great many people have helped me in a variety of ways over the three years that I was researching and writing this book. Peter Reynolds assisted me greatly with the research, and supported me throughout; he and Asheley Griffith, Hazel Sheeky Bird, and Nick Tucker read and gave valuable advice on the text at all stages. Lynne Vallone was my writing companion and constant source of inspiration and advice, and Jane Rosen has been a marvellous guide through the intricacies of left-wing history and collections relating to it, as well as an indefatigable finder of obscure facts. Julia Mickenberg's research has been seminal to this study, and her interest in my own project has been generous and stimulating. Phil Nel similarly nurtured and believed in the project. I am very grateful to Catriona Nicholson for reading the manuscript before submission and offering advice and encouragement. Jenny Kelly of the North of England Institute of Mining and Mechanical Engineers loaned me books and introduced me to Kitty Barne. Martin Kettle and Michael Rosen gave up time to talk to me about their experiences as readers of radical children's literature. Joan Venditto searched through the Lawrence and Wishart papers at Yale on my behalf. I am grateful to Julian Reid, Archivist at Merton College Oxford, for his help and hospitality while I was working in the Blackwell Archive, and to Rita Ricketts, who shared her knowledge of the history of Blackwell's. Martin Sanders facilitated my time in the Gollancz Archive at the Modern Records Centre, University of Warwick. Brian Rance, recently retired Archivist of King Alfred School, Natalie Wood, former Archivist-Librarian at Abbotsholme School, and Jenny Woodland, Archivist at Bootham School welcomed me into their archives, gave thoughtful advice, and fact-checked. Dawn Sinclair, Archivist at HarperCollins and Emma Yan in Archive Services, University of Glasgow helped with my questions about the William Collins archives. Mark Turner provided the image for Figure 1. Others who aided me in various ways are Pete Biller; Ron Floethe; Josef Keith from the Library at Friends House, London; Dan Jones; Sarah Lawrance and the Collections staff at Seven Stories, National Centre for Children's Books; Kika and Jehane Markham; Jane Powell, Librarian and Archivist at the Marx Memorial Library; staff at the People's History Museum; Special Collections staff at the Robinson Library, Newcastle University; Andy Simons of the British Library; Tara Sutton and her colleagues at the Working Class

Movement Library; and Lou Taylor. Jacqueline Baker, my editor at Oxford University Press, believed in this project when it was no more than an idea. Turning that idea into a manuscript was made possible by a Major Leverhulme Fellowship for which I am extremely grateful. Finally, thank you to my colleagues in the School of English at Newcastle University—and particularly to Linda Anderson, Kate Chedgzoy, and Matthew Grenby—who cheered me on my way.

Part of Chapter 1 first appeared in '"A prostitution alike of matter and spirit": anti-war discourses in children's literature and childhood culture before and during World War I' in *Children's Literature in Education*, November 2012 120–39.

Part of Chapter 3 first appeared in 'The Forgotten History of Avant-garde Publishing for Children in Early Twentieth-Century Britain' in Elina Druker and Bettina Kümmerling-Meibauer (eds), *Children's Literature and European Avant-Garde*. Amsterdam: John Benjamins, 2015.

# Contents

# List of Figures

Every effort has been made to contact those involved in creating the images reproduced in this volume. In a number of cases it has been impossible to locate any individual(s) with a possible copyright interest. Anyone who has information about images reproduced here should contact the publishers. OUP will be happy to rectify any errors or omissions at the earliest opportunity.

# List of Definitions and Abbreviations

In this study a distinction is made between *picture books*, in which illustrations repeat information contained in the text, and *picturebooks*, in which the images augment the text.

# Introduction

## Radical Children's Literature and the Attempt to Rewrite Britain

> So to your books, comrades! Read, study, learn.... Thus only will
> you be able to hew down successfully the deeply-rooted ancient trees
> of ignorance and superstition, and in the clearing make the wheat
> and rose of a saner system to ripen and to blossom.
>
> (*The Revolution*, 1.10, April 1918 162)

Between 1910 and 1949 a number of British publishers, writers, and
illustrators included children's literature in their efforts to make Britain a
progressive, egalitarian, and modern society. Some came from privileged
backgrounds, others from the poorest parts of the poorest cities in the land;
some belonged to the metropolitan intelligentsia or bohemia, others were
working-class autodidacts, but all sought to use writing for children and
young people to create activists, visionaries, and leaders among the rising
generation. As the following pages show, together they produced a significant
number of both politically and aesthetically radical publications for children
and young people. This 'radical children's literature' was designed to ignite
and underpin the work of making a new Britain for a new kind of Briton.

Social transformation is not simply a matter of desire and legislation; it
requires new visions which themselves depend on new forms of knowledge
and new ways of seeing the world. Radical children's literature drew on the
latest ideas from the spheres of science, politics, economics, pedagogy,
social policy, literature, and the fine and applied arts to encourage readers
to look with fresh eyes at how people were living, interacting, and
organizing themselves. It offered readers a vision of the children and
young people who would inhabit a new world and who were at the centre
of efforts to reform and regenerate society; indeed, the twentieth century
was to be 'the century of the child' (Key, 1909) and shaped in the image
of its hero, the adolescent (Aries, 1996 29). Radical texts assumed an
audience of intelligent, capable, socially aware young readers and set about

providing them with the skills, information, and inspiring social visions they would need to find solutions to the many problems confronting the world; problems that would result in two world wars, a global financial crisis, and mass social unrest and protest over this period.

Producers of radical children's literature did not come together to form a coherent group—there was no orchestrated movement to generate radical texts and no manifesto of the kind so popular among avant-garde groups at the time, where aims were set out and targets identified. Nevertheless, the individuals whose publications for children make up this study had similar aspirations, and their spheres of activity and networks of influence overlapped and intersected (Figure I.1). Though their authors, illustrators, and publishers represent a spectrum of opinion, from unaffiliated liberal to hard-line communist, radical texts share a socially progressive outlook and promote the attractions of a more just, equal, and modern society for all. Radical writing for children works to break down stereotypical attitudes to gender, race, class, poverty, ethnicity, nationality, and childhood. Mainstream children's literature, by which I mean both popular works and those that feature in histories of the subject, tended to construct an idealized version of childhood separate from and superior to adulthood, making the process of growing up something diminishing, to be regretted, and staved off for as long as possible. The books featured in this study, by contrast, focused on helping their readers mature into rational, fulfilled, capable adults by arming them with the skills and information they would need to interrogate their surroundings and decide what they wanted to think and believe.[1] As will be seen, the majority of those who produced radical works for children and young people also supported experimental work in the fine and applied arts and in literature. They saw children's books as vehicles through which taste could be changed in ways that would lead to the radically different kinds of buildings, furnishings, infrastructure, production practices, and social spaces that would underpin a new kind of society. These works stand apart from the majority of children's books of this period in that they are future orientated; concerned with where society is heading rather than nostalgic for Britain's imperial past.

Almost none of the writers, illustrators, publishers, or any of the more than 249 radical books, periodicals, pamphlets, and newspapers they

---

[1] For a discussion of the relationship between childhood innocence, maturity, and mainstream children's literature see Jacqueline Rose (1984), Trites (2000), and Reynolds (2007). Beauvais (2015) offers an interesting alternative in her discussion of European children's books that celebrate children as 'potential adults' (20).

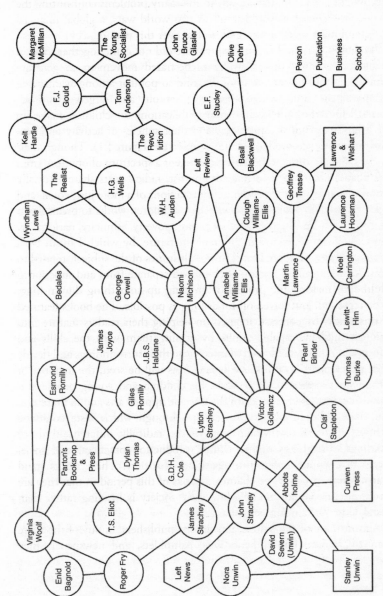

**Figure I.1.** Indicative network of radical connections

produced feature in standard histories of children's literature (the Appendix provides a list of radical titles). The following chapters consider the effects of the hole in the cultural memory that has been created by the longstanding tendency to overlook the radical strand of children's publishing in the first half of the twentieth century. This study is an attempt to mend that hole and to look with fresh eyes at the history of publishing for children, from the end of the Edwardian period to the start of what is often referred to as the 'second golden age' of British children's publishing in the 1950s. The aim is not simply to recover forgotten material but also to begin the work of assessing how engaging with this material affects understanding of both the history of children's literature and of these years in British arts and letters more generally. It offers explanations for why these texts and many of the figures who produced them were so rapidly and insistently dismissed after the Second World War, and the years in question singled out as a peculiarly fallow time in children's publishing.

## CRITICAL CONSENSUS AND SOCIAL FORGETTING

A survey of the small amount of criticism devoted to this period reveals the consistent and yet paradoxical nature of how the history of British children's publishing in the first half of the last century has effaced this area of publishing for children and young people. In children's literature criticism the years leading up to and often including the First World War are normally treated as part of the long nineteenth century. For the purposes of this study, however, it is useful to begin at the start of the new Georgian period because some key examples of both political and aesthetic radicalism are found in juvenile publications produced as Britain moved closer to joining in the war with Germany. Referring to the literary and artistic merits of writing produced for children, Robert Leeson describes the years between 1914 and 1949 as an 'age of brass between two of gold' (Leeson, 1985 Chapter 12); John Rowe Townsend deems this a dreary and backward-looking time (Townsend, 1965 163), while for Marcus Crouch, these were years when the effects of war and its aftermath meant that much of what was published for children was 'derivative and stale', though he made an exception of the 1930s (Crouch, 1972 17). The low production values of the many annuals and reward books produced between the wars and the rise of series and genre fiction are regularly offered by children's literature critics and historians as evidence of systemic mediocrity. Taking her cue from the characterization of children's publishing during these years as risk-averse and conservative, Jacqueline Rose (1984) claims that modernism, the foremost literary and artistic movement of the first half of the twentieth century, was consciously rejected by makers and publishers of children's literature. Her verdict was readily accepted. Modernism, it was agreed, had been eschewed by the children's literary establishment on the grounds that it was too closely associated with bohemia and both too stylistically complex and too eager to overturn literacy and literary rules that its readers were still acquiring to be suitable for the young. Recently Rose's conclusion has been shown to be exaggerated, particularly with regard both to individual high modernist writers and to publishing for children in Europe and North America across the last century (see Higonnet, 2009; Hodgkins, 2007; Natov, 2003; Reynolds, 2007, 2011; Westman, 2007; Kümmerling-Meibauer, 2013; Olson, 2013). One facet of this study involves identifying and considering modernist and/or avant-garde publications for children in early twentieth-century Britain.

It is not only in the areas of modernism and avant-garde experimenta-tion that historians and critics have traditionally found the children's literature of these years wanting; for more than half a century it has also been accused of inhabiting a culturally disengaged backwater at a time of profound and wide-ranging upheaval in politics and culture. According to Geoffrey Trease, before the Second World War children's books failed to reflect 'the changing [social and ideological] values of the age' (Trease, 1964 21). For Peter Hunt, the children's books published between the two world wars offer a comfortable, middle-class, and apolitical version of childhood which gave rise to a time of 'pervading quietism, a retreat from the realities of the world surrounding the child and the book'. 'Children's literature', he continues, 'did not register the attitudes of Auden or Caud-well, or notice the founding of *Left Review* (1934) or John Lehmann's *New Writing* (1936), and it largely ignored class and political struggles until they were too overwhelming to be ignored' (Hunt, 1995 193). Although he goes on to discuss a few 'dissenters', Dennis Butts concurs, concluding that,

> The children's literature of this period tends to reflect the values of the prosperous and untroubled part of the population, not really noticing the often violent struggles of the General Strike and the rise of communism and fascism . . . it is as if children's writers deliberately chose to ignore them and retreat into comedy or pastoral fantasy. (Butts, 2010 120)

Leaving aside for the moment the radical texts featured in this study, the problematic nature of this dismissive consensus is immediately apparent when it is set against the equally widespread acknowledgement (including by many of the same critics) that many important writers and illustrators for children were active during this period, among them Edward Ardizzone (1900–79), Enid Blyton (1897–1968), Walter de la Mare (1873–1956), Eleanor Farjeon (1881–1965), Eve Garnett (1900–1), Kathleen Hale

(1898–2000), W.E. Johns (1893–1968), Hugh Lofting (1886–1947), John Masefield (1878–1967), A.A. Milne (1882–1956), Mary Norton (1903–92), Arthur Ransome (1884–1967), Noel Streatfeild (1895–1986), J.R.R. Tolkien (1892–1973), P.L. Travers (1897–1996), Geoffrey Trease (1909–98), Alison Uttley (1884–1976), T.H. White (1906–64), and Ursula Moray Williams (1911–2006). Such a list confounds labels such as 'dull', 'derivative', and 'stale'. By any measure this is a substantial and significant group whose members have left an indelible mark on British children's literature. It would be hard to find a larger, more versatile or enduring cluster of talent in either of the highly vaunted golden ages of children's publishing.[2] Although for the most part these are not the writers and illustrators whose work features in this study, the fact that they are so numerous is significant since it belies the characterization of these years as exceptionally dull and disengaged.

## A CASE IN POINT: *AN OUTLINE FOR BOYS AND GIRLS AND THEIR PARENTS* (1932)

The extent of the misrepresentation can be established in a single example, which also provides a useful prelude to this project as a whole since it gives a sense of who was producing radical children's literature for what audiences and to what ends. *An Outline for Boys and Girls and Their Parents*, edited by Naomi Mitchison, must rank as one of the most ambitious books for children of all time. It was the brainchild of the left-wing publisher Victor Gollancz. Gollancz's 1932 spring catalogue announced its imminent publication with great fanfare. The catalogue, like the elaborate pre-publication pamphlets he circulated to potential stockists, purchasers, and reviewers, explained that this book was meant 'to help forward the new world' by introducing the 'citizens of the future' to the many branches of knowledge they would need to solve the problems then confronting Britain and the world (MSS. 318/4/7a); (Figure I.2).

Gollancz's excitement about the *Outline* was both politically and economically motivated. His allegiance to the Left was the foundation of his publishing business and it underpinned his determination to make high-quality publications of all kinds available to the masses by producing them at affordable prices. Like most on the Left, he believed passionately in the role of education in bringing about social change, and felt that people of

---

[2] The years 1870–1914 are usually identified as the first 'golden age' of children's literature; those between 1950 and 1970 as the second. The 1990s, which saw the publication of Philip Pullman's His Dark Materials trilogy and J.K. Rowling's Harry Potter books, have been mooted as a possible third 'golden age' (see Pearson, 2013).

**Figure I.2.** Title pages from Naomi Mitchison (ed.) *An Outline for Boys and Girls and Their Parents*. Illustrated by William Kermode and Ista Brouncker. London: Victor Gollancz, 1932

every background, sex, and age should have equal access to the best thinkers, teachers, and writers. But Victor Gollancz was also a supreme businessman, and he was convinced that the *Outline* would be a bestseller. The previous year he had published the first book in what was to become a series of Gollancz 'Outlines': *An Outline of Modern Knowledge*. In the same catalogue that announced *An Outline for Boys and Girls and Their Parents* he claimed the first *Outline* had 'probably enjoyed . . . a more immediate success than that achieved by any serious work published at a similar price [8 shillings and 6 pence], selling a steady 2,000 copies a week, or nearly 50,000 in three months' (MSS. 318/7/4 6). Those sales boded well for the new book, as did those of the other children's books Gollancz had published.

Where the average print-run for a new Victor Gollancz book was between 1,000 and 3,000 copies, for children's books print-runs began at 4,000 and could extend to 10,000 if there were a US co-edition. At the beginning of the 1930s Gollancz was actively developing this side of the business. Works such as *The Moon on My Left* (1930) by Caryl Brahms; Sylvia Lynd's edited collections, *The Children's Omnibus. A Storybook for Boys and Girls* (1932) and *The Christmas Omnibus* (1932); Eleanor and Herbert Farjeon's *Kings and Queens* (1933) and *Heroes and Heroines* (1933); *The Modern World—A Junior Survey* (1933) by Hubert Clinton Knapp Fisher, and Helen Mary Sidebotham's *The Whipsnade Animal Book for Children and Others* (1933) were all either published or in production when Gollancz was launching *An Outline for Boys and Girls and Their Parents*. He had every reason to believe that sales of the *Outline* would surpass anything he had yet produced. In anticipation of a bestseller Gollancz splashed out on big-name contributors, ordered an initial print-run of 50,000, and prepared for translations and large overseas sales.[3] This was, he trumpeted, 'the Book which all Parents and Teachers, since the War, have wanted for their Children' and, at nearly 1,000 pages with 166 illustrations, he hailed it as 'the cheapest book of our generation' (MSS. 318/4/7a 2, 3). Reviewing the book for *The Bookman*, Geoffrey West endorsed Gollancz's claims. *An Outline for Boys and Girls and Their Parents* was, he said, one of those books 'which every home with children should possess as a matter of course . . . a forward-looking book to attract to itself the intelligence, and to its clear ideal of a planned world society the loyalty, of the younger generation' (West 60). The *British Medical Journal* too welcomed the volume (how often have children's books been reviewed

---

[3] Although Naomi Mitchison was disappointed by the amount her contributors earned, Gollancz was generous with his advances, another sign of his confidence in the volume. The 1932 production book shows this as a major investment from him not least in the amount paid out to contributors.

in that august journal?). Gollancz, it concluded, had published 'an amazing and abundant and provocative store of knowledge . . . and all for 8s. 6d' (1932 61).

The fate of Gollancz's ambitious project is set out below; for now, what is significant about *An Outline for Boys and Girls and Their Parents* is that it was bold, politically radical, actively promoted—and has been entirely forgotten. All of the works featured in this study similarly defy the received view of children's literature from this period. They too are variously adventurous, experimental, and/or politically engaged, sometimes all at once, and like the *Outline*, they have disappeared from history so thoroughly that it has now become a commonplace that such writing never existed. In the context of what was a time of upheaval, change, and conflict, however, this view is perplexing. These were years when, in Britain and across Europe, political parties on both the Right and Left vied to capture the minds and sympathies of the young, for the young were associated with 'energy, vitality, faith, strength, vigour' and credited with the capacity to overturn or revitalize decadent domestic politics (Pomfret, 2005 27). Children were equally important to modernism and to a range of avant-garde experiments that placed spotlights on youthful creativity on the one hand and art and design activities aimed at children on the other. As recent studies have shown, between 1910 and 1949 radical writers across Europe and North America were producing new kinds of children's books that acknowledged the dynamic political, cultural, and social changes that were taking place (see Mishler, 2003; Mickenberg, 2006; Kinchin and O'Connor, eds, 2010; Mickenberg and Nel, eds, 2010; Kümmerling-Meibauer, 2013; Druker and Kümmerling-Meibauer, eds, 2015). How could British children's literature have gone unmarked by the clashes, challenges, and revolutions of these decades?

The books and publications discussed in the following chapters demonstrate that it did not. As the only medium specifically targeted at the young, children's literature was inevitably caught up in competing attempts to capture young hearts and minds by writers from all backgrounds and of all political persuasions. Radical children's literature urged young readers to be excited by the prospect of social change and to engage with rather than retreat from modernity. It encouraged readers to learn about, question, experiment with, disassemble, and refashion ideas, systems, and institutions. In a complicated interaction between liberation and control, at the same time that they stirred readers up to challenge the status quo, radical texts generally tried to recruit and direct them, not just as readers but as individuals who embodied and performed the radical message. This is a variation on the process of 'enscripting' readers that Robin Bernstein writes about in relation to children's literature and racism in *Racial Innocence: Performing American Childhood from Slavery to Civil Rights* (2011). Bernstein is interested in the way children's books from the past function both as texts that convey meaning through literary modes and as 'scriptive things' or objects that prompt certain kinds of behaviours. Scriptive things, which include the merchandise, images, artworks, and performances that often evolve around popular texts, are at the centre of her efforts to locate aspects of history for which there are no formal records or substantial amounts of other kinds of corroborating evidence. For Bernstein, books and other kinds of writing are of particular interest for the way they 'enscript' readers, meaning that they combine the literary device of interpellation (calling the reader into a text) with the scripts/ directions for physical responses associated with them as objects: open the book/magazine, turn the pages, study and colour the pictures, enact the scenes (2011 77).

Examples of the way radical children's literature enscripted young readers are given below and throughout this book, but there are important differences between the enscripting activities in the examples Bernstein discusses and those at work in radical children's literature. The most important of these is that Bernstein looks at strategies associated with those who were enslaved and so had to deflect and misdirect the attention and understanding of oppressors while the groups and individuals who produced radical children's literature did so openly and were often socially influential. Nor did their readers have to conceal their responses. They donned uniforms, mounted performances, and created texts and artworks all in the cause of promoting the ideas they encountered in their reading. Where they are similar is in the extent to which both bodies of material have been subject to what Bernstein calls 'social forgetting' (8), resulting in holes in the cultural memory. Despite differences in who produced radical children's literature, for whom, why, and how they were used, Bernstein's 'tool for analysing incomplete evidence... to make responsible, limited inferences about the past' (2011 79) has been as relevant for this study as for her own since little information about some key aspects of the production, distribution, and reception of radical children's literature has been preserved.

## CREATING A POPULAR FRONT OF READERS

Radical children's literature was the product of three areas of life in early twentieth-century Britain: left-wing politics, modernist and avant-garde art and design, and progressive education (these were the decades when most progressive or 'modern' schools—Beacon Hill, Bedales, Dartington, and Summerhill among them—came into being). As Figure I.1 shows, often the three areas overlap as individuals move between them and interests converge; for example, many of the first progressive schools had their roots in the early socialist philosophies and practices of William Morris and Edward Carpenter, and Morris's influence was equally strong on avant-garde developments in the arts, including illustration for children (Kümmerling-Meibauer, 2013 16; Olson, 2013 83). Similarly, pupils who attended progressive schools tended to be the offspring of the liberal intelligentsia and so grew up in milieux where it was customary to oppose war, to champion political and intellectual freedom, to favour modern design and ways of living, and to be sympathetic to left-wing causes. So, for example, members of the Unwin and Curwen families who attended or worked at Abbotsholme School became involved in aesthetically and intellectually significant publishing houses, groups dedicated to placing traditional crafts in the service of modern design principles, and creating such new living environments as garden cities (see Chapter 6).

The interconnected nature of these three broadly progressive areas is nowhere more apparent than in the area of left-wing publishing for children, which was also the earliest and largest of these three spheres of publishing activity. The following overview of left-wing children's publishing sets the scene for the remaining chapters, which look in more detail at the way modernist art and design, progressive education, and literary responses to the Left played out in radical children's literature. In the process of introducing left-wing children's publishing from this time, the story of Victor Gollancz's monumental *Outline for Boys and Girls and Their Parents* is also brought to its conclusion.

For those on the Left, print, whether in the form of books, magazines, or pamphlets, was central to creating the social will and conditions necessary for remodelling society within people of all ages. Reading armed activists with information, analytical skills, and arguments that could be used to convince others of the necessity for change and the benefits it would bring, while books and other printed materials could be used to reach out to the population at large, helping to spread new ideas and build a broad progressive consensus. From the end of the nineteenth century there had been a steady trickle of socialist publications aimed at readers both young and old; typical examples for children include Keir Hardie's letters to children in the *Labour Leader* (from 1896), Walter Crane's *The Child's Socialist Reader* (1907), and Edward Carpenter's *St. George and the Dragon: A Play in Three Acts for Children and Young Folk* (1905). After the First World War, momentum began to build. Publishers, writers, and artists sympathetic to progressive and/or left-wing politics determined to build a Popular Front of readers; this was to be a book-based coalition of individuals who, whether or not they were affiliated to any political group, were like-minded in their opposition to many official government policies and associated ideologies. That their vision for this coalition included children is clear from a review of left-wing literature in a 1938 number of the *Daily Worker*: 'What is significant about the books that people are now reading in ever increasing numbers is the fact that they deal with matters that, whether we like it or not, are everyone's close concern, the intellectual's and the manual labourer's, the mother's, the father's, *and the boy's and girl's*' (quoted in Croft, 1990 11, emphasis added).

Until the 1930s, however, there was little in the way of a recognized and available body of left-leaning children's literature, and much of what existed was specifically designed for use in Socialist Sunday Schools (SSSs) or similar teaching environments. Gradually publishers began to see that there might be money in appealing to a broader audience of young readers and their parents by including some books about or for working-class children. The push for demotic publishing is usually associated with two men. The first has already been introduced: Victor Gollancz, whose unambiguously left-leaning publishing house was established in 1927 with the initial aim of producing inexpensive editions of accessible books about economics and topical social issues. The second is Allen Lane, who in 1935 launched what rapidly became Britain's leading paperback publishing house, Penguin Books. Although Penguin too reprinted and commissioned many works that reflected the views of the Left, Lane's business model was less ideologically driven than Gollancz's, and to avoid being pigeon-holed as a left-wing publisher and so possibly limiting the market for his books, he ensured that Penguin's list contained contrasting voices.[4] This strategy, and the much larger scale on which he published for children, have given Lane and his children's imprint, Puffin Books, a pre-eminence in the history of twentieth-century British children's publishing that has effaced the activities of Gollancz and the others who catered more overtly for an audience of the liberal Left. The story of Puffin books has been told often (see, for instance, Baines, 2010; Carrington, 1957, 1979; Gritten, 1991; Rogerson, 1992; Somper, 2001) and it will feature at times in this alternative history too, but Gollancz's less

---

[4] Lane's decision to distance Penguin from the Left for business reasons anticipated the more general tendency described above. Initially, however, there was no such concern. According to one-time senior Penguin editor, Jack Morpurgo, in the early years there was a perception that 'Penguin were designed as propaganda for the Soviet Union and Allen [Lane] himself a paid-up member of the Communist party' (quoted in Hare 1995, 71). For more information about Penguin's relationship with the Left see Wootten and Donaldson, eds, 2013.

recognized contributions to children's publishing are a more valuable initial source of insights into the radical children's publications that appeared between the two world wars.

## VICTOR GOLLANCZ AND LEFT-WING CHILDREN'S PUBLISHING BETWEEN THE WARS

It is difficult to be sure exactly how many titles for children were published by Gollancz's firm before Britain entered the Second World War (a defining moment in the company's history), but on the basis of catalogues and production books it appears that between 1928 and 1939 there were approximately twenty Gollancz children's books. As evidenced by the production books and Victor Gollancz's professional correspondence relating to these years, children's books were not a sideline to the business but part of the total operation.[5] Although none challenged the supremacy of Gollancz's bestselling author Dorothy L. Sayers, as has already been noted, the children's titles were printed in relatively large numbers and were often reprinted subsequently. At least two books for children were also offered through the Left Book Club (LBC) (1936–48), a Gollancz project that both tapped into and fed popular opinion, making it a useful barometer for measuring the climate for Left activism.[6] In the 1930s that barometer was set fair. It is not wishful thinking on the part of the *Daily Worker*'s reviewer when he identifies the extent to which concerns traditionally associated with the Left had entered the mainstream of British

---

[5] Children's titles listed in Gollancz's production books and catalogues between 1928 and 1939: 1928: *The Diary of a Communist Schoolboy* by N. Ognyov (pseud. Mikhail Grigor'evich Rozanov); 1930: *The Moon on My Left* by Caryl Brahms; *Tal* by Paul Fenimore Cooper; 1931: *Children be Happy* by Rosalind Wade (a crossover school story that less than happily resulted in a libel case when it turned out to be autobiographical rather than fictional); *The Monkey Moo Book* (fairy stories) by Professor Leonard S. Hill; 1932: *The Children's Omnibus. A Storybook for Boys and Girls* and *The Christmas Omnibus* edited by Sylvia Lynd; *An Outline for Boys and Girls and their Parents* by Naomi Mitchison; *Kings and Queens* by Eleanor and Herbert Farjeon; 1933: *Heroes and Heroines* by the Farjeons; *The Modern World—A Junior Survey* by Hubert Clinton Knapp Fisher; *The Whipsnade Animal Book for Children and Others* by Helen Mary Sidebotham. No new children's books appeared from 1934–6. 1937: *The Adventures of the Little Pig and Other Stories* by F. le Gros and Ida Clark; 1939: *The Children's Historical Atlas* by J.F. Horrabin; *The Junior Week-end Book*, written and compiled by J.R. Evans; *A World to Win (An Intelligent Child's Guide to Socialism and Capitalism)* by Major Jeffrey Marston.

[6] Gollancz conceived and managed the LBC with the Marxist political campaigner John Strachey and Harold Laski, Professor of Political Science at the London School of Economics. Already admired as both a publisher and an entrepreneur, Gollancz here again displayed his business acumen: all LBC books were published by Victor Gollancz Publishing.

life. Although only a minority of the population were paid-up members of left-wing parties and organizations, these were no longer the preserve of the disgruntled, the disenfranchised, or the kind of idealistic 'cranks' in the Edward Carpenter mould previously associated with socialism or more extreme leftist ideologies (Croft, 1990 11; Joannou, 1999 3). As seen in the discussion of Naomi Mitchison below, a number of those from middle and upper-class backgrounds joined in peace rallies and distributed leaflets about unemployment, opposed fascism, campaigned for birth control, and argued for social and economic reform and planning. By the late 1930s the children of pacifist Bloomsbury were fighting alongside the Republicans in Spain. Communist cells could be found in public schools, some of whose pupils also raised money for hunger strikers, showed the latest films from Soviet Russia, and published their own radical magazine (discussed in Chapter 1).[7] It was to this audience as well as to the more traditional working-class socialist core that the LBC appealed.

And appeal it did. There were just 5,000 subscribers for the first LBC offering, *France Today and the People's Front* by the leader of the French Communist Party, Maurice Thorez. By the end of 1936, so in the space of seven months, membership had risen to 20,000. It continued to rise steadily over the next two years as the threat to peace increased, unemployment continued to cause mass hardship in parts of the country, and the activities of Oswald Mosley's British Union or 'Blackshirts' (largely based on the youth section of Mosley's earlier New Party) began to spread the ideologies and tactics of fascism. These were the concerns at the heart of LBC publications, many of which were written by the left-sympathizing intellectuals with good social networks and access to the media who Gollancz cultivated as supporters and contributors. By April 1939 LBC membership had reached 57,000, generating a wide range of ancillary activities including 1,500 Left Book Club Discussion Groups, a monthly newsletter, *Left News*, and summer camps where members met to study and debate topical issues. Amidst all these activities for adults Victor Gollancz had not forgotten his younger constituency: the editorial for April 1937 acknowledges the need for a Junior Left Book Club and promises to deliver it as soon as the workload allows.

[7] Reviewing Peter Conradi's *A Very English Hero: The Making of Frank Thompson* (2012), Jeremy Harding (2013) offers some insights into the extent of left-wing activity in public schools of the 1930s and the surprising compatibility of the ethos imbibed as part of a classical education and the values of the Left. Brother of the historian E.P. Thompson, educated at Winchester and Oxford, Frank Thompson was a member of the Communist Party, and fought in Spain. As a Major in the Special Operations Executive he was executed in Bulgaria in 1944.

Members have insistently pointed out, in ever increasing numbers, that we are neglecting half, and perhaps the most important half, of our task if... we ignore those who hold the future in their hands. The Junior Left Book Club will be a separate organisation—though it will, of course, interlock with the Left Book Club at many points: every book will be specially written for the Club, and our present intention is to make the price of the monthly book one shilling. (*Left News*, April, 1937 305)

While waiting for him to deliver on this promise, young people began forming unofficial book groups, a sign of the importance placed on reading by politically aware youth. In fact, throughout these years reading was a favourite recreational activity among children of all classes: according to a 1921 leader in *The Times*, 'The modern child... read ten times as much as his grandparents had done' (McAleer, 1992 133, 136).[8] It was also widely promoted, supported, and monitored through new activities such as a national 'Boys' and Girls' Book Week' (founded in 1932), touring exhibitions of children's books from overseas, exhibitions of illustrated children's books at major museums, regular reviews and features in the national press, and a range of surveys and studies of what the young were reading and why.[9] The majority of what was being read spanned mainstream information books and popular fiction, whether in the form of comics and annuals or series books. The radical texts at the centre of this study, by contrast, tended to be the choice of a minority of children and young people of the kind who attended SSSs and progressive schools such as Abbotsholme in Staffordshire, from where students wrote to the LBC offices to say that they had set up their own LBC group (*Left News*, November, 1938 1057). The limited nature of its audience is clearly one reason why radical children's literature has not featured in histories of children's publishing from this period.

No information about the background of the young Londoners who formed an unofficial LBC youth group in 1937 is available, but their enthusiasm was such that by September of the following year that group was able to report having held a meeting in Kingsway organized 'with the assistance of Mr. Trease' (*Left News*, September, 1938 984). The Mr Trease referred to is surely the writer Geoffrey Trease, whose work, as will become clear, was central to the development of left-wing children's publishing in the 1930s. These initiatives together with continued requests from children

---

[8] McAleer's *Popular Reading and Publishing in Britain 1914–1950* summarizes the findings of a number of surveys of young people's reading habits which show both the appetite for reading and variations by class and sex (1992).

[9] McAleer (1992) provides a good overview of the coverage, surveys, and events associated with children's literature in the years covered by this study.

and their parents produced a long article in the September 1938 number of *Left News* by staff members Sheila Lynd (who edited two children's omnibuses for Gollancz) and Jane Conway. Although obviously keen to encourage young readers, they are cautious about when they can deliver the promised supply of books specially created for younger readers, explaining that they need 'a really considerable number of Youth Groups' to be flourishing before they can undertake so large a task on top of the current workload (*Left News*, 1938 983). Meanwhile, they note that 'A surprising number of young people already read the [LBC] books.'

Chapter 1 considers the extent to which some older children and adolescents were drawn to reading about the problems of the day—and possible solutions to them—in works not specifically aimed at a juvenile readership. (It is worth remembering that until 1918 the school leaving age was twelve, meaning many of those who were 'children' in terms of age were also part of the workforce and so the adult world.) This tendency points to an important difference between young people's reading in the first half of the last century and today that has also affected how histories of children's literature have viewed these years. Since the 1950s fiction has been the mainstay of children's lists, but between 1910 and 1949 information books and other kinds of non-fiction constituted a much larger, livelier, and more influential part of the children's publishing scene than is currently the case. The carefully categorized lists of books for children and adolescents produced by organizations ranging from religious and political groups to local authority libraries over these decades clearly show the preponderance of non-fiction titles. For instance, the lists contained in *The Public Library and the Adolescent* (Leyland, 1937) are almost entirely concerned with information and self-help titles. More wide-ranging is Lilian Stevenson's *A Child's Bookshelf*, five editions of which appeared between 1917 and 1922. Sixty-one of the 116 pages of annotated booklists in the 1922 edition, with their 'suggestions on children's reading with an annotated list of books on heroism, service, patriotism, friendliness, joy and beauty' (7), are given over specifically to information books. The remaining sections comprise a mixture of fiction and non-fiction.

*A Child's Bookshelf* illustrates why young people looking for radical reading matter would have been attracted to LBC titles. Stevenson in fact connects reading with social change, but while she aims to support the work of young people as the 'builders of a new world' and to cultivate in them an inclusive, internationally aware, anti-war spirit, her perspective is both Christian and her recommendations mainstream (Stevenson, 1922 11).[10]

---

[10] There was no reason why a Christian reading list should have been exclusively mainstream; indeed, there is a pronounced overlap between Christian and socialist ethics

Although there were a number of radical bookshops around the country and left-wing organizations, newspapers, and publisher's newsletters such as *Left News* and *The Eye: The Martin Lawrence Gazette* provided some reviews of children's books they regarded as ideologically sound, these were not always easy to source. For socially engaged adolescents, the LBC brand identified books with the kind of content they were seeking and, perhaps just as important, identified readers with the LBC.[11]

Adolescents might have been prepared to read LBC titles, but as the requests for Junior Left Book Clubs indicate, parents, teachers, and children themselves wanted books specifically for children that encouraged even the very youngest readers to start engaging with the concerns and debates that preoccupied their left-leaning elders. Victor Gollancz identified *The Adventures of the Little Pig and Other Stories* by F(rederick) Le Gros Clark and his wife Ida as just such a book (Figure I.3). Initially published in 1936 as one of two collections of *Little Leopard Stories* by Lawrence and Wishart, whose role in left-wing children's publishing is discussed below, the group of stories about the Little Pig was warmly praised by Harry Pollitt, General Secretary of the Communist Party of Great Britain. In a review in the *Daily Worker*, Pollitt congratulated the Clarks for taking on the important work of writing for children and for the collection's beautiful storytelling and unobtrusive didacticism (16 December 1936). The following year Gollancz repackaged the stories as an LBC 'supplementary' title, meaning it was offered alongside that month's featured book. At the same time, Victor Gollancz announced a deal with Lawrence and Wishart which meant that all the firm's children's books were advertised to LBC members. This arrangement went some way towards fulfilling Gollancz's promise to supply appropriate books for younger readers without the need to commission and produce them himself.

*The Adventures of the Little Pig* does what George Orwell complained that writing on the Left failed to do—especially when aimed at the young. In his often-quoted article on 'Boys Weeklies' (1939), Orwell blames the pious preachiness of left-wing writing for failing to appeal to young readers in the way the popular papers published by the right-wing establishment were doing. Orwell's criticisms are not unfounded, but there is an extent to which he sees what he expects to see. This means that he either ignores or misses, for example, the popular adventure stories of

in much of what was published for SSSs. Stevenson's book is, however, highly conventional in its politics as well as Christian in its orientation.

[11] Details of the number and distribution of radical bookshops for this period can be found at: http://www.leftontheshelfbooks.co.uk/images/doc/Radical-Bookshops-Listing.pdf.

**Figure I.3.** Cover, Frederick Le Gros and Ida Clark's *The Adventures of the Little Pig and Other Stories*. London: Lawrence and Wishart, 1936. Image courtesy of Lawrence and Wishart and The Bodleian Library, University of Oxford, Opie AA320

Herbert Allingham in the working-class paper *The Butterfly* (Amalgamated Press, 1904–40) featuring Polly Perkins and her friend Maximilian Trent who each week set out 'to right cases of social injustice—sweated labour, slum housing, police stitch-ups, adulterated food, poverty in old age' (in Jones, 2012 168). Nor does Orwell mention the Clarks' story, or any of the other children's books by then available, including those advertised in *Left News*, mentioned in children's papers published by groups such as the Co-operative Movement (its children's paper, *Our Circle*, ran from 1907–60) and reviewed in left-wing papers such as the *Daily Worker*, which frequently called attention to suitable publications for children. Harry Pollitt's piece, for instance, appeared under the banner 'Stories We Can Gladly Give Our Children' and ran alongside a review of Geoffrey Trease's *Missing from Home* (1936). Many of these works were as preachy as Orwell claims, but some writers were working hard to produce exciting and appealing stories that reflected the ethos of the Left.

*The Adventures of the Little Pig* exemplifies the kind of writing Orwell had in mind, and the fact that it is in a slim paperback format that looks very like a comic would have made it easy to include in a piece focusing on weekly papers. It avoids the sermonizing he deplored while still pointing out the inequities of capitalist society and the benefits of abolishing the exploitative master class, redistributing wealth, and creating a welfare state (none of these terms is used, but their sense infuses the collection). The stories also praise community and the satisfactions to be gained from honest work of any kind, and stealing of the Robin Hood variety). So, for instance, the first two tales centre on the hardships endured by the mother of the eponymous Little Pig who is in thrall to a cruel, lazy farmer. The farmer not only makes her and all the other animals work too hard, but also charges them rent. When she becomes too old to work, the mother pig has nothing to live on until her son arrives for a visit with a fabulous necklace he has been given by a 'kindly robber'. In Robin Hood fashion the robber has stolen it from a duchess but gives it to the Little Pig to provide for his mother's old age. After the adventures he experiences on the way to visit his mother, the pig returns to his carpenter's shop 'cheerfully to work for his living'; as the last line of this socialist story and at the height of the Depression, this is equivalent to living happily ever after (Clark, 1936 64).

Orwell's failure to mention *The Adventures of the Little Pig* stands out in part because Gollancz was Orwell's publisher and Orwell contributed to *Left News*.[12] Additionally, in 'The Dual Purpose of *Animal Farm*', Paul

---

[12] Frank Richards (the pseudonym used by Charles Hamilton when writing his stories about Greyfriars School) publicly criticized Orwell's attack on the boys' papers as ill

Kirschner traces a series of connections between children's stories, including *The Adventures of the Little Pig*, and one of Orwell's best-known works, *Animal Farm* (1946). Kirschner points out that Orwell almost certainly read the Clarks' stories since *The Road to Wigan Pier* was published by the LBC in the same year as *The Adventures of the Little Pig* and Orwell was already convinced of the importance of childhood reading (Kirschner, 2004).[13] Neither Orwell's failure to mention *The Adventures of the Little Pig* nor the fact that it has largely been forgotten can be blamed on its authors' lack of credibility or informed opinion. Frederick Le Gros Clark (1892–1977) was a distinguished social scientist who investigated the relationship between malnutrition and poverty, specializing in the effects of undernourishment on children's development. His work meant that he saw many children of the poor at close quarters.

Presumably aware that in the Soviet Union there were heated debates about whether the fairy tale was a bourgeois form of story that was infused with elitist values (see Rosenfeld, 2003), while the Clarks borrowed fairy tale elements such as tricksters and talking animals, they combined them with other forms (fables, animal stories, picaresque tales, short stories) to create tales that avoid the dull lessons and catechisms of which Orwell was so critical.[14] At the same time, they steered clear of the politically suspect areas of magic and the cult of pretty children that had come to the fore in late-Victorian and Edwardian England. Reviewing the book for *Left News*, Sylvia Townsend Warner praises both the Clarks' refusal to bow to the cult of fairies that had followed the success of *Peter Pan* and the fact that their stories 'are not an insult to the intelligence of children' (*Left News*, September 1937 514).[15]

informed. He and others pointed out that there were good left-wing writers that Orwell ignores, among them Geoffrey Trease. When he subsequently read some of Trease's work, Orwell approached him to suggest producing a quality left-wing boys' paper. Nothing came of the project (GT/10/02/03 189).

[13] Kirschner credits Nicholas Tucker (b. 1936), who attended a progressive school and grew up reading left-wing books, with pointing out the similarities between Orwell's novel and the Clarks' stories.

[14] If this was a deliberate strategy, it was too subtle for even some well-informed critics. In a 1937 round-up of books for Socialist children that appeared in *The Worker's Monthly* under the title, 'What Shall Our Children Read?', Geoffrey Trease refers to the Clarks' 'little sixpenny books of fairy stories for the younger children, under ten, *The Enchanted Fishes* and *The Little Pig*' [sic] (GT/07/04/01 51). The Clarks' stories can also be seen as a British variation on the kind of cultural critique known as 'Aesopian language' then popular in the Soviet Union. The term 'Aesopian language' is found in 'innocent-seeming tales' which use parables, animal fables, double meanings, and other devices in ways so overt that they compel readers to recognize that they contain hidden meanings (Maslen, 139).

[15] Warner was either unaware of or disagreed with the Soviet mistrust of fairy tales as the review praises their subversive potential and her own work is infused with elements from traditional folk and fairy tales.

The Clarks' collection of stories has the distinction of being one of just two children's books offered as LBC titles—the other was *An Outline for Boys and Girls and Their Parents*, bound in an LBC edition at the reduced price of 5 shillings in 1936. This was not, as might be assumed, a new edition, but surplus stock remaining from the first 1932 printing. The reasons for the surplus go some way to explaining why Victor Gollancz was so uncharacteristically slow to respond to demands for a Junior Left Book Club and his decision to promote Lawrence and Wishart's children's books in place of publishing more politically engaged children's books under his own imprint.[16]

## OUTCRY OVER THE *OUTLINE*

> There had been nothing like the *Outline*. It was not an encyclopedia but a critical stock-taking of contemporary knowledge. It was up-to-date; indeed it presented the advanced thought in each of its subjects. It was written for intelligent people of all ages. The simplification lay in the way in which difficult concepts were presented by means of illustration and example, not in artificial restriction of language or an avoidance of complexities.... Above all it encouraged the reader to think for himself.
>
> (Crouch, 1962 81)

So reads Marcus's Crouch's evaluation of the *Outline* thirty years after it was first published. There is nothing in Crouch's description to indicate that the volume was anything other than a welcome addition to the home library. In fact, its reception was turbulent at best. Gollancz had the idea for *An Outline for Boys and Girls and Their Parents*, but its shape and content were the work of his editor, Naomi Mitchison (Figure I.4), then a young writer who was beginning to garner a reputation for her historical fiction for children set in the classical world. Mitchison was an interesting but not obvious choice as editor. At the time she was in her early twenties and had little in the way of a public presence. She was, however, a friend of Gollancz's and he knew that their backgrounds and sympathies were

[16] Both were offered at the peak of LBC activity; catastrophe followed soon after. Disturbing news from Stalin's Russia and Britain's entry into the Second World War saw membership crash. Gollancz was pushed to explain and maintain his commitment to the Left and his vision for a programme of changes that would result in 'peaceful, gradual change to a Socialist Britain' which would have oversight over international reconstruction at the end of the war (Gollancz, 1941 xvii). By then the LBC was no longer driving this vision. It ceased operating in 1948, by when it had for some time been too enfeebled to have much effect on public opinion.

**Figure I.4.** Wyndham Lewis portrait of Naomi Mitchison (1939). Image courtesy of National Galleries Scotland

well aligned. Both Mitchison and Gollancz had been born into solidly middle-class families and were well connected. During the 1920s both had embraced the cause of the radical Left, and both regarded publishing as part of political praxis. Mitchison's daily life reflected her progressive ideals. She took her children on rallies, distributed leaflets for left-wing causes, went to Vienna with funds for beleaguered socialists, and was friends (and sometimes more than that in her open marriage) with bohemians, homosexuals, communists, and dissidents.

Naomi Mitchison's children's books are imbued with her ideological beliefs. For instance, her first novel, a book for children called *The Conquered* (1923) set during Ceasar's Gallic Wars, deals with issues of colonization and exploitation in ways that make it a mirror for the 'troubles' in

Ireland. Read in this way it expresses sympathy for the Republican cause, as the political scientist Ernest Barker, then Principal of Kings College London, notes in his Preface to the 1927 edition (hailing from Scotland, Mitchison was familiar with both sides of the colonial experience). *Cloud Cuckoo Land* (1925) uses the backdrop of the classical world to explore the conflict between democracy and repression in Mitchison's own time. In it she also writes openly and sympathetically about homosexuality (her progressive views on sexuality and contraception were to play a crucial role in the fate of the *Outline*). She set many of her stories in antiquity and undertook meticulous research to ensure the accuracy of the world in her books, but Mitchison's historical novels are not directed at an élite readership. She avoids Ancient Greek or Latin constructions and vocabulary and insider references to the classical world, choosing instead a modern vernacular style and plots centred more on people, relationships, and behaviours than historical events.

The example of Naomi Mitchison illustrates that some areas of children's literature *were* part of the literary scene occupied by W.H. Auden, Christopher Caudwell, and others on the literary Left; she also represents those writers and works for children who were engaging with class and political struggles in the way histories of children's literature suggest children's writers and their work did not. Although young, Mitchison was already thoroughly involved with both the activities of the Labour Party and the literary elite. She was, for example, on the editorial board of *The Realist*, a short-lived (March 1929 to January 1930) intellectual monthly journal edited by Arnold Bennett that sought to inform readers about developments in the arts and sciences. Other board members included the editor of the science journal *Nature*, Richard Gregory; the biologist Julian Huxley (brother of Aldous and later the first Director of UNESCO); Bronislaw Malinowski, then a pioneering anthropologist based at the London School of Economics; and the writers H.G. Wells and Rebecca West. As this list suggests, as well as being close friends with many major literary figures, she was also well connected in the scientific community. Her father and brother were both influential scientists, and Mitchison herself started to read for a science degree at Oxford, though this was disrupted when she became a Voluntary Aid Detachment (VAD) nurse during the First World War.[17] Her political networks were equally well developed, and not just because her husband, Richard (Dick) Mitchison, was a Labour MP who helped draft the Beveridge Report. Naomi

---

[17] Mitchison maintained her scientific interest throughout her long life and always saw it as compatible with her literary work. She edited *The Double Helix* (1968), James D. Watson's account of discovering the structure of DNA. Watson dedicated the book to her.

Mitchison was a Labour Party activist in her own right and was invited to stand for office, though she declined.

Mitchison made effective use of all these networks in compiling the *Outline*. She wanted it to be 'a book for the next generation, reflecting the best of the leading liberal thinkers of the day, challenging many of the more conventional social and cultural assumptions' (Calder, 1997 105). Instead of turning to children's writers for contributions, Mitchison coerced notable figures from many different disciplines to write for children about their areas of expertise; for example, the up-and-coming Labour politician Hugh Gaitskell provided the chapter on economics, W.H. Auden the one on literature, Clough Williams-Ellis covered architecture, and the writer Richard Hughes, author of two radical children's books (*The Innocent Voyage*, 1929; *The Spider's Palace*, 1931), contributed the section on 'Physics, Astronomy and Mathematics'. Lecturers from all the major universities and arts institutions across Great Britain were also represented in essays on topics ranging from population control and modern dance to an analysis of war and revolution in the first three decades of the twentieth century.

The *Outline* aimed to teach 'boys and girls' and, through or alongside them their parents, 'how power and knowledge and order are organised, and how the organisation can be altered' (*Outline* 11). In the nearly 1,000 pages that make up the *Outline*, Mitchison and her contributors take well-informed swipes at the national diet, organized religion, unjust laws, inequalities between the sexes, marriage, patriarchy, the commandeering of the world's resources by the West, abuses of power including those affecting children, patriotism, capitalism and private profit, industry, and much more. They also vaunt the virtues of kindergartens, communal living, global communication, science, technology, engineering, and the undisputed heroes of the volume, the Russian people, the Soviet Union, and the Russian Revolution.

The *Outline* was intended to be controversial, and it was. Despite being praised in many quarters, notably by Mitchison's influential friends, it was vigorously attacked by conservative institutions. Members of the Anglican establishment in particular were outraged by Gollancz and Mitchison's project; an open letter to the press signed by 'one Archbishop, two Bishops, the Headmasters of Eton and Harrow, and fourteen other prominent men' denounced the *Outline* both for undermining traditional Christian values (not least through its open discussions of sexuality and birth control) and for approving developments in communist Russia (Benton, 1990 83). The influential Catholic apologist Arnold Lunn attacked it in *The English Review* for the same reasons: Lenin appears in the index, he complains, but not Jesus Christ. Lunn was also offended by what he regarded as the *Outline*'s neglect of cultural history and a vacuous eagerness to admire 'the last thing' (Lunn, 1932 471–84). His attack was the more devastating because the review also praised both Mitchison, whom he calls a 'brilliant writer', and the lucid and interesting nature of many of the contributions. Comparing the volume to a meal hosted by the Borgias (every course was perfectly prepared and only marred 'by a slight touch of poison in the wine', 483), he condemns it as a book that could do 'immense and irreparable harm' in the hands of 'elementary school teachers, and of the vast company of ill-informed, but intelligent clerks and shop assistants of both sexes' (483). These are exactly the kinds of readers Gollancz was committed to reaching, and the slight to their right to knowledge or ability to manage it the kind of attitude he loathed.

Although by the standards of most books, and even by that of Gollancz's other children's books, the *Outline* sold well (25,000 copies were sold in 1932; a further 2,000 by 1934, and the remainder of the original print-run of 30,000 in the form of cheap editions offered through the LBC), the book was mortally damaged at home and it failed to find overseas publishers who were willing to take it on.[18] Gollancz had invested considerably, both financially and personally, in this project. While he might have taken some comfort from the fact that the book was clearly regarded as powerful—why else would so many big establishment guns be aimed at a single book for children?—from that time his appetite for producing children's books was tempered, contributing to the failure to deliver a Junior Left Book Club and the decision to join forces with Lawrence and Wishart, the original publishers of *The Adventures of the Little Pig*.

The relationship with Lawrence and Wishart was caught up in the dramatic collapse of the LBC following Britain's entry into the Second World War. In December 1939 *Left News* announced the termination of their relationship. Only Gollancz's part of that story has so far been told, however. A full picture of left-wing publishing for children in Britain and its place in a wider, more accurate history of children's literature from these years must take account of the contribution of Lawrence and Wishart and some other singular left-wing children's books and periodicals.

[18] The figures all appear on the page 61 spread of the 1932 production book. These detail how many sets of printed pages were bound at a given time and when new bound copies were ordered. They also list the fees paid to Mitchison and her contributors (MSS 318/2/1/5).

## READING FOR YOUNG REBELS

Although they are the best remembered of the left-sympathizing publishers, Allen Lane and Victor Gollancz did not have a monopoly on left-wing publishing for adults or children and were far from being the first to cater for this audience. As the following chapters show, contributions to the stock of radical writing for children were also made by a range of left-leaning but more commercially orientated publishers such as Basil Blackwell and William Collins and some small independent firms. But to round off this introductory discussion of children's literature and its relationship with left-wing politics, attention needs to be given to the publishing house that produced the greatest range and number of uncompromisingly left-wing children's books of all: Martin Lawrence. Although it bears a man's name, it is unclear whether there was an individual named Martin Lawrence at its head, so here I refer to the firm.

Closely associated with the Communist Party in Britain, Martin Lawrence merged with the liberal, anti-fascist publishing house Wishart Ltd to form Lawrence and Wishart in 1936; the new company continued to provide the children of the progressive and left-wing sections of British society with the kind of politically relevant publications that Martin Lawrence had initiated with *The Red Corner Book for Children* (1931) (Figure I.5). Geoffrey Trease called this miscellany addressed to 'rebel children' 'the very first attempt in England to produce a Socialist story book for boys and girls' (1937 *Worker's*, n.p.). As its editor explains, it set out to 'stir in [young readers] an understanding of the worker's life, the social struggles and the goals which the workers have set themselves' (n.p.). Modelled on the format of popular children's annuals, the volume contains a mixture of stories, poems, articles, cartoons, and puzzles, all promoting liberal-to-hard-line Left values and insisting on the need to contest the status quo. Like all of Martin Lawrence/Lawrence and Wishart children's books, *The Red Corner Book for Children* urges young readers to recognize the congenital faults in class-based capitalist countries and to start imagining better ways to organize society. It also places a spotlight on children, telling them that they are capable of hard work and heroism, and that the future is in their heads, hands, and hearts.

A similar volume, *Martin's Annual* (1936), was published jointly by Martin Lawrence and International Publishers, its equivalent Communist Party press in the US. Starting with the editor, Joan Beauchamp, most of the contributors were British, including Geoffrey Trease (the volume contains three pieces by him); the socialist, pacifist illustrator, and writer Laurence Housman; the communist newspaper editor and

WE'RE marching towards the
         morning,
We're struggling, comrades all ;
Our aims are set on victory—
Our enemies must fall.
With ordered step, red flag unfurled,
We'll build a new and better world !

**Figure I.5.** Title page and verso: *The Red Corner Book for Children*. London: Martin Lawrence, 1931. With permission of Lawrence and Wishart. Image courtesy of National Library of Scotland

founder-member of both the Socialist Party of Great Britain and the British Communist Party T.A. 'Tommy' Jackson; Marxist politician and writer T.H. Wintringham; and the left-wing writer and artist Pearl Binder, whose children's books and illustrations about Soviet Russia are discussed in Chapter 2. Together they provided stories about young freedom fighters and those who oppose fascism; lessons from nature in how the small and weak outwit the large and strong; a warning against the seductions of military recruiting regiments; accounts of Soviet heroes; the pleasures of what Russian children who have grown up in exile in the US discover when their families return to the new Soviet Union; cartoons deriding the Blackshirts; and a detailed critique of Britain's national anthem. There were also comic poems, a revolutionary alphabet, recipes for healthy eating, and a competition to find juvenile proletarian writers.

As the list of contributors to Martin Lawrence's second experimental volume shows, many of those who produced radical children's literature were political activists and professional writers for adults rather than children's writers. While they may have felt it important to address the rising generation, their lack of experience in writing for a juvenile audience often results in the kind of uneven, propagandistic writing that so irritated George Orwell. A typical example is Gertrude Ring's poem 'Marion has a Doll' in which wealthy Marion's privileged life is set against those of the poor children who live around her and who provide the collective voice of the poem. Marion, it seems, has not just *a* doll but 'One, two, three, four, five, six, seven dolls. / Dark, fair, curly haired and black' who sleep in comfort while the poor children sleep on the ground. Marion also has a dog who eats better than they; she has fine shoes for every occasion while they run barefoot; she has 'a Fraulein, a nurse, a governess' and many other people who give her attention and time. By contrast, the poor children say, 'No one cares for us': their parents are too busy working while their teachers are disengaged. Marion travels the world while the poor children stay in their tenements and have to work. The poem ends with a promise of change that is also a threat:

> Still we proletarian children learn how things will change,
> How our big Red brothers will conquer the power in the world;
> We will also become fighters,
> With one, two, three, four, five, six, seven thousand children. (20–1)

The writing in these early collections is often clumsy and so sectarian that it addresses only the converted and may, perversely, have alienated them since most of the items are examples of what socialite and Left-activist Ivy Elstob, in a 1936 review of children's books for the *Daily Worker* that anticipates Orwell's attack in 'Boys' Weeklies', condemns as 'bad books' for young socialists. Such books, she says, are overly didactic and simplified 'to the point of fatuity' (Elstob, 1936). Elstob's complaint about the lack of literary merit in much writing intended for the children of the Left needs to be seen in the context of the socialist writing of the 1930s as a whole. In his overview of socialist fiction in the 1930s Gustav Klaus both records the frustrated comments of Edgell Rickword, editor of *Left Review*, on the poor quality of much of the 'proletarian' writing the journal tried to foster, and observes that the socialist writing of the 1930s (the most active period for socialist fiction) was always variable in quality (in Lucas, 1978 5, 14). Martin Lawrence's first attempts to create proletarian writing for children were similarly uneven and underestimated the literary taste of a significant part of their audience. The contents assumed that 'proletarian' children would be familiar with and respond to comics and other more popular forms of writing. On the evidence of surveys of young readers from the time, this was certainly true of some working-class children, but the section of the working class who read widely and so were likely actively to be seeking out material for their children to read objected to being written down to and expressed themselves 'disappointed by lack of literary quality in left books' (Rose, 2001 317). The uneven quality of much of the politically radical children's literature has helped to tarnish the view of writing from this period. Nonetheless, while there is no need to resurrect it on the grounds of literary merit, its existence needs to be remembered and its sentiments and goals examined.

Working-class readers often read widely, including among the classics which had the merit of giving them some of the same frames of reference as those who had the advantages of upper and middle-class educations.[19] The fact that working-class readers enjoyed and appreciated canonical works did not mean that they aligned themselves with the dominant culture, however. There is a long tradition of working-class autodidacts who were both well read, including in the classics, and who used their reading to feed their radical views. This tradition is reflected in the recommendations made to the children who attended SSSs: *Socialist Sunday Schools: A Manual* (1923), for instance, contains a list of 'Books Recommended by "Young Socialist" Education Bureau' in which authors such as R.M. Ballantyne, George Eliot, Rudyard Kipling, and Sir Walter Scott stand alongside those by Edward Carpenter, F.J. Gould, and William Morris. It is also found in the recommendations by 'Mr. Wiseacre', whose column on

---

[19] Another reason for turning to the classics was that, due to the efforts of left-leaning publishers such as Victor Gollancz, Basil Blackwell, Allen Lane, and perhaps especially J.M. Dent with his Everyman's Library (1905–), such books were readily and inexpensively available.

reading for young people appeared in *The Young Socialist*, and in features in the *Daily Worker* by noted academics such as Arnold Kettle (e.g. A. Kettle, 1951). A similar tendency to encourage young people to read across the progressive bourgeois literary canon prevailed in most better-off left-wing households and progressive schools too (M. Kettle, 2012; Rosen, 2012).

The fact that, in keeping with much socialist-inspired writing of the time, many of the contributions were crudely executed probably explains why both *The Red Corner Book for Children* and *Martin's Annual*, although intended to be the first in a series of annual numbers, were one-off productions. The failure is particularly noteworthy given the enthusiastic support of the Children's Corner of the *Daily Worker* for *The Red Corner Book for Children*, and belies an announcement from the publishers in that paper that 'Owing to large pre-publication demand we have been able to revise the price downward' (*Daily Worker*, 5 December 1931).[20] As will become apparent, many radical texts were more subtle, better written, and more attractively produced than these two volumes, but here it is worth thinking again about these materials as scriptive things, noting how they combine textual and visual material that references the comics and magazines popular with working-class children and young people to direct how readers interacted with them. 'ABC for Martin' in *Martin's Annual*, for instance, adopts the same 'A is for . . .' formula of alphabet books to initiate readers into its particular version of the world that Robin Bernstein identifies in E.W. Kemble's 1898 *A Coon Alphabet*.[21] Beginning with 'A stands for Armaments', this alphabet for young revolutionaries too uses repetition (the pattern is, of course, repeated for all the characters in the alphabet), accumulation, rhythm, rhyme, and graphic images to accompany each letter to direct readers to the next text in sequence and prompt them to guess how the rhyme will be completed. All this is part of making the text something they have internalized and can reproduce. As something inserted in a miscellany, 'ABC for Martin' is a simpler use of the alphabet form than Kembles's; there are no page turns or jokes, but the familiar pattern nonetheless guides readers through 'Y is for You who will know how to fight' and 'Z is the Zeal that will add to your might.' The direct address to 'you' is both the culmination of the interpellating

---

[20] Although George Orwell seems not to have known about Martin Lawrence's volume, *The Red Corner Book* displays most of the faults that Orwell hypothesized would make a 'normal' boy reject any new left-wing publication for boys: 'dreary uplift . . . Communist influence . . . adulation of Soviet Russia' (Orwell, 1940).

[21] Bernstein is drawing on Patricia Crain's work on alphabets (2000) to show how the alphabet format helps underscore the racist messages in the text.

strategies and a direction to readers to join in the revolution that 'R' promises 'we're going to win'.[22]

Whatever their status as literature, radical texts such as *The Red Corner Book for Children* and *Martin's Annual* are significant as landmarks in the attempt to create a body of left-wing writing for children. They bear the hallmarks of proletarian writing; they include high genres such as historical fiction and popular forms such as comics; and like the more impressive publications being produced in Soviet Russia and discussed in Chapter 2, they delight in the belief that the work of transforming society along socialist lines is unstoppable.

Although of the contributors to *Martin's Annual* only Binder, Housman, and Herminya zur Muhlen continued to write for children, in everyday life the paths of writers who contributed to the volume would have crossed frequently (as illustrated in Figure I.1). All were involved in left-wing organizations, most with left-leaning publications (Wintringham helped establish the journal *Left Review*), and several travelled in Russia in the 1930s. Together they represent one cross-section of those who made up the Left and unaffiliated but progressive circles in Britain after the First World War; notably only Jackson had working-class roots. The middle-class nature of this group is not unusual; as has already been seen, both Naomi Mitchison and Victor Gollancz came from upper middle-class backgrounds and, as Mitchison frequently explained, it was precisely her comfortable circumstances and the presence of domestic help that made it possible for her to take on the work of challenging social injustice (Mitchison, 1979 182).[23]

While the two annuals were Martin Lawrence productions, the firm also published children's books that originated in other countries, usually in co-editions, normally with International Publishers based in the US, who were similarly bound up with the Communist Party there. A typical example is 'Alex Wedding's' *Eddie and the Gipsy. A Story for Boys and Girls* (1935; published in the US without the subtitle) (Figure I.6). Alex Wedding was the pen-name of Grete Weiskopf, a children's writer then based in Berlin where the book was first published as *Ede und Unko* (1931). *Eddie and the Gipsy* is illustrated with photographs by John Heartfield (Helmut Herzfelde). Photography was a relatively new form of illustration

---

[22] In *Tales for Little Rebels* (2008) Julia Mickenberg and Philip Nel discuss 'ABC for Martin', noting, for instance, its emphasis on violent action and its reference to topical figures, events, and ideas of the period.

[23] Klaus notes that middle-class intellectuals were also responsible for much socialist fiction for adults (1978, 14). See Lethbridge (2013) for a discussion of the dependence of wealthy socialist radicals on their servants. Virginia Nicholson makes the same point in *Among the Bohemians: Experiments in Living, 1900–1939* (2002).

**Figure I.6.** Cover, Alex Wedding's *Eddie and the Gipsy. A Story for Boys and Girls* showing one of John Heartfield's photographs. London: Martin Lawrence, 1935. Image supplied courtesy of The Bodleian Library, University of Oxford, Fic. 27842 e.444, Front Cover

for children's books and though, as discussed in Chapter 3, it sometimes featured in experimental works, its first application, as here, tended towards realism and documentary. Marcus Crouch criticizes a tendency for photographic illustrations to be too literal, but in *Eddie and the Gipsy*, this quality becomes a strength (Crouch, 1962 85). In combination with the pointed nature of the story, Heartfield's photographs of real children working together and enjoying each other's different family lives is in the same spirit as his better-known anti-fascist montages and bitterly satirical images of Hitler. Set during the Nazis' rise to power, *Eddie and the Gipsy* tells the story of a German boy whose comfortable life and assumptions are transformed when his father, formerly a company man and strike breaker who disapproved of communists, loses his job to 'rationalization' in the form of new machinery. The eponymous Eddie finds a job selling newspapers with the help of a friend whose father is a communist and union activist, thus beginning his political education. His stereotypes of society—and ultimately those of his father—are overturned when Eddie's father is betrayed by one of the investors in his former firm, while his family benefits from Eddie's new friendship with a Romany girl. The themes of trade union activism (forbidden under the Nazis) and friendship across the racial divide, compounded by a positive depiction of the Romany family and photographs featuring real children, led in due course to the book's being burned by the Nazis. Both Wedding and Heartfield were forced to flee Germany when Hitler came to power.

*Eddie and the Gipsy* posed several challenges for its British translator, Charles Ashleigh. To deal with them the book includes an unattributed Foreword, presumably by Ashleigh, which points out the similarities between the lives of children in Germany and Britain. The comparison was not unproblematic as Britain was casting a watchful eye on the increasing influence of Nazism in Germany:

> although the people in the book are Germans, and the city is a German city, you will notice that, really, there is very little difference between the way in which working people live there and in Britain. They work in plants or factories—or, as Betty [Eddie's older sister] does, in a hairdresser's shop. They get the sack just as they do here, and they draw relief—when they can!—too. And they have strikes, and also—I am sorry to say—strike-breakers, just as in Britain and, in fact, every other country where there are capitalists and working people. (in Wedding 9)

The problems of workers who are oppressed by capitalism are also at the heart of novels by the first specialist children's writer published by Martin Lawrence, Geoffrey Trease. Trease, a young man in his twenties during the 1930s, had left Oxford without matriculating to earn his living in

London, where he turned from a brief period as a Christian journalist and writer to leftist activities and interests. Ultimately, however, both Christianity and left-wing politics were secondary to his primary ambition, which was to become a professional writer. Trease put his writing skills in the service of his causes, but he also used causes to find audiences and opportunities, a factor that becomes important when examining his decision to detach himself from left-wing publishing. Before looking at his rejection of the Left, however, it is necessary to plot the path by which Geoffrey Trease became the public face of socialist children's literature in 1930s Britain.

## GEOFFREY TREASE AND THE RETREAT
## FROM THE LEFT

The comprehensive scrapbooks of reviews and articles Geoffrey Trease kept throughout his long writing career show him to have been a determined and professional writer who understood the benefits of having a public identity for building a readership.[24] Once in London he quickly succeeded in getting an impressive number of articles and other contributions published in Christian magazines and newspapers. As he was to do for many years, he turned his hand to almost any relevant topic and writing task (sometimes taking on *noms de plume* suited to the job in hand). He learned much about the craft and built a network of publishing contacts while working as a reviewer for a commercial publishing firm. At this time he and some colleagues set up what they called the Promethean Society, a group for pacifists, humanists, and devotees of Freud, Marx, Wells, Shaw, Lenin, Trotsky, Gandhi, and D.H. Lawrence. They read Havelock Ellis (as discussed in Chapter 5, an open-minded attitude to sex and sexuality was a hallmark of progressive thought in the period) and watched foreign films, including some from Russia 'with rows of tractors churning up the collectivised black earth' (GT/10/02/03 161). In other words, they were typical of both LBC members and the left-wing idealist-activists of the period, doing everything they could to question, defy, and reform what they referred to as the 'Olympian establishment'. Looking back as a man in his seventies on this period in his life, Trease recalled, 'We believed, Social Credit being the latest gospel, that the world's poverty could be cured by a simple change in the financial system. War

---

[24] Trease's scrapbooks can be viewed at Seven Stories, the National Centre for Children's Books, Newcastle, UK.

could be abolished by disarmament, if necessary unilateral, and by non-violent demonstrations such as lying down in front of troop-trains' (MS GT/O5/01, 161). The slightly rueful tone here and throughout *A Whiff of Burnt Boats* (1971), the first of the three volumes that make up Geoffrey Trease's autobiography, reflects his older self's awareness of the Prometheans' youthful naivety, but it also gives voice to the sense of disillusion felt by those who, like him, had hoped for so much, when they began to realize that, far from changing the world for the better, the Soviet experiment had ended in show trials, the Great Terror, and the Cold War.

During his Promethean phase Geoffrey Trease took up the cause of the Left, and in doing so found a way to re-launch his writing career. He successfully approached Martin Lawrence with his idea for a Marxist re-telling of the Robin Hood story for children; the national and international critical success of *Bows Against the Barons* (1934) (Figure I.7) among progressive educationalists and reviewers began a partnership that lasted several years (Chapter 2 covers more about Trease's work during this period). Trease was immediately commissioned to write several more books for the firm, and within a year had two novels in print, contributions in *Martin's Annual*, and a number of articles about left-wing children's literature in a wide range of journals and newspapers. Being published by Martin Lawrence and his efforts to spread the socialist gospel through his children's books and journalism quickly established Trease as the leading writer of politically radical children's literature. Although impressively industrious, he continued to struggle financially. Eventually he concluded that the platform that had launched his career was now holding him back. 'I was not', he notes, 'helped by my publisher's reputation as a specialist in left-wing literature' (MS GT/O5/01 188). The point was driven home when a single piece in the *Boy's Own Paper* earned him more than any of his Lawrence and Wishart novels, and Trease began to refashion his public face to suit a mainstream audience (MS GT/O5/01, 189). The distance he put between his early time as the leading left-wing writer for children in Britain and his later more mainstream (though always liberal) career is reflected in his accounts of early twentieth-century British children's publishing, and contributed to the 'social forgetting' of radical children's literature, his own included (Reynolds 2016).

Trease's contribution to erasing the history of socially radical writing for children is surprising because it was he who, six years before Orwell's attack on boys' magazines, set alarm-bells ringing in the heads of liberal and left-wing parents and teachers when he denounced mainstream children's literature for purveying 'suggestions and influences' that worked to make their young readers subscribe to 'the present system' rather than to 'build the new world' (GT/07/04/01/17). He followed that charge with

**Figure I.7.** Cover, Geoffrey Trease's *Bows Against the Barons*. London: Martin Lawrence, 1934. Image courtesy of Girls Gone By Publishers

articles supporting the kinds of books he had started to write, and also praising similarly left-wing offerings by others, including *The Red Corner Book for Children*. Trease did his homework and knew there were such books, some of them both pre-dating and surpassing his own efforts, as in the case of F. Tennyson Jesse's 1927 historical novel for children, *Moon-raker*. Set in 1801–2 during the Haitian Revolution, it features a cross-dressing (female-to-male) pirate, what appears to be a homoerotic plotline, a failed but heroic uprising by former slaves whose successful state is attacked by Napoleon, and the suicide of a woman who can only fulfil her ambitions by posing as a man. With its concern with human rights, liberty, and the way society deforms the minorities it oppresses, *Moonraker* is a quintessential example of radical children's literature.[25] But having turned his back on left-wing children's books, Geoffrey Trease seems to have cultivated a blind spot about left-leaning writing for the young. In reviews and books about children's books he does not mention the contribution of writers such as Richard Armstrong, Pearl Binder, Thomas Burke, Marjorie Fischer, Janus Korczak, Bill Naughton, and Amabel Williams-Ellis, to name just some of those who were producing radical texts during the 1930s and 1940s (see Appendix). As the series of critical evaluations of writing for children during these decades cited at the beginning of this Introduction makes clear, Trease was not alone in dismissing and ignoring radical writing for children, but the following chapters show that doing so significantly undervalues the efforts of those, among whom Geoffrey Trease clearly features, whose visions of how society needed to change were expressed to children and young people in the form of radical children's literature.

As evidenced by the examples already discussed, the charge that this was an era when children's literature was operating outside the concerns of literary and intellectual culture needs to be revised, and with it the view put forward by critics and historians that this was a period paralysed by legacies from the past and fear of the future. In adult writing this view is supported by the literary trope of arrested youth and expressed through fictions of failure, despair, and decline (see Esty, 2012; Harris, 2010; Overy, 2009); however, radical children's literature had no truck with paralysis. Its creators were bent on turning young readers into successful agents of all kinds—scientists, engineers, architects, and artists. The writers, illustrators, and publications discussed in the following chapters are reminders that during what is often characterized as an anxious and

---

[25] The following year saw the publication of John Womack Vandercook's *Black Majesty: The Life of Christophe, King of Haiti* (1928), which charts the same events though without Tennyson Jesse's interesting take on sexual politics.

even a 'morbid age' in Britain, some children's writers and illustrators were deliberately and optimistically using the medium of children's books to shape opinion and refashion society (Overy, 2010). Before moving on to look at how this was done, it is necessary to say something about the readers of radical children's literature.

## RADICAL READERS

The extent to which the phenomenon that was radical children's literature has been forgotten means that tracing its readers and ascertaining how numerous they were, how much they read, and what they thought about radical children's literature is a complicated process. More important than details of print-runs, range of titles, or numbers of editions of individual publications (although where possible these are given) is the extent to which these works shaped their collective imaginations. Starting with Maurice Halbwachs's *On Collective Memory* (1950), memory theorists have shown that individual memories are influenced by elements such as families, organizations, and communities and the memories each of these generates. As the following chapters show, the original readers of radical children's literature tended to belong to families with strong left-wing political and/or artistic allegiances. Many were also part of organizations, institutions, or social groups such as SSSs, the Co-operative Movement, left-wing youth organizations, progressive schools, and bohemia. Together these created a context in which children were growing up that was also shaping what would become individual and group memories of this turbulent period in British and world culture. The memories associated with these works and their readers are particularly interesting because, as activists and members of the avant-garde, creators of radical children's literature were consciously representing the present while keeping one eye on the future. Reading these works, therefore, means encountering what might be called 'future memory', for it connects us with what people hoped was being called into being as well as with what they knew at first hand.

Memory theory tends to be concerned with recovering memories that have been lost over the passage of long periods of time or as a consequence of trauma. The hole in the cultural memory created when radical children's literature was pushed to the back of library stacks, left to go out of print, and ignored by historians is relatively recent and cannot compare to the mass trauma associated with genocide, war, or environmental catastrophes. In many ways it is more analogous to the kind of forgetting that affected didactic writing of the eighteenth and nineteenth centuries and so was judged by generations of critics to be tedious, misguided, and a betrayal of childhood. Recently much has been done to restore the reputation of early didactic writers (see, for instance, Mitzi Myers, 1986, 1989, and M.O. Grenby, 2005), and this study begins a similar process of re-reading the work of writers of radical children's literature. In trying to strip away preconceptions and attempt to understand how readers originally received these works, it has been productive to think of the effects of two world wars, economic crisis, widespread disillusion with Stalinist Russia, and the threat represented by atomic weapons as constituting a collective trauma leading to social forgetting. That makes it possible to separate differences between public and private memories: radical children's literature may have been forgotten at a cultural level, but books read in childhood often linger in the memory, and for at least some children who grew up in households where commitment to the Left was strong and enduring, these books demonstrably had an effect and for some they have retained their appeal.

It is possible to deduce something about the popularity and legacy of the earliest examples of radical children's literature from print-runs, the number of editions of individual books, and contemporary reviews, but the best way to understand the appeal and impact of the many kinds of publications that were produced—particularly with regard to politically radical works—is found in the memories of those who made up the original target audience and their children; the generation who were children in postwar Britain. I have sought to access readers' memories in a variety of ways: through conversations and correspondence, by reading biographies, autobiographies, memoirs, and histories of organizations, and by consulting the Mass Observation archives. Often such documents are written by adults, and though they may reveal what writers, artists, and illustrators were attempting to do, they say little about how children's books were received or remembered. Occasionally, however, a memoir has proved to be a rich resource. This was the case with Independent Labour Party (ILP) MP Jennie Lee's (1904–88) *Tomorrow is a New Day* (1939). Lee's father, a miner, was chair of the local ILP party in Fife and her childhood was shaped by her parents' left-wing politics. She attended an SSS, her father was a Conscientious Objector in the First World War, every Saturday night she joined in discussions with visiting speakers who would address the big Sunday public meetings run by the ILP, and she undertook tasks for the party such as collecting membership dues each week. Lee was an exceptionally clever child who became a notable public figure, but as the following chapters will show, the shaping forces of her childhood were very much in keeping with those of other left-wing families of the time.

*Tomorrow is a New Day* (1939) begins with a detailed account of Lee's early life, which was published by Puffin in an abridged version for children in 1948. Reading was a prominent feature of her childhood and youth, and she gives details of the works she read when young that stayed in her mind as an adult. Although such accounts are likely to be partial and faulty, her experience chimes closely with other evidence of what children of the Left and middle-class liberals found or were given to read; it includes the mixture of fact and fiction, children's and adult publications that feature throughout this book. For instance, after doing their chores on Saturday mornings, she recalls that she and her younger brother 'were given our Saturday pennies and could dash off to buy our weekly quota of one penny fairy-tale and two comic-cuts. I chose the fairy-tale, my brother the comics. We each devoured our own, then eagerly swapped' (20). Such publications were obviously for an audience of children and, as has been discussed, they were popular with working-class youth. Lee's family's bookshelf contained classics including *The Arabian Nights*, *The Count of Monte Cristo*, *White Fang*, and *The Three Musketeers* alongside adult books such as *Das Kapital*, *The Family Physician*, *Ingersol's Lectures and Essays*, and *Science History of the Universe* (20). By the age of eight she remembers reading across its contents, and soon after she read aloud to a blind adult friend the books that make up *The Story of the Working Class throughout the Ages* (45).

Jennie Lee exemplifies the target audience for radical children's literature, and just as she represented her constituency in parliament, so she can be seen as representative of a generation of readers of politically radical children's literature. The affection with which she recalls childhood reading is mirrored in a less exalted reader (Lee eventually became Baroness Lee of Asheridge): Ruth Bloom, born in 1932 and raised in a left-wing household in London, remembers choosing *The Red Corner Book for Children* from a bookshop in Hackney 'and loving it' (J. Rosen, 2013). The volume was shared by the three children in the family and handed down to their children. It remains in the family and continues to be valued.

While many of the books discussed in this study never featured in public collections, they too remained in families and their legacy is found in the next generation whose parents were reading radical children's literature at the same time as Jennie Lee. Children growing up in left-wing households in postwar Britain not only had access to the wave of books that soon were being said to constitute a second golden age in children's publishing; they also continued to read radical works. The tendency to pass books down and across families meant that they read the radical children's literature written for their parents as well as more recent works. Like their parents, they came across the descendants of radical children's literature in a variety of ways including through political party branches and fund-raising events such as annual *Daily Worker* bazaars. It is through such second and third-generation readers of radical children's literature that it is possible to capture the sense of pleasure, engagement, and belonging these works gave to their first readers. The writer and broadcaster Michael Rosen (1946–), for instance, remembers the satisfaction of talking about 'their' books he and other children of the Left had when they got together or joined in family discussions (Rosen, 2014). Similarly, author and journalist Martin Kettle (1949–), whose father, Arnold Kettle, was both a left-wing academic and contributed regularly to the *Daily Worker*, describes reading in childhood and youth as part of what identified someone as an insider, a member of a community. The comedian Alexei Sayle is another public face of the postwar generation of radical readers. He writes about reading, holidays, and social life as a child growing up in a communist household in *Stalin Ate My Homework* (2010).

The books that shaped Rosen, Kettle, and Sayle in childhood were often the same as those read by their parents or given to them by parents, meaning radical children's literature lived on for another generation. Other legacies of radical children's literature and evidence about how it came to be forgotten are set out in the chapters that follow. The chapters are thematic and broadly chronological in organization. Together they give a sense of what radical children's literature told children about themselves, their bodies, the world they were growing up in, their contribution to culture, the future, and the ways in which they could bring about change. Recovering these works is about change, too; changing how we think about publishing for children in Britain in the early twentieth century by learning what a substantial part of Britain wanted to tell the next generation about its past, present, and future.

# 1

# War and Peace in Radical Writing for Children

## TOY STORIES: OPPOSITION TO WAR IN THE SHADOW OF THE FIRST WORLD WAR

In 1915 some British children opening the pages of a new picturebook will have encountered a full-page photograph showing a blindfolded figure standing before a firing squad in the moment before the signal to 'fire' is given (Figure 1.1). The soldiers are in full uniform, and their red coats and busbies clearly identify them as British, though in the story they are referred to as Wooden Heads—or 'Pudd'n Heads' by their enemies. The image appears in *War in Dollyland (A Book and a Game)* (Figure 1.2), an example of the strand of radical writing for the young with which this chapter is primarily concerned: works that oppose war and criticize the politicians, arms dealers, and institutions responsible for military conflicts. It is also a useful reminder that radical texts were not exclusively produced by left-wing or small independent publishing houses. Ward Lock and Co., founded in the middle of the nineteenth century, had a long tradition of publishing children's classics, including *Alice's Adventures in Wonderland* and *Tom Brown's School Days*. In this case, author Harry Golding was a regular and prolific Ward Lock writer, editor, and compiler, best known for a popular series of 'Wonder' books and mass-market compilations with names such as *Our Darlings* (1905) and *Day Dreams* (1910). *War in Dollyland*, then, was more widely available and would have reached a broader constituency than most of the books produced by Martin Lawrence and Victor Gollancz.

As far as can be ascertained from the scant information about Harry Golding available, it was only in this collaboration with photographer Albert Friend (about whom there is even less information) that Golding broke away from the kind of bread-and-butter work he produced for the company over several decades. Friend's photographs set the radical mood and tone for a satire reminiscent of the Lilliputian episode in *Gulliver's Travels*. Just as Jonathan Swift establishes the pointlessness of the war

**Figure 1.1.** Execution of a spy, from Harry Golding and Albert Friend's *War in Dollyland (A Book and a Game)*. London: Ward, Lock & Co., 1915. Princeton University Library

**Figure 1.2.** Cover, *War in Dollyland (A Book and a Game)*. Princeton University Library

between the Big and Little-Endians, so Golding explains that there is no basis for the war in Dollyland. The antagonists, the Wooden Heads and the Flat Heads (Fat Heads), are fighting about the shape of their heads, although 'all their heads were precisely the same, so there was nothing whatever to quarrel about' (Golding, 1915 11). Like all the other publications discussed in this chapter, the radical nature of Golding and Friend's picturebook sets it apart from the dominant trend in writing about war for juvenile audiences typified, for example, by the work of G.A. Henty and Percy Westerman. Steeped in patriotic nationalism, these often had titles such as *With Clive in India* (1884), *Under Wellington's Command* (1898), or *The Dreadnought of the Air* (1914), and featured military heroes and brave British campaigns. It is books such as these that led Paul Fussell to conclude in *The Great War and Modern Memory* (1975) that mass enlistment in 1914–16 by adolescents and young men was linked to boyhood reading.

That some boys enlisted in response to the image of the battlefield as a place of camaraderie, heroism, and self-sacrifice perpetrated by such books is indisputable: several of the men who as boys fought in the First World War that Richard van Emden interviewed for *Boy Soldiers of the Great War* (2004), for instance, confirmed that reading war stories and comics influenced their decision to join up. In *Kitchener's Lost Boys: From the Playing Fields to the Killing Fields* (2009), John Oakes concludes that 'the mind-set of the boys who offered themselves for sacrifice in the First World War, w[as] profoundly influenced by the juvenile fiction of the day' (Oakes, 2009 45). What such accounts ignore, however, is the fact that these were not the only stories in circulation and that not all young readers read them uncritically, unconsciously absorbing their messages. Both before the First World War and in the years before the Second World War there were many counter-narratives, counter-discourses, and counter-contexts that would have created readers likely to resist the world view of popular pro-war writing even if they enjoyed reading war stories. Precisely such readers feature in Jonathan Rose's *The Intellectual Life of the British Working Class* (2001), among them Percy Wall, who was a Conscientious Objector (CO) in the First World War. As a boy, Wall enjoyed reading mainstream writing for children such as the *Magnet* and Henty's novels, but he also 'studied the *Clarion* (a weekly socialist newspaper), the *Freethinker*, *The Struggle of the Bulgarians for Independence* and *The Philippine Martyrs* for their politics' (Rose, 2001 332). Wall does not refer to any children's books, but radical children's literature had for decades offered young readers alternative perspectives and discourses. Among the first pacifist stories in wide circulation was Leo Tolstoy's 'Ivan the Fool', which was available in English translation as early as 1895 and republished regularly across the period of this study. It tells what happens when the good ruler Ivan's peaceful kingdom is attacked by his wicked brother's army. Ivan and his people 'offered no resistance, but only stood by and wept' (1896 71). Eventually the soldiers can no longer bear to keep abusing Ivan's people and desert their leader, leaving Ivan's kingdom to live in peace and prosperity. Golding and Friend's picturebook is typical of radical writing about war in the way it set in motion a multitude of clashing ideas and associations that worked to discredit the military mythos developed by writers such as Henty and Westerman. Often radical stories do this through questioning the wisdom, skill, and veracity of those responsible for waging wars.

In *War in Dollyland*, questions are stimulated by the tension between the subject—war—and Albert Friend's use of toys as models, photographed against the kind of cardboard, paper, and string backdrops associated with children's art and games. Although they look childish, the images are infused with meanings that are far beyond the experiences and understanding of most children, making this a book that speaks simultaneously though differently to adult and child readers. At the same time, the toys and backdrops implicate children in the action of the story, reminding readers of whatever age that battles frequently feature in children's play and fantasy lives, and toys and costumes made and purchased for them are often miniature versions of adult weapons and uniforms.

In *War in Dollyland*, the relationship between children's imaginative play and war is intensified by the subtitle *(A Book and a Game)* and the encouragement in the preliminary pages for children to try their hands at making additional scenes for their own toys:

> This is at once a book and a game. The book has been made for you: the game you can make for yourselves. Nearly all the toys required you probably have or can model from plasticene; the other odds and ends Mother or Nurse will be only too glad to get you.... (Golding, 1915 n.p.)

The fact that the text refers to readers' nurses and assumes cupboards are stocked with toys such as Noah's arks and plasticine indicates a mainstream, middle-class readership rather than a specifically left-wing or progressive niche audience, but *War in Dollyland* shifts the register of both mainstream stories about war and war-games. Instead of providing a fictional context and set of activities that young reader-players can use to practise for the time when they will be required on the battlefield, it establishes an equivalence between children and military commanders. The parallel implies both that those in charge of fighting troops have failed to learn that war is not a game and that their grasp of the complexities and ethical dilemmas posed by war is no better than a child's.

Albert Friend's toy models are far from elaborate, and in many ways it is the ubiquity and crudeness of the dolls in the photographs that make them so disturbing, at least to present-day eyes. In the absence of reception evidence relating to *War in Dollyland*, the effect can usefully be compared to a more recent series of artworks that also uses toys to make a statement about officially sanctioned murder in a wartime context: Polish artist Zbigniew Libera's Lego Concentration Camp Set (1996). In Libera's Lego scenes (which come complete with replica boxes), the discordancy between ideas of childhood innocence, play, and toys on the one hand, and Nazi death-camps on the other, has provoked heated debate in fine art and Holocaust circles. Some viewers regard these as profound works of art that defamiliarize images of the Holocaust in ways that add impetus to acts of witnessing; for others, however, the conjunction of toys and death-camps is trivializing and disrespectful (Feinstein, 2000 n.p.; Warner, 2005 78–9). Responses to Libera's work are helpful for thinking about how Golding and Friend's picturebook might have struck its original readers; particularly adults who purchased it for or read it aloud to children assuming it would be more traditional in its attitudes to soldiers and war. Turning again to the execution scene, for instance, what would in any case be an incongruous image for a juvenile audience must for many have become increasingly contentious over the remaining years of the war when hundreds of soldiers were shot as 'cowards' and 'deserters'; especially since many of those required to form firing squads and some of those who stood before them were only teenagers who not long before would have been playing with their own toys.

*War in Dollyland* is not in fact about those who defy authority or desert after signing up or being conscripted: the figure before the firing squad (who in the way of games with toys appears to be a female doll standing in for a male soldier) is meant to be a spy. Instead, it features ordinary (toy) soldiers caught up in a pointless war but nonetheless being brave, saving the day and clearing up messes caused by inadequate, war-mongering leaders. When reporting to his buffoon of a General, for instance, the Sergeant Major deliberately looks through the wrong end of his telescope to make everything smaller:

'Very tiny force, sir,' he reported. 'They'll run directly.'

'Then forward!' cried the General, and waved his arms so violently that he nearly fell off his horse again. (12)

As well as caricaturing those in charge, *War in Dollyland* shows the bodies of dead and injured soldiers, and features a monument that clearly fails to compensate for the sacrifices of those it memorializes. Golding and Friend's picturebook is one of a cluster of children's books and stories about toy soldiers that subvert traditional attitudes and ways of writing about war for children. Reinserting these and the other radical works discussed in this chapter into the account of early twentieth-century children's literature puts the spotlight not just on texts, but on whole categories of children and the publications produced for them that have been overlooked by historians of children's literature. As in the case of Percy Wall, for boys who reached military age during the First World War, reading could play a role in decisions to oppose war as well as to enlist.

The best known of the toy soldier books is *Little Wars: A Game for Boys of Twelve Years to One Hundred and Fifty and for that More Intelligent Sort of Girl Who Likes Games and Books* (1913) by H.G. Wells. Published two years before *War in Dollyland* and also illustrated with photographs of toy soldiers, it is likely that Wells's book inspired the Golding-Friend collaboration and predisposed Ward Lock to assume there would be a market for such a picturebook. As its title indicates, *Little Wars* was not written exclusively for children, though it is usually classified as a children's book in catalogues, collections, and criticism. In it, as in its precursor, *Floor Games* (1911), Wells regularly addresses adults, assuming that they too will enjoy and benefit from play of the kind he describes. There is, in fact, a notable absence of children in the photographs that illustrate *Little Wars*. These show Wells himself, occasionally with friends including co-creator Jerome K. Jerome, crawling among toy soldiers arranged in complicated tactical formations on carpets and out of doors. Nor is the play described in the book the kind of play associated with the young. Although the 'little wars' Wells describes to some extent take place outside the time of everyday life in that they span several days during which no work appears to take place, they do not represent a fantasy interlude. There is, for example, no attempt to animate the toys or to project emotions onto them in the way Susan Stewart identifies as characteristic of children's play with toys (Stewart, 1984 32). Neither is this about regressing to a childish state of unruliness and the freedom associated with children's unrepressed psyches (ideas discussed in relation to Surrealism in Chapter 3). Rather, the scenarios depicted are all highly strategic and based on battles played out by Wells and his friends.

Far from featuring ways to escape from the demands and constraints of everyday life through play, Wells's book has serious objectives. The first is didactic: based on his own experience he maintains that playing wargames soon exposes the 'inevitable consequences of war'. Since, he says, even members of the armed forces, from captains to commanders, 'presently get into difficulties and confusions' when making Little Wars, the games provide important insights into 'just what a blundering thing Great War must be' (Wells, 1913 99). A second objective reflects Wells's interest in the role played by genetics in the evolution of the human psyche and the drives and instincts that shape male responses to war. A pacifist at the time, he concluded that there must be an instinct for war since, against his wishes, he himself was fascinated by it. Reasoning that an instinct cannot be eradicated—at least in the short term—he concluded that ways must be found to satisfy and redirect males' predisposition to fight. The games of military strategy played out on miniature battlefields populated by toy soldiers that make up *Little Wars* were intended to assuage the aggressive instincts and simulate the thrills of war.

> How much better is this amiable miniature than the Real Thing! Here is a homeopathic remedy for the imaginative strategist. Here is the premedita- tion, the thrill, the strain of accumulating victory or disaster—and no smashed bodies, no shattered fine buildings or devastated country sides, no petty cruelties, none of that awful universal boredom and embitterment, that tiresome delay or stoppage or embarrassment of every gracious, bold, sweet, and charming thing, that we who are old enough to remember a real modern war know to be the realty of belligerence. (Wells, 1913 97)

As a children's book, *Little Wars* is radical in combining scientific and psychological knowledge with play in an attempt to influence how society works; in this case by challenging the assumption that military engage- ments are the only way to ensure access to resources and solve disputes between nations.

Wells was far from the first to see books about toys as a way of cultivating an interest in alternatives to war in the young. The last of the stories about toy soldiers to be discussed here, *The Toy Soldier: A Children's Peace Story* (n.d.) by the otherwise unknown E.J. Hawley, is so typical of such stories that it may have been the inspiration for 'The Toys of Peace' (n.d.), a parody of pacifist children's writing and child rearing by 'Saki' (H[ector] H[ugh] Munro).[1] Both stories feature a boy called Bertie who indulges in aggressive games about war with toys, but to very different ends. Saki's story is about progressive parents whose best efforts to raise their children as pacifists are in vain. It ends with the children, who have

---

[1] The date of neither story is certain, but since it is set in the Boer War Hawley's story probably appeared before 1910. It may also have been published by a number of other Peace Societies, but the only example I have located was published by the Leicester group. Munro died fighting in France in 1916; 'The Toys of Peace' was included in a 1919 collection of his short stories published with an accompanying memoir by John Lane.

been left to their own devices, using pacifist toys to conduct a battle. The pacifist aunt in Hawley's story, by contrast, succeeds by joining in the boy's game and reaching out to his imagination.

Having observed her nephew staging a battle with his toy soldiers and delighting in the death of an 'enemy', she agrees to help him hold a funeral. In her role as 'parson' she tells this salutary story.

> This man, whom we have just buried, lived in a farmhouse on the veldt. He was a very good husband and father. All his children loved him very much. When he went away to the war his little girl threw her arms around his neck and hugged him tight, and said she hated war because it took father away. Then her mother cried, and said she hoped father would come back again for, if not, who was to see to the farm, and get food for the children to eat? The eldest boy, who was named Bertie, after an English man who had been kind to the farmer, stood very quiet and still, and when his turn came to say 'good-bye,' he clenched his little hand and vowed that if ever he became a man he would not let people fight. He would make them all be good, and then there would never be any war at all to take little boys' fathers away. (Hawley, n.d. 6)

Bertie's aunt drives home the lesson by saying a prayer for 'all the little children who have not got any fathers' and writing on the tombstone, 'Here Lies Somebody's Father'. Before bedtime the boy asks to disinter his soldier and restore him to the bosom of his family and, now understanding that in life soldiers are real people with families, declares himself to be against war.

## THE PACIFIST TRADITION IN SOCIALIST WRITING FOR CHILDREN: *THE YOUNG SOCIALIST* AND *THE REVOLUTION*

*The Toy Soldier: A Children's Peace Story* was published by the Leicester Peace Society, one of the many local branches of the International Peace Society (founded 1816) that produced pacifist literature for all ages which their members distributed freely or at greatly subsidized rates. As the prospect of war with Germany seemed increasingly likely, left-leaning organizations followed the example of the peace societies by using writing for children to oppose militarism and promote the merits of peace and pacifism to the rising generation. This reflects the fact that the ninth of the Ten Commandments learned in Socialist Sunday Schools (SSSs) is, 'Do not believe that he who despises other nations and desires to wage wars against them is a good patriot. War is a remnant of Barbarism. Fight only in defence of your country' (Hazell, 1907 1). Unsurprisingly, socialist organizations were a particularly active source of anti-war writing for the young. The foremost organ for reaching a readership of socialist children and youth was *The Young Socialist*, which used editorials, features, fiction, verse, music, and illustrations to drive home the message that the only war worth fighting is 'the war against poverty, against slumdom, against children going to work, when they ought to be in school: against unemployment, over-work, low wages' (*The Young Socialist*, 1912 219). Like the other examples of pacifist writing for children featured here, the magazine strongly opposed the aggressive militarism, stockpiling of weapons, and Germanophobia that had begun to dominate public discourse in the months before Britain entered the First World War.

*The Young Socialist* was distributed through SSSs, and SSS classes and activities underpinned both its pacifist message and its enscripting strategies. On the first Sunday of 1913, for instance, the Schools held a National Socialist Peace Service at which all scholars sang 'A Hymn of Futurity', about a time 'When all mankind shall be/Bound in fraternity;/ When works of strife shall cease,/And deeds of love increase,/And universal peace/Bless all humanity' (1913 4). 1913 also saw the launch of the Young Socialist Citizen Corps, the magazine's peace movement. The military overtones in the name were not accidental: just as SSSs made use of many of the trappings of Christianity (as well as attending Sunday Schools, children sang hymns and learned a Socialist catechism), so the organization borrowed strategically from both the military and successful uniformed organizations such as the Boy Scouts. The logic behind the military trappings in an anti-military organization is exemplified in a short story that appeared in a 1916 number of *The Young Socialist*, 'The Bugle Call. How the German lad answered it' by Russell Everett. Set in Berlin, it describes twelve-year-old socialist Karl and his mother encountering a military regiment marching behind an unfurled banner. Karl knows 'what soldiers and martial music really meant' because his father has told him how the fathers and brothers of French and German children like himself, who have never met or quarrelled, have been ordered to fight by their rulers. Nevertheless he is moved by the spectacle and asks, 'Is there no bugle-call for me, mother? Is there no banner I can follow?' (1916 52). In the story, Karl has to be content with metaphorical bugles and banners, but the editors of *The Young Socialist* provided more tangible symbols and trappings for their readers. The Young Socialist Citizen Corps had uniforms, a banner, and opportunities to march. The Corps's emblem which, like so much Socialist print material from this period, was designed by Walter Crane, depicts an 'olive wreath crested with a civic crown, encircling the cap of freedom, and enclosing the heart of love and life, over which hovers the dove of peace' (1913 219). The motto reads: 'The children of all lands shall unite for Peace' (Figure 1.3).

252     THE YOUNG SOCIALIST.

OUR YOUNG SOCIALIST CITIZEN CORPS

"The Children of all Lands Shall unite for Peace."

THERE were so many reports held over from last month, that I shall have to limit myself to a very few words this time. Let it suffice to say that the movement is spreading rapidly.

Enquiries have reached me from "Bonnie Dundee," Kilmarnock, and Gorton, and three Corps are in process of being formed in these places. Good luck to them! We hope to hear from them next month. Birmingham is very quiet. What is the matter?

Here is the Glasgow report:—

> 34 Aberdour Street, Dennistoun,
> 23/10/12.
>
> Dear Comrade,—Glasgow No. 1 is still developing. Our course of dry land swimming instruction has been completed (all our members can swim on dry land) and we are now taking up semaphore signalling. Our Citizens are quite enthusiastic about it. One of our speakers on a recent Sunday threw out a very useful hint, which we intend to discuss, and as it may be useful to the other Corps, I pass it on. The suggestion is that we rent an allotment garden in the name of the Y.S.C.C., and take up gardening as a subject. It might be a practical method of expressing our citizenship, and the products would help to beautify our schools. Our "First Aid" is progressing. We have mastered the "bones" and "fractures," and will now proceed to the "blood-vessels." We are also taking up "Flower Drill," for spectacular purposes. Corps now number 35. I am glad to note that Corps are springing up everywhere.
>
> Yours fraternally,
> DUNCAN JACKSON.

Bravo Glasgow! Dry land swimming, and gardening. The Glasgow Corps intends to be ready in good time for the coming commonweal, evidently.

Paul West writes from busy Lancashire as follows:—

> Dear Comrade Young,—I am almost smothered in work. Part of that work just lately has been the attention I have been paying to the Y.S.C.C. I have been doing what I can in my

area, which, as you will admit, is a large one. Also I have been pushing forward my local comrades here at Nelson, with the object of inducing them to form a Y.S.C.C. I was glad that they did not require much convincing about the benefits of a Corps. They gave me the privilege of introducing the subject at one of our Quarterly Teachers' Conferences. The result was a good discussion, and a unanimous decision to form a Corp. I am hoping to persuade other schools in a like manner, and I should be pleased to give my services for expenses. The greatest difficulty with schools is the unsuitability of their rooms, but where this barrier does not prevail, I should urge schools to pay serious attention to this new phase of S.S. School activity.

Then there is the question of a suitable Instructor; every school has not such a person in the ranks of its workers. In this case the members of the branch must be gone through, and failing this, someone outside who is sympathetic to the cause, and then, if no one can be found, one or two workers should be prevailed upon to attend physical culture classes, in order to qualify. If there are no classes of this character, there are plenty of books of instruction, from which any person of moderate intelligence could become fairly proficient. I would like to give hope and encouragement to all my comrades North, South, East, and West, to do their best in this matter, if only for the sake of the children; and there is no doubt that the Y.S.C.C. will form a link to bind and attach them to the school. We

**Figure 1.3.** Emblem of the Young Socialist Citizen Corps. Image courtesy of the Working Class Movement Library

Encouraging SSS members to put on their uniforms and march around their neighbourhoods was not simply about giving them a sense of identity or stirring children's emotions. Through their activities SSS pupils performed their affiliation, strengthening bonds with the SSS while spreading the socialist message and providing entertainment for locals. The same was achieved when SSSs mounted pageants and public performances of short plays such as *Paddly Pools: A Little Fairy Play* (1916). One of several similar short plays by actor, pacifist, and reformer Miles Malleson, *Paddly Pools* was frequently performed by SSS children during the First World War. As its subtitle suggests, *Paddly Pools* is rooted in the fascination with fairies, the mystical, and hope in a spirit world and afterlife that became particularly widespread at a time when families were losing sons, fathers, and brothers at a catastrophic rate. The play's appeal to SSSs lay in its depiction of children as the hope for the future, a future founded on socialist principles. Though adults are shown as deaf to promptings towards peace, Malleson's child hero understands that if war is to be avoided, the next generation will need to create a more just and equable world, a world that 'might belong to everyone . . . without any barbed wire or quarrelling' (14).

Although critical of the current conflict, *Paddly Pools* is respectful of fighting men. In this, Malleson's play is typical of wartime socialist publications for children; while these never ceased to disapprove of war or champion peace, once Britons were on the battlefield they supported and empathized with the fighting troops and respected the sacrifices they were making. The strongest support in SSSs, however, went to members who were incarcerated or otherwise suffered for being COs: socialists made up a significant proportion of the approximately 16,000 British subjects who identified as COs during the First World War. Following the introduction of conscription in 1916, *The Young Socialist* increasingly relates stories of socialists who suffer for their beliefs. Often these take the form of detailed accounts of the tribunals of SSS members who were approaching or had just attained military age and 'who held true to the principles of internationalism, the wrongness of shedding human blood' and the conviction that 'arbitration of the sword' is futile (1916 50). Time and again readers encounter young people from backgrounds like their own who have gone to tribunals armed with SSS literature as evidence of their 'Socialist faith' (1916 67). These sit alongside first-hand accounts of how conscription was experienced by readers, usually in the form of letters to 'Flora', editor of the correspondence pages, from child readers with family members who had been incarcerated for refusing to serve. 'Annie Swallow of Honley, near Huddersfield' is one of those who shared her experiences:

> Dear Flora,—I attend the Honley Socialist Sunday School, which began on August 4th, 1918. I have had a 'Young Socialist' magazine for three years, and I look forward to it every month. My father has been away for nearly two years as a conscientious objector and he has now come home. It feels a treat, I can assure you . . . . (1918 118)

Also included are contributions from former members who, being old enough to be called up, have refused to serve on the grounds of conscience. Writing from prison, Sidney Warr (jun), Fred Tait, William Morris Duff, and David Guffie among others greet young readers and underline the importance of the values and ways of thinking they learned when they were members of their SSSs. Sidney Warr tells readers, 'The S.S.S. movement can be proud of the fact that it has helped so many young people to become Conscientious Objectors to warfare and its causes' (1916 35). While they do not dwell on their hardships, CO contributors to the magazine make sure these are understood. William Morris Duff tells of comrades who have suffered so much that they have given in because 'only the strongest can survive all the threats and tortures which are meted out to those who are fighting (passively) for freedom of conscience' (1916 112). In a poem called 'Thoughts from a Cell' written in June 1916, Fred Tait (at the time serving six months' hard labour) explains that he spends his time trying to imagine the natural world since he is so cut off from it. The poem reassures readers that he is sustained by his socialist convictions, and though trapped 'between four gloomy walls' he is 'Without regret or sorrow, or impatience with my lot' because 'I dream of lands where LOVE shall reign, and war and hate be not' (front page, October 1916). His equanimity was sorely tested; news from the Tyneside Union SSS later that year includes the announcement that

> Our comrade, Fred Tait, is now undergoing a second term of imprisonment. He was not allowed at liberty after serving his first term, even for a few days, but had to go through the mill again without a respite. Never mind, Fred, the Sunday School is proud of you! (1916 156)

One of the most detailed accounts of life in prison as experienced by COs is found in a letter written in May 1916 by Comrade Littlefield, of Willesden School, an SSS teacher imprisoned in Felixstowe:

> Well, it is over three weeks since I left you, and it seems years. Shut up in a cell with nothing to do, with only the four walls and bare boards, time indeed passes slowly. I walk round and round my cell sometimes to pass the time. Our punishment rations are a round and a half of dry bread three times a day. I am not allowed any books or papers, so don't know what's going on in the outside world.... To all good comrades I extend the hand of fellowship. 'Carry on,' as the Army says, and we will save England from the nightmare of unrestricted militarism which exists in Germany, France, and Russia.... (1916 100)

The conditions he describes would have been familiar to readers since COs who refused to take up non-combatant roles such as driving ambulances were often held in solitary confinement, had their diets restricted to bread and water, and were given prison sentences of up to ten years. A few, notably the 'Richmond Sixteen', were threatened with execution.[2] Unsurprisingly, then, contributions to *The Young Socialist* present COs as martyrs to the cause of peace and the project to build a global commonwealth of workers. This tendency is even more pronounced in *The Revolution: A Magazine for Young Workers* launched in 1917 by SSS founder Tom Anderson for his more radical Socialist School. *The Revolution* includes many features about COs as well as correspondence from some about their experiences. However, as its title indicates, *The Revolution* was not objecting to the war on pacifist grounds. Articles such as 'Don't Shoot Your Class' assume that one day workers will have to fight, but that this was the wrong battle and would only be injurious to themselves and those like them:

> you, a slave, a member of a subject class, are ordered to don uniform and march away to slay.
>
> To slay whom? The people who oppress you, the people who live in luxury whilst you toil and starve all your days?
>
> NO! You will march away to shoot your own class your brothers who under another flag and speaking another tongue, will likewise march to war at their masters [sic] bidding to meet and fight you. (*The Revolution*, 1918 197)

*The Young Socialist* remained staunchly anti-war throughout the 1920s and 1930s (*The Revolution* ceased publication in 1918) and regularly highlighted writers, from Leo Tolstoy to F.J. Gould, whose stories and books furthered the cause of peace. The magazine did not, however, assume or desire that its young readers would read only socialist writing—about conflicts or any other topic. As discussed in the Introduction, socialist and other left-leaning educators and leaders also encouraged reading of the classics, most literary genres, and scientific works (science being the byword for most forms of serious study at the time). The recommendations of *The Young Socialist*'s Mr Wiseacre, whose column was introduced in 1934, span adventure and island stories, historical fiction, folk tales, animal stories, travel writing, books about explorers, machines, and inventions as well as the classics. Good home libraries, he told readers, should contain poetry, plays, and criticism, while 'There is no excuse on the grounds of expense for any home library not containing the plays of Shakespeare or the novels of Walter Scott' (1934 98).

[2] Held at Richmond Castle in North Yorkshire, the Sixteen were forcibly taken to France where, because they refused to participate in war work, they were court-martialled and sentenced to death. At the last hour the sentence was commuted by the Prime Minister.

While war stories do not feature in Mr Wiseacre's recommendations, there are plenty of battles in both Shakespeare and Scott, not to mention Homer. The implicit assumption is that, like Percy Wall, readers of *The Young Socialist* will know their socialist commandments and be sufficiently well versed in socialist philosophy and arguments to prevent them from unthinkingly accepting bourgeois/capitalist ideological assumptions in what they read. In *The Tasks of the Youth Leagues* (1920), Lenin officially identified learning as the main job of the young and the most important tool for rebuilding the world. Knowledge could be acquired from a range of sources, so reading widely was regarded as an important means of tempering and developing ideas as well as of becoming familiar with the mind-set and frame of reference of the groups in society socialists opposed. This view is anticipated in *The Revolution*'s feature, 'Books and the Young Socialist' which demands that its readers 'Read, study, learn' because reading, and particularly books, provide the route to the 'mental evolution' necessary to bring about social revolution (Starr, 1918 161).

Socialists were not alone in educating groups of young people to resist the ideologies and assumptions that dominated society and found expression in mainstream writing for children: the progressive schools that reached their heyday in the 1920s and 1930s were equally committed to creating a group of young people capable of reading across the grain of mainstream texts. Progressive schools produced little in the way of writing for children themselves; certainly nothing so clear or sustained in its mission as *The Young Socialist*, *The Revolution*, or the many other magazines, pamphlets, newspapers, and stories produced by other left-wing organizations (between 1921 and 1943 there were at least sixteen such publications for young communists: see Appendix). However, pupils at progressive schools were an obvious and influential audience for radical publications, as seen in the incident discussed in the Introduction, when pupils from Abbotsholme School set up a Left Book Club.

## ALTERNATIVE READING CULTURES IN BRITAIN'S PROGRESSIVE SCHOOLS

Pupils at progressive schools belonged to a very different social strata from those who attended SSSs, and there were fewer of them. Although insignificant in terms of numbers, pupils from progressive schools wielded a disproportionately high level of influence during the years of this study through their work as publishers, policy makers, professionals, and public thinkers. To give an example, among the pupils who attended

Abbotsholme in Staffordshire (founded 1889), King Alfred School in London (1898), and Bootham School in York (1822) were Lytton Strachey; the architect Edwin Landseer Lutyens's children; the Rowntree children; and offspring of two prominent publishing families: the Curwens (The Curwen Press) and the Unwins (Sir Stanley Unwin founded the publishing house George Allen & Unwin in 1914).

In comparison to socialist and communist organizations, progressive schools did not produce a notable body of writing for children (though as discussed in Chapter 6, they did contribute to writing about sex education). Schools are not in the publishing business, of course, and they rarely have access to the kind of presses and distribution systems available to socialists and other political organizations. Moreover, though their pupils were often comfortably off, during these years progressive schools were generally operating close to their financial margins. This meant that not only was there little in the way of publishing directly associated with progressive schools, but also that for most of the period covered by this study, progressive schools tended to spend very little on books or libraries. In fact because they relied largely on donations and had no dedicated specialists seeking out specifically progressive books, the contents of libraries in progressive schools were generally more limited than, but otherwise very like, those at traditional schools. Popular books in the run up to the First World War included those by G.A. Henty, Gordon Stables, Ernest Seton Thompson, H. Rider Haggard, Alexander Dumas, Edward Bulwer-Lytton, Charles Dickens, and Baroness Orczy (*Abbotsholmian*, 1906 113–14; *The Abbotsholme School Magazine*, 1907 13).

Stephen Humphries (1981), Anna Davin (1996), and Jonathan Rose (2001), among others, have pointed to the importance in relation to working-class readers of distinguishing between what is read and how it is read. The same pertains to progressive school pupils. The fact that they were immersed in non-traditional educational environments and came from families that supported progressive education (some of the parents had themselves attended progressive schools) made it unlikely that they would read books about war, colonial expansion, or revolution in the same way as those from conservative backgrounds. Between 1910 and 1949, peace, pacifism, equality, and internationalism were as central to the educational philosophy of most progressive schools as they were to SSSs, creating an educational context that nurtured radical readers and thinkers. While SSS scholars were always on the margins of society, pupils at progressive schools were often well off and well connected. They carried the radical message into middle and upper-class environments where it could be stirred into the mix of British culture. As readers and disseminators of radical children's literature, these pupils may have read differently from young working-class socialists, but they had many shared aims, ideals, and political positions, not least their opposition to war.

A sense of how some progressive school pupils reshaped narratives in the light of their schools' ethos can be gleaned from their writing, for the schools 'published' pupils' work in the form of school magazines and similar publications. The 1914–19 numbers of *The King Alfred School Magazine* (*KAS*) show that as the war progressed, events on both the home and Western fronts began to be reflected in pupils' writing. Some of this was in a traditional vein: the volume for 1916 includes a poem about the British scaring off a cowardly Kaiser, a drawing of an air ship, and a short story about 'How Smith Won the VC', but it also includes examples of writing clearly informed by progressive ideals and codes of conduct. For example, in the next year's bound volume a story set during the Civil War begins with the pronouncement, 'John hated boys' games, swords and war & he missed his Father who was rampageous and sports-loving though he always had a kind word for his timid son' (1917 85). The timid son proves to be a hero in the progressive school mould when, having pondered the condition of a recently captured prisoner ('has he any little boys like me?'), he secretly releases him. The act of compassion is vindicated when the boy's father in turn is captured and the former prisoner is able to return the favour and spare him. Although the story uses war as a backdrop, it displays the core values of progressive schools in its emphasis on empathy, humanity, and doing good for the sake of good. It also demonstrates how familiar genres such as the historical novel, the war story, and fables about good deeds could be re-fashioned in the minds of non-traditional readers.

Similar stories and essays appear in *The Observer*, the equivalent pub-lication at Bootham School, both before and after the First World War (the war itself is a recurring motif). The bound volume for 1922–4, for example, contains a time-travel story ironically titled 'The Glory of War' about a peace-loving man who falls asleep and 'wakes up' amidst the carnage of a medieval battlefield. In the course of the dream he experiences fighting in the First World War, which makes him cry aloud 'against the foolishness and hideousness of war', and witnesses a future London under assault from a bombing campaign that prefigures the Blitz. 'Surely', the narrator asks, 'man would not spoil the beauties of nature and peace of the world by another and infinitely more terrible war?'(1922 408). The volume for 1927–9 includes a profile of Mussolini as part of a critique of fascism, and a tale about the courage of a young man who, having been forced by his family to enlist, deserts and escapes to France, where he subsequently lives a long, satisfying, and peaceful life.

Perhaps one of the most consistent aspects of opposition to war in progressive schools during the First World War was the determination not to construct Germany and its people as the enemy. Most progressive schools were founded on German pedagogic principles and had close ties with that country. Typically there were school exchanges between pupils and staff, and holidays spent in the two countries of the kind frequently described in school publications. The 1908–9 number of *The Abbotsholmian*, for instance, includes a student piece comparing 'School Life at a German Gymnasium and Abbotsholme' that concludes with the statement that Germans are 'true and trusted friends' (3).[3] The complicated position in relation to Germany of Britain's progressive schools during the First World War is captured in an obituary published in the December 1916 number of *The King Alfred School Magazine*:

> Maurice Basden (Lieut. Royal Flying Corps.)
> K.A.S., 1904–1908
> Maurice Basden was at King Alfred School for four years . . . in the Spring of 1914 he went to Germany . . . where he was treated with marked kindness because he was an Englishman. He left Hamburg for the summer holiday in England one week before war was declared, without the slightest suspicion of approaching events, and with every hope of returning there in September . . . . He was killed on May 20th, 1916, in aerial combat . . .
>
> His great desire, if he had lived through the war, was to return to Germany the day after peace was declared. (182)

Like many of those who founded and managed the new progressive schools, King Alfred's Headmaster, John Russell, had spent time in and admired Germany and refused to renounce his strongly positive feelings about that country even when Britain and Germany were at war and pupils like Maurice Basden were dying in battle. In 'The School of War', a public address to young people that Russell gave in London in November 1914, when 'war fever' was at a peak, he testified to his affection for Germany, German culture, and the German people, including German soldiers, who, he noted, were dying as pointlessly and as horrifically as British troops. Russell's Headmaster's report of 1916 lists the names of old boys and girls who were involved in some kind of war service and those who had died and/or been honoured on the battlefield. While proud that

---

[3] Admiration for Germany was not confined to that country's art and culture. The 1908–9 number of *The Abbotsholmian*, for instance, includes an encomium of the 'German Military System' which is described as 'a marvellous organization' to which the British Army and Royal Navy are compared unfavourably (3). O'Sullivan (1990) provides a relevant discussion of Germanophilia.

former pupils were serving their country, he concludes the report by saying, 'It is impossible for me to feel more strongly than I have always felt that war, in the absolute sense, is wrong, a prostitution alike of matter and spirit' (n.p.).

This conflicted attitude was replicated across the progressive schools then in existence and created a confusing context in which the importance of service and protecting the nation vied with repugnance for war and affection for Germany as a place, people, and culture. Maurice Basden's obituary, the substance of which is reinforced in a letter from the young man's mother published in the same number of the *KAS Magazine*, is a powerful reminder that the fact that a boy enlisted at a very young age did not mean that he had absorbed militaristic, nationalistic, or anti-German messages from boys' fiction or, indeed, from any other source. Deciding to fight in defence of one's country when background, education, and belief make war anathema is quite different from enlisting in the naïve belief that war will offer the kinds of adventure featured in popular boys' fiction.

## THE RADICAL DILEMMA: PACIFISM VERSUS FASCISM

The interwar years saw opposition to war spread across large parts of the population, generating many different kinds of writing designed to build resistance in the young to any future epidemic of war fever. One target of radical writers, illustrators, and publishers was the patriotic war-as-adventure story, large numbers of which were still in circulation. Radical children's writers frequently sought to expose the false view of war in such stories by providing young readers with material that stripped away romantic myths about the battlefield. *An Outline History of the Great War* (1928), G.V. Carey and H.S. Scott's best-selling history of the First World War for young people, for instance, aimed to give young readers a powerful sense of 'what the War *felt like*'. This, the authors maintained, is 'more important than to know its events in outline' in helping them resist 'the false glamour which is apt to be shed on war, when viewed from a distance' (Preface). Carey and Scott's counter-narrative took the form of an information book, but fiction, with its capacity to create a strong sense of place, events, and empathetic bonds with characters, was particularly suited to the work of discrediting the traditional war story.

Helen Zenna Smith (Evadne Price)'s *Not So Quiet: Stepdaughters of War* (1930), a novel written, as its title indicates, in response to Erich

Remarque's *All Quiet on the Western Front* (1929), speaks directly to the young. Its central character, Nellie Smith, a young voluntary aid detachment (VAD) ambulance driver, demands that those who come after her see through the blandishments of the older generation that has sent them to war. 'My generation', Nellie writes, 'watches these things [parents who encourage their children to kill the children of other parents] and marvels at the blindness of it . . . helpless to make its immature voice heard above the insensate clamour of the old ones who cry: "Kill, Kill, Kill!" unceasingly' (Smith, 1930 164–5). Nellie's first-hand experiences of battle are set against the pronouncements about the nobility and value of the war made by her parents and other adults safely at home. When *Not So Quiet* was published, the category now known as Young Adult (YA) fiction did not exist and so it was published as general fiction, but the novel's point of view and address clearly imply a youthful reader. Price also makes use of tropes familiar from the school story, including midnight feasts, punishments, communal sleeping arrangements, and bullies. The Commandant resembles a harsh teacher, and the girls live according to an imposed routine and code of behaviour, endure terrible meals, are known by nicknames, speak in an insider's slang, and have crushes on each other. Like boarding school pupils writing home under the watchful eyes of tutors, Smith's VADs' letters must pass through the censors so they write what they are expected to write and tell their parents at home what they want to hear: '*It's such fun being out here, and of course I'm loving every minute of it; it's so splendid to be really in it*' (original italics, 30). Price's use of first-person address, the confessional nature of the writing, and its dependence on colloquial speech, often in the form of reported conversations, became standard characteristics of YA fiction.

No doubt in part because it was not categorized as being for young readers, Price's novel had considerable impact in its day. It was awarded the Prix Severigne in France as 'the novel most calculated to promote international peace' and became an immediate bestseller (Hardy, 1988 8). Its anti-war message is unmistakeable, but as a novel it is conveyed through empathetic characterization. A more characteristically socialist/ leftist means of discrediting traditional narratives about war was to focus on facts, figures, and logical arguments about the wasteful and destructive nature of war. Often the publications for young people where such facts and arguments were set out took the form of newsletters, pamphlets, and photojournalism. Distributing, reading, and sometimes contributing to such materials by those involved in peace activism and/or left-wing youth organizations formed an integral part of radical youth identity. The scale of production of such items can be seen in a publicity announcement for the International Peace Congress held in August 1934 in Sheffield.

Prospective delegates are assured that a 'comprehensive selection of anti-fascist and anti-war literature will be on sale' and given details of titles regarded as particularly important. Among these is *20 Years After!* (meaning after the First World War), the 'best-selling photo-essay against war and fascism' (Figure 1.4). According to the publicity material, more than 20,000 copies of *20 Years After!* had been sold, and delegates to the Congress are urged to promote it there as 'The most powerful blow against War.' To make its case against war the pamphlet uses a combination of moving photographs and statistics to highlight the kind of social and economic conditions that feed war fever: unemployment, social divisions, exploitation, nationalism, and armament sales. At the same time, it argues that those on the margins of society and so most likely to find themselves on the front line have least reason to serve: running alongside a photograph of a homeless young man sleeping on the Embankment are the questions 'Fight for your country? What country has he?'

Most items in *20 Years After!* concentrate on explaining to the young why they are the targets of war propaganda and why they should resist it. A typical example is a feature on youth crime that provides statistics about the rise in juvenile crime and quotes from a 1933 speech by the President of the National Association of Probation Officers that identifies the cause of juvenile crime as unemployment and goes on to predict that 'At the present rate, half a million of the adults of the next generation will have been before the courts before their 21st birthday.' The piece concludes, 'War leads to unemployment! Unemployment leads to crime!' (*20 Years After!* 4). One full page is given over to quotes from prominent figures from Britain and Europe including Lloyd George, General Goering, Marshal Petain, and Mussolini. All assume a second world war is inevitable. The quotes are juxtaposed to show how the young will once again be expected to sacrifice limbs and lives but will gain nothing from doing so. Perhaps the most chilling is one from Robert Baden-Powell that invokes the Scouting motto: 'Are you prepared to lose a limb or two if need be; to die, if need be, as Boy Cornwell did in Jutland? Think it over—and BE PREPARED!' (7).[4]

Even more hyped in the Congress literature than *20 Years After!* is Henri Barbusse's fifteen-page account of the previous year's Paris Congress, *You Are the Pioneers*. Barbusse was the founder of the World Movement Against War and a leading figure in anti-war events across Europe. Using the vocabulary of revolution, *You Are the Pioneers* (1933)

---

[4] Jack Cornwell, a working-class boy from Essex, was the youngest recipient of the Victoria Cross, awarded posthumously for his courageous feats during the battle of Jutland in 1916.

**Figure 1.4.** From *Twenty Years After!*. London: Youth Council, British Anti-War Movement, 1934 4–5. Image courtesy of the Working Class Movement Library

identifies the young people who gathered in Paris as the 'shock-brigade of humanity' and urges them to lead the way to international and lasting peace by refusing to participate in any future war. Like most of the information publications aimed at this audience, *You Are the Pioneers* is highly polemical and stresses the importance of young people being well informed about political developments so that they cannot be misinformed and manipulated into enlisting as had happened to the previous generation.

More than 600 young people attended the Sheffield Congress. They represented a diverse body of groups from across the UK including the Youth Anti-War Council (94 delegates), the Young Communist League (74), the Woodcraft Folk (9), the Jewish Lads' Brigade (2), various Student Societies (45), and the Clarion Cycling Club (1). By attending the Congress they were performing radicalism; much of this performance was predicated on having learned arguments, areas of concern, strategies of opposition, and goals through reading publications such as *20 Years After!* and *You Are the Pioneers*. Such works made up an important aspect of young people's reading in the interwar years and formed a lens through which other works would have been read and understood. Often they were also instrumental in identifying more substantial reading for committed young radicals.

Throughout the 1930s publications for young members of the Labour Party, the Young Communist League, and similarly left-orientated organizations carried reviews and recommendations about what to read to help understand the causes of war (and so how to avoid it) and the case for social change. *Challenge, the Fighting Fortnightly Newspaper for Youth* (launched March 1935, re-launched as *Challenge, Youth Weekly* in 1940), for instance, encouraged its young readers to read *The Road to War*, an analysis of the government's foreign policy by the New Fabian Research Bureau (1937). The Labour Party's *League of Youth Organizations Bulletin* (*Bulletin*) for May 1938 suggests that organizations will find performing suitable plays a good way of helping young people engage with issues. Recommended plays include A.A. Milne's *The Boy Comes Home* (first performed in 1918 and still being recommended to youth organizations in the approach to the Second World War), J.M. Synge's *Riders to the Sea* (1904), and all the plays of Henrik Ibsen. The books endorsed by the *Bulletin* were usually published by organizations known to be sympathetic to the Left and aimed at both the young and readers new to subjects (often implicitly those assumed to have left school at a young age). Typical examples are the 'Plebs Outlines' to subjects such as Economic Geography, Finance, and the British Empire, published in affiliation with the National Council of Labour Colleges from 1921.

During this period left-wing youth papers assumed that their audience read not to escape to the idyllic riverbanks or mythical pasts evoked in mainstream children's literature, but to improve their knowledge, learn from past mistakes, and prepare for adulthood. In the middle of the Second World War, for example, the *Bulletin* takes it for granted that 'young folk will find great interest' in '*Government by the People* and *Intermission 1919–1939* by [Mary Eleanor] Beggs and [Darlow Willis] Humphreys' (both published in 1941). This view of the seriousness attached to reading by increasing numbers of young people is acknowledged by the publisher Stanley Unwin in his reflections on *Publishing in Peace and War* (1944). Despite problems for publishers caused by paper rationing and the loss of books during the Blitz, he observed, war-time publishing was booming. 'The most pleasing feature of all', he writes, is that 'young people are buying books . . . for the acquisition of knowledge and the enjoyment of good literature, and not merely as an escape from war' (Unwin, 1944 25).[5] Booksellers who contributed to a Mass Observation survey during the war also commented on the new interest in book-buying by the kinds of (working-class) young people who 'aren't used to buying books' (in Rose, 2001 233).

Young people were not just *buying* books, pamphlets, and newspapers, however. During the 1930s those involved with left-wing organizations also became involved in producing materials for members and events. Newsletters and leaflets became so much a part of left-wing activism that eventually the *Daily Worker* produced an instructive insert in the style of a comic strip for quite young readers about how newspapers are made. *Little Tusker's Own Paper* (1945) teaches Little Tusker the elephant how to make a newspaper for his mates so that he can 'talk to lots more' (1945 2). One interwar publication stands out as an example of radical writing by young people for young people.

## RADICAL READER-WRITERS: THE CASE OF *OUT OF BOUNDS*

One morning in the early summer of 1934, a hand-picked group of public school pupils received an anonymously produced circular announcing the birth of an anti-establishment magazine written by pupils for pupils. The

[5] By the time Stanley Unwin was writing, reading had become part of the British war-time identity; Britons of all ages were encouraged to identify themselves as readers in contrast to the book-burning Nazis. A 1941 Ministry of Information Film even characterized the Second World War as 'The Battle of the Books', associating reading in Britain with the 'freedom to speak our minds' unlike the 'Nazi robots' with their restricted access to books and ideas.

circular invited its readers to become involved as contributors, distribu-tors, sources, and readers to *Out of Bounds: Action Against Reaction in the Public Schools*. The magazine was the brainchild of delegates to a confer-ence organized by the Federation of Student Societies (FSS), a group of university students, mainly from Oxford and the London School of Economics, formed in April 1933 and committed, as they put it, to 'the immediate mobilization of forces to join the counter attack on militarism, reaction, fascism and war' (in Marwick, 1970 47). University students already had radical journals such as *Youth: An Expression of Progressive University Thought*, founded in Cambridge in 1920 by the British Feder-ation of Youth, and the National Union of Students' journal, *The University* (1922–39). *Out of Bounds* was intended to provide a similar forum for younger readers by introducing them to left-wing political ideas, largely through focusing on what the FSS regarded as the primary forces of militarism and oppression in the public school system: the Officers' Training Corps, fagging, and corporal punishment. The fact that pupils from schools were attending a conference organized by a coalition of university students reflects the emergence of youth as a social category after the First World War, when many officers and soldiers went from the classroom to the battlefield. Some survivors resumed their educations at universities after the war, and it was the youngest of these, still little more than teenagers, who helped found organizations such as the FSS.

*Out of Bounds* was masterminded by two brothers, Giles and Esmond Romilly, nephews of Winston Churchill and pupils at Wellington Col-lege. The Romilly brothers headed an editorial board made up of other pupil-delegates who had attended the FSS conference. A photograph of the board, published in the *Sunday Graphic* for 15 April 1934, identifies other members as H.F. Bartlett (St Paul's), P. Jeffries (University College School, London), and Miss M. Hartland (North London Collegiate School for Girls). Other 'conspirators', as a *Daily Mail* article about the 'Red Menace' in Britain's public schools labelled the pupils who contrib-uted to *Out of Bounds*, were drawn from a range of public and progressive schools including Wellington, Bootham, Charterhouse, and Rugby.[6]

It was the Romilly brothers whose energy and commitment brought the magazine into being. Esmond's involvement with *Out of Bounds* eventu-ally led him to run away from school and install himself in the back rooms of Parton's Bookshop. The bookshop in Parton Street, London was well known as both a centre for left-wing activists and British modernists (its owner, David Archer, published writers including Dylan Thomas and

---

[6] The *Daily Mail* article, 'Red Menace in the Public Schools', anticipated the first number of the magazine, appearing on 3 February 1934.

George Barker through the Parton Press).[7] There, while self-consciously living 'down and out' in London (Orwell's *Down and Out in Paris and London* had been published the year before), Esmond met and learned from some of the leading literary figures of the day. In addition to Barker and Thomas (who thought Esmond a fraud) these included James Joyce, Virginia Woolf, and T.S. Eliot, some of whom gave practical advice and financial support to the enterprise.

When, inspired by the circular announcing *Out of Bounds* to run away and join the group behind the magazine, Phillip Toynbee tracked the sixteen-year-old down in Parton Street, where he found 'a short, square, dirty figure with a square white face and sweaty hair' who was 'dramatically on his guard, conspiratorial, prepared for violent aggression or ingenious deceit' (Toynbee, 1980 14). This is the Esmond Romilly who, with Toynbee, joined the anti-fascist protest against Oswald Mosely's mass rally at Olympia on 7 June 1934 where they were battered by Mosely's Black Shirts (Toynbee 32). Esmond cuts a very different figure in the photograph of the Romilly brothers taken in 1935 to mark the publication of their joint memoir, *Out of Bounds: The Education of Giles and Esmond Romilly*. The photograph shows two clean-cut teenagers immaculately dressed in white shirts, ties, and waistcoats (a slightly more casual, knitted one in Esmond's case), looking for all the world like upstanding members of the Tory family into which they had been born.

In his half of the brothers' memoir, written while he was spending time in a remand home, Esmond describes how he and Giles used reading to educate themselves away from the teachings of home and school. Giles's opposition to war and the militarism of school, for example, was fuelled by Norman Angell's argument in *The Unseen Assassins* (1932) that military power was obsolete in an age of free-market capitalism but that economic separatism would inevitably lead to another war. Esmond's reading encompassed studies of communism and Marxism and a wide range of socialist and communist newspapers and magazines. He augmented his reading by joining a peace correspondence group, attending meetings and rallies, seeking out 'real live Communists', and spending time in left-wing haunts, including David Archer's bookshop (Romilly, *Education* 184; 192).

All of these activities and books associated with them find their way into the pages of *Out of Bounds* through polemical editorials and opinion pieces, critiques of public schools individually and as a system of

---

[7] In the brothers' memoir, Esmond invents names for Archer and his bookshop, presumably to disguise Archer's role in what was widely regarded as an unsavoury interlude; the mother of Philip Toynbee, one of Esmond's closest friends at the time, referred to Esmond as 'rotten meat' (Toynbee, 1980 32).

education, and reviews of left-wing books. Although *Out of Bounds* was for and about public schools, not all the original contributors were public school pupils. Esmond also involved two of his new London acquaintances, a pair of teenage working-class communists, in writing for and distributing the magazine. Unfortunately, R.E.D. (or Ruddy) Stanley and his brother Sidney (probably the same Sidney Stanley who came to public notice in a 1948 tribunal into government corruption) were something of a disappointment. It transpired that both were involved in criminal activities, and *Out of Bounds* 3 carries the emphatic disclaimer: 'We wish it to be known that neither S. Stanley, our Distributing Manager, nor R. Stanley, are any longer in any way connected with us' (3, 1934 2).

Unlike the long-lived *The Young Socialist*, with its modest production values, affordable cover price, and constant struggle to build its readership, the considerably more expensive *Out of Bounds* (costing a shilling an issue, it was not inexpensive even for well-to-do pupils) ran for only four numbers, but by number two had an impressive print-run of 3,000 and even carried some advertisements.[8] Reflecting the centrality of reviews and reading to the magazine, most of the advertisements are for books and bookshops, while the editors offer to supply 'political books or pamphlets of any kind' that readers found it difficult to obtain. They also announce plans to start a lending library (2, 1934 30). Unsurprisingly given the limited number of left-wing publishers and booksellers, despite the differences in their audiences, there was considerable overlap between the books recommended to readers of *Out of Bounds* and those of other left-leaning youth publications.

Reviews in *Out of Bounds* are reasonably lengthy (running to approximately 800 words) and in line with the discussion about shared reading by adults and youth in the Introduction, they move without comment between books aimed at an adult audience and those classified as children's literature. Among the reviews in the first number of *Out of Bounds* is *Memoirs of the Unemployed* (1934), a Victor Gollancz volume edited by Lance Beales and R.S. Lambert, both contributors to Gollancz's and Mitchison's *An Outline for Boys and Girls and Their Parents*. *Memoirs of the Unemployed* is a series of interviews with individuals who had lost their jobs. The young reviewer, L. Shinnie of Westminster School, calls it 'one of the most terrible indictments of the present form of society that it is possible to make' and identifies the volume as valuable to 'the public

---

[8] Eight hundred and fifty of the initial print-run of 1,000 were sold in twenty-three public schools; the rest were sold outside the public school network including, after any press coverage, in Piccadilly, where Esmond hawked it to passersby. How many copies were eventually sold is unclear.

school boy' not only for what it reveals about the conditions under which the unemployed live, but also because it shows 'that he too may suffer in the same way; for in this book are included two accounts from men who have no doubt been at public schools'.[9] Although he writes from the opposite side of the class divide, the lesson Shinnie draws from the book would have been at home in a review in *The Young Socialist*: 'members of the public schools', he concludes, 'can only make certain that they will not suffer the conditions depicted in this book if they join with the working classes to achieve a better society' (*Out of Bounds*, 2 35–6).

The need to improve society in ways of particular interest to those still at school is equally central to *Progressive Schools* (1934) by L.B. Perkin, also warmly received in *Out of Bounds*. The reviewer (P.D. Wellington) compares progressive schools' emphasis on freedom and trust with the system of control through oppression and suspicion in public schools, ending with the sombre reflection that 'It is depressing ... to read how one *might* have been educated, and to realise how much one has missed through an "orthodox" education' (3, 1934 36). Other reviews endorse John Strachey's *The Menace of Fascism* (another Gollancz publication), and two works are specifically for young readers: the Young Communist League pamphlet *Ten Points Against Fascism* ('Everyone interested in the fight against Fascism should not only buy this pamphlet, but learn the contents by heart' (41)) and Geoffrey Trease's *Bows Against Barons* [sic] (1934), published by Martin Lawrence. Trease's book found favour with the soon-to-be discredited R.E.D. Stanley, who 'wholeheartedly' recommends it as 'an enthralling study of England in the Middle Ages' that shows 'that every uprising has an economic cause' (2, 1934 41). Not all publications were so warmly received: predictably, *The Greater Britain* by Sir Oswald Mosley (published by the British Union of Fascists Headquarters, 1932) is derided for its 'fallacious jargon', 'untruthful economics', and 'idiocy' (2, 1934 39).

As well as reviews, *Out of Bounds* carried advertisements for books by left-wing publishers and radical bookshops, including an announcement for new books aimed at left-leaning readers published by Wishart & Co, soon to merge with Martin Lawrence. Other advertisements feature an offer from New Plan Books to supply books at trade prices to small groups and to help readers of *Out of Bounds* start up libraries; a magazine called *FIGHT* which covered 'the struggle against Fascism and War'; and an announcement by the League Against Imperialism for *China News* and *Indian Front*, two works described as 'important anti-imperialist publications'.

---

[9] Unlike the editors, who operated anonymously, except when writing articles or other contributions, presumably with a view to being able to continue publishing, reviewers and their affiliations tended to be given, though with varying levels of detail.

It is not clear how much revenue advertisements generated or what the advertisers' relationship with the magazine was. For example, an advertisement in *Out of Bounds* 2 for a book called *That's Sedition—That Was!* gives the name of its publisher as Sidney Stanley (the other discredited Stanley brother) of 4 Parton Street, the address of the bookshop where Esmond Romilly was based.

Reviews and advertisements sit alongside features including reports on events such as the 1933 Youth Congress in Paris (all the resolutions from that congress are covered and its 'Manifesto To the Youth of the Whole World' is reproduced). Contributors to *Out of Bounds* would have been familiar with Barbusse's pamphlet *You Are the Pioneers*, and his influence is evident in the magazine's rhetoric and concern to help the current generation avoid being drawn into a war that would not be of their making and that would benefit institutions, interest groups, and individuals of whom they disapproved. Shortly after the last number of *Out of Bounds* appeared in 1935, however, views about whether war could be legitimate took a marked turn in response to the spread of fascism in Europe.

## FIGHTING FASCISM: CHILDREN'S LITERATURE AND THE SPANISH CIVIL WAR

Although determined not to fight in a capitalist war, many of those on the Left had always accepted that it might be necessary to fight in a class war to liberate workers. Their position is embodied in the figure of Ellen Wilkinson, the Labour MP for Jarrow and a pacifist in the First World War who argued in her prophetically titled 1934 pamphlet *Why War?: A Handbook for Those that Will Take Part in the Second World War* that a war on behalf of the working masses would be justifiable (Overy, 2010 188). She identified the civil war in Spain as precisely such a conflict and, like many on the Left, gave her support to the International Brigades. It was not only those from working-class sections of the Left who took up the Republican cause: many writers, intellectuals, and liberals from all backgrounds not only supported the Republicans but also went to Spain in different capacities. Among them were both Romilly brothers, with Esmond serving as a solider in an International Brigade. In the closing lines of *Boadilla* (1937), which recounts his experience as one of only two survivors from his brigade during the defence of Madrid, Esmond explains his reasons for joining up and how he came to accept that defeating fascism required military action.

> I am not a pacifist, though I wish it were possible to lead one's life without the intrusion of this ugly monster of force and killing—war.... And it is not with the happiness of the convinced communist, but reluctantly, that

I realize that there will never be any peace, or any of the things that I like and want, until that mixture of profit-seeking, self-interest, cheap emotion and organized brutality which is called fascism has been fought and destroyed forever. (Romilly, 1937 286)

As the Romilly brothers' decision to become involved in the events in Spain suggests, there was much to capture the interest of children and young people in Britain about the conflict unfolding there; especially when 4,000 Spanish children who had been evacuated following the assault on Guernica arrived in Southampton in May 1936. It is perhaps surprising, then, how little was written about the Spanish Civil War for children and youth at the time.[10] Much of what *was* published did not agree with the Left's interpretation of it as a battle between ordinary people and fascist authority. Percy Westerman's *Under Fire in Spain* (1937) sides with the government, and so does Peter Dawlish's *Captain Peg-Leg's War* (1939), set in the fictional country of Savonia (clearly recognizable as Spain) where the elected government is under attack from a group of rebels mostly made up of foreigners. Captain W.E. Johns's *Biggles in Spain* (1939) is less partisan, and its complicated plot, full of misconstructions and unstable alliances, goes some way towards capturing the murky reality of the war. Though Biggles and his pals are accidentally drawn into the fighting and do not have an easy time trying to fulfil their task of carrying intelligence to the British government, being in the thick of the action is nonetheless made to seem exciting and purposeful.

As these stories suggest, a new war revived old war-story formulae so it is somewhat misleading that the best-remembered children's book associated with the Spanish Civil War, American Munro Leaf's picture book, *The Story of Ferdinand* (1936, published in Britain in 1937), is about a figure who refuses to fight. The eponymous Ferdinand is a bull who likes to sit under a cork tree and smell flowers and cannot be provoked into attacking the matadors in the bull ring, no matter what they do. Since the book was released a few months before the war in Spain broke out, Leaf and his illustrator, Robert Lawson, were giving expression to dwindling hopes for peace rather than advocating pacifism in the face of fascism. The war was still raging, however, when Walt Disney turned Leaf's story into an Oscar-winning animated film in 1938, by when it was known as a pacifist fable.

The Left Book Club (LBC) was unusual in producing a pamphlet for young people in conjunction with the British Youth Peace Assembly.

---

[10] Writing about the youth magazines produced in Britain's universities during the 1930s, Marwick too notes that 'the Spanish Civil War is given rather less prominence than one might expect', especially given the fact that some of the most distinguished of those who joined the fighting were, like Esmond Romilly, very young men (49).

Called *Unite for Peace* (1936), it shows rebel planes flying over Madrid and points to the international law 'which binds nations to assist friendly governments faced with revolt', meaning that Britain's non-intervention stance is 'a direct contravention of international custom and law... thus placing the legal government on an equal footing with the rebels' and providing a screen for aggressors' (MSS. 946/37/201-xvix 4–5). The majority of the pamphlet is geared towards mobilizing youth to join with youth from around the world to work for peace, but it ends with an appeal to raise funds to send relief to Spain. The appeal raised 110,000 tins of milk for the children of Spain which were delivered on a specially commissioned ship and delivered by a youth delegation representing a range of youth organizations (946/39/42i, 1936 4).

With so little in the way of writing specifically for them, children had to look elsewhere for information about the war in Spain and the children who had fled from the conflict and were now in their midst. Many would have learned about the presence of the Spanish youngsters through fundraising events made necessary by the British government's refusal to support the young refugees. The churches, charities, and trade unions that had called for and agreed to maintain the young Spaniards mobilized local communities to help look after the children. At least eighty-eight 'colonies'—locations where groups of *niños* were billeted—were established across the country; the scale of the undertaking meant that many British children would have been involved in supporting and caring for the young Spaniards until the majority were repatriated in 1939. Few of the refugees spoke English, and so the only book that told their story for them would have been key reading for radical families and all those involved in the care of the refugees. Although not marketed as a children's book, *The Basque Children in England; An Account of their Life at North Stoneham Camp* (1937) by 'Yvonne Cloud' (pen-name of the writer and left-wing activist Yvonne Meyer Kapp) is not only well within the abilities of competent young readers but, like *Not So Quiet:Stepdaughters of War*, it strongly resembles a children's book (Figure 1.5). *The Basque Children* is short, the print is large and clear, and the many photographic illustrations mostly feature children.[11] It was also the only book specifically about the Spanish children available while they were trying to make a new life in Britain.

---

[11] The photographs were by Bauhaus-trained Edith Tudor-Hart, Austrian-born communist and anti-fascist activist now remembered primarily as the Soviet agent who recruited British spies including Kim Philby. In 1936 her British husband, Dr Alex Tudor-Hart, joined the British Medical Aid Unit in Spain. Edith Tudor-Hart went on to become a notable photographer of children.

**Figure 1.5.** 'Basque and English school boys', North Stoneham Camp, Hampshire (1937) by Edith Tudor Hart. Image courtesy of National Galleries Scotland

Yvonne Cloud's text largely consists of a series of letters from a Spanish father to his three sons who are about to be evacuated. The language and style of the letters are simple, and because they are directed at real children, their sentiments and advice are entirely suitable for young readers. The letters tell the boys to look after each other and love all the other children travelling with them as if they were brothers. Understandably the boys' father is concerned about the reception they will receive in Britain, so the first letter coaches the boys on how to present themselves to their hosts:

> if they ask if you are Red, say plainly that you are proletarian, poor, human, and Christian. Say that you love best those who are workers, earning their bread with the labour of their hands, that you love the sacred mandates of the law of God, that I, your father, and the fathers of the other children ... do

not kill in aggression, but defend themselves; that all we ask for you is bread and peace.... (Cloud, 1937 10–11)

'Bread and peace' refers to Lenin's 1917 justification of revolution and identifies Britain as a country with a vested interest in wars that victimize the poor:

Two questions now take precedence over all other political questions—the question of bread and the question of peace. The imperialist war, the war between the biggest and richest banking firms, Britain and Germany, that is being waged for world domination, the division of the spoils, for the plunder of small and weak nations; this horrible, criminal war has ruined all countries, exhausted all peoples, and confronted mankind with the alternative—either sacrifice all civilisation and perish or throw off the capitalist yoke in the revolutionary way, do away with the rule of the bourgeoisie and win socialism and durable peace. (Lenin, 1917 n.p.)

As the reference to Lenin indicates, *The Basque Children in England* is a radical text that not only teaches children about how war might affect them, but also reflects the thinking of many on the liberal Left in Britain that the cure for war would involve new forms of social organization and an economic model other than capitalism. Many believed the way forward was being mapped in post-Revolutionary Russia and so, as Chapter 2 sets out, radical children's publications took up the cry that *Moscow has a plan*!

# 2

# Moscow has a Plan!

*Representations of the Soviet Union in Radical
Children's Literature*

During the 1930s and 1940s a cluster of radical children's books appeared
in Britain that depicted the Soviet Union as a grand experiment in which
technology and the sciences (at the time most disciplines aspired to the
condition of being a science) were being used to plan and deliver a new
way of managing society. As has already been noted, this was a time when
large parts of Britain were what E.M. Forster described as 'bitten with
Communism' (in Overy, 2010 288); in their depiction of life in the Soviet
Union these children's books capture the hope that the Soviets were
developing systems that could cure the booms, busts, and inequities of
capitalism that had disenfranchised and oppressed huge numbers of
people around the world, and which many blamed for the series of wars
that had punctuated the first decades of the twentieth century.[1] In these
books the Soviet experiment is regarded as the 'most exciting adventure in
the history of the world' (Stapledon in Mitchison, 1932 565), and writers
and illustrators used stories, characters, themes, and settings from or in the
USSR to create the desire in young readers for Britain to become a
Socialist state. As this and later chapters will show, radical children's
literature was deeply committed to internationalism, but in the case of
the Soviet Union, the task of getting young Britons interested in a distant
country and its people and politics was made easier because children and
childhood were proclaimed to be central to Soviet policies and propaganda. While the reality for most children was far from ideal, as Catriona
Kelly documents in *Children's World: Growing Up in Russia, 1890–1991*

---

[1] Britons' fascination with developments in the Soviet Union and communism more
generally was not unique. Mishler (2003), Mickenberg (2006), and Mickenberg and Nel
(eds) (2010) document the same phenomenon in the US. English-language texts often
migrated between the UK and the US and many were generated in a number of other,
mostly European, countries.

(2007), from the moment the Bolsheviks came to power they identified children as the future. It was soon widely reported in the USSR and abroad that Soviet children were happier, healthier, better educated, and had more opportunities for play, creativity, and genuine participation in the affairs of the country than they did anywhere else in the world (Kelly, 2007 61). A vision of the Soviet Union as a utopia for children became a staple of radical children's literature in Britain.

There were three principal ways in which radical children's books spread the good news about the Soviet Union in Britain. The first was through novels by Anglo-American writers about the Soviet Union; the second took the form of books by Soviet writers that were available in translation, while the third featured some of the outstanding picturebooks that were created in the USSR during the 1920s and 1930s. The quality and invention of these picturebooks were celebrated beyond the nursery and the classroom, and in Britain they were held up as evidence of the success of the Soviet system and its investment in the young. For example, in a 1934 article about 'Children's Books in Russia' for *Design for Today*, Russophile artist and writer Pearl Binder urged Britain to follow the Soviet example in the area of children's publishing: 'one of the lessons we might take to heart is their decision that only the very best is good enough for the future men and women of the world' (Binder, 1934 26). This chapter examines the three kinds of radical children's books that spread an image of the Soviet Union as an ideal world in the making, where children, childhood, and youth were valued and given important roles.

## DREAMING IN RED: CHILDREN'S BOOKS SET IN THE USSR

Throughout the 1930s, British children's books about life in the Soviet Union were infused with the desire for socialism to succeed, which means that they show the country in the best possible light. Nowhere is the Soviet story told in more glowing terms than in Naomi Mitchison and Victor Gollancz's *An Outline for Boys and Girls and Their Parents*. Its contributors subscribed wholeheartedly to the Soviet experiment, and Mitchison was an early visitor to the USSR. She travelled there for the first time in 1932, the same year that the *Outline* was published, as part of the Society for Socialist Inquiry and Propaganda. A 1981 memoir describes the high hopes she and her companions had when they set out. They travelled, she writes, in a

state of excitement and a kind of hope which probably none of us has ever quite experienced again. I think we should remember that this is how the

Russian revolution seemed to many of us, an awakening from a bad dream to
a clear day. (Mitchison, 1981 61–2)

It was in this spirit that Mitchison edited the *Outline* and, although at the
time of writing neither she nor any of her authors had actually been to the
Soviet Union, it was in the same spirit that many of them wrote for it. For
example, in his chapter on 'The Last Thirty Years or War and Revolution:
Why?' London School of Economics (LSE) lecturer Lance Beales is
fulsome in his praise for the way the Russian people had taken charge of
their own destiny, were rebuilding their country using the latest machinery and ideas, and had begun the work of redistributing wealth to make a
society where all were treated equally. 'Their example', he proclaims,
'provides a living inspiration to the working classes of other countries
and an unmistakable challenge to the defenders of the existing order in the
rest of the world' (in Mitchison, 1932 565). In the same vein Charles
Skepper, also at the LSE, extols Soviet adjustments to the institution of the
family for breaking down patriarchy and other traditional nexuses of
power, while Olaf Stapledon's vision of how society would work in the
future (discussed in detail in Chapter 7) is largely based on the 'new
models and machinery of government' being piloted in the USSR (in
Mitchison, 1932 723). The version of the Soviet Union put forward in the
*Outline* contrasts greatly with portraits of Russia found in mainstream books
for children written before, during, and after the Revolution. While often
critical of the Tsarist regime, no mainstream books support the idea of
revolution or the efforts of the Bolsheviks. For example, Bessie Marchant's
*Hope's Tryst* (1905) focuses on the oppressive surveillance culture in Tsarist
Russia while her *A Girl and a Caravan: the Story of Irma's Quest in Persia*
(1915), which despite its title is preoccupied with pre-revolutionary Russia,
warns against anarchy. Herbert Strang's *Brown of Moukden* (1906), set
during the Russo-Japanese war of 1904–5, is highly critical of the weak
Tsar and his officials; F.S. Brereton's *With Our Russian Allies* (1916)
supports the Tsar and shows Russian peasants as yokels who need to be
ruled, as, for the most part, does Charles Gilson's *In Arms for Russia* (1918).
Bessie Marchant's *A Dangerous Mission: a Tale of Russia in Revolution* (1918)
captures the widespread belief that, with a few adjustments, the old regime
could have been made good. When Russia withdrew from the First World
War, Escott Lynn's 1918 *Knights of the Air* captured the mainstream
attitude that the Tsar's rule had been replaced by one even more tyrannous.[2]

---

[2] Jane Rosen's 'In Darkest Russia' (2014) discusses all of these texts in more detail.
Rosen also points out that a sympathetic treatment of a character who has suffered under
the Tsar is found in E. Nesbit's 1906 *The Railway Children*.

The *Outline* is typical of the pro-Soviet tone and rhetoric found in radical writing for children, whether information books and biographies about Soviet leaders produced in Britain or novels based on child characters who travel to and across the country. The seeds for the first of these novels were sown when Geoffrey Trease and Martin Lawrence learned that Trease's *Bows Against the Barons* had been translated into Russian and was in its fourth edition there, with sales exceeding 100,000 copies (Trease, 1971 208). Although international copyright laws did not pertain in the USSR, the Soviet publisher had no wish to deny a fellow traveller his rightful earnings; however, payment could only be made in roubles which had to be spent in the USSR. Trease and his wife decided to go in person to collect his royalties and spend them on a five-month residency (at 75 per cent, the generosity of the royalty payment gave Trease the idea of returning to settle in Moscow if he could not make a better living in the UK) (GT/05/01 208). The trip formed the basis for *Red Comet: A Tale of Travel in the U.S.S.R.* (1936).

From the 1920s the Soviet Union was visited by numerous official trade delegations, trade union excursions, political and scientific expeditions, and independent travellers from both the UK and the US (Nicholson, 2009 57). Most were ideologically predisposed to like what they saw; as the travel writer Robert Byron commented disparagingly, there was a high degree of predictability about both the trips and the accounts they generated. Most visitors, he complained in 1933, spent 'three weeks gaping at belt conveyers...and return[ed] to proclaim the dawn of human happiness' (Byron, 2011 61). *Red Comet* belongs to the large body of writing from the 1920s and 1930s for both adults and children that features accounts of travel around the Soviet Union. In works for adults the focus tends to be on centralized planning, collective agriculture, and industrialization (all those conveyer belts). Children's books such as Trease's focus more on the breaking down of social barriers, opportunities for work, and facilities specially catering for the young.

Since Geoffrey Trease is remembered as a writer of historical fiction, *Red Comet* stands out for its focus on the future and the use of a framing story featuring a wholly invented amphibious flying machine, the eponymous Red Comet. The plot begins when brother and sister, Peter and Joy, prevent the theft of Red Comet, the prototype for a revolutionary flying machine developed by their neighbour, Jim. Jim invites the pair to accompany him on a trip to the Soviet Union, where he hopes to sell his plans for Red Comet to the forward-looking Russians since Britain is too backward to appreciate it. Making an advanced airplane the fulcrum of the story is a nice gesture to Soviet pride in 'Stalin's Eagles', the aviators who were celebrated across the country for breaking flying records and undertaking heroic rescues (Fitzpatrick, 1999 72). They fly from city to city so that Jim can attend meetings, and while he is talking business the children explore.

Although stylistically and at the levels of plot and characterization *Red Comet* is far from Trease's most accomplished novel, it is nonetheless significant as the first book by a British writer to attempt to convey what it was like to grow up in the Soviet Union in the 1930s. The novel's weaknesses can in part be attributed to the fact that it was commissioned and published by International Publishers, the Moscow-based state publishing house that was sponsoring the Treases' visit; together with his pro-Soviet bias at the time (he modified his ideas considerably by the end of the 1930s) this would no doubt have inclined him to be uncritical. *Red Comet* was also written at speed: it was completed within the five-month residency while Trease was also undertaking official duties for his sponsor and writing about the trip for a number of newspapers and journals back home. The Author's Note indicates that the book was tested on young readers in Yalta in the Crimea, a practice Trease had observed in some of the children's libraries he visited on the trip. It is unclear whether he read his story to them in English or if his young Soviet audience heard it in a translated version; either way, *Red Comet* flatters local listeners more than it questions official accounts of life in the USSR.

Although Trease always claimed that he and his wife were free to choose where to go and what to see, they evidently stuck closely to the kinds of destinations favoured by the official state tourist agency, Intourist. Founded in 1929, Intourist was designed to promote an image of the Soviet Union as a thriving, technologically advanced society run for the good of the people. Officially approved travel itineraries for visitors tended to feature visits to crèches, maternity homes, parks of rest and culture, factories, and collectivized farms as well as the more usual tourist fare of theatres, museums, and galleries. This explains the frequency with which certain places, amenities, and aspects of life in the USSR recur in books set there. The Intourist influence on Trease's account of life in the Soviet Union should not be underestimated. On Naomi Mitchison's first visit she was firmly discouraged from visiting some of the ancient archaeological sites she had read about and which were well off the regular tourist route. When she finally succeeded in gaining permission to visit some ancient tombs on the southern steppes, she was left to fend for herself. This meant travelling 'like a Russian', including on a boat which she found to be dirty, flea-ridden, uncomfortable, overcrowded, and hierarchical (Mitchison, 1981 64). As a feminist she was particularly disappointed that although women were allowed to do men's work, attitudes were in other ways still very patriarchal and sexist. As will become apparent, this episode makes a useful point of comparison with radical children's books about travelling in the USSR, most of which include very different accounts of boat journeys. A lengthy journey by boat up the Volga provides an extended episode in *Red Comet*, an example of how Trease introduces a number of what were to become stock-in-trade features of children's and youth fiction about contemporary life in the Soviet Union.

Everything Peter and Joy do on their travels is in line with an Intourist-approved itinerary. They meet a plethora of friendly English-speaking locals who serve to demonstrate the enthusiasm for learning among the Soviet population and make Peter and Joy feel ashamed of their inability to speak any language other than English. The Soviet youngsters they meet proudly tell them about their fulfilling lives and show the two British children how a better new world is emerging from the ruins of the old. Soon Peter and Joy begin to make unfavourable comparisons with their lives at home and particularly the way opportunities are circumscribed on the basis of class, sex, and economic exigency. As they fly over St Petersburg, they see 'thousands of modern flats' for the workers and factory chimneys rising amidst the palaces and cathedrals of 'bygone days'. The conjunction deliberately makes the factories analogous to palaces and cathedrals in their grandeur and status while the text goes on to explain that the new cities have been designed for the convenience of the workers and to benefit the country by reducing time spent travelling to work and rationalizing facilities in given areas. Peter and Joy are impressed to discover that instead of neighbourhoods determined by the wealth of the people who live in them, in the Soviet Union people of all backgrounds and professions live in the same kinds of houses and the same parts of cities. This egalitarian way of managing housing becomes one of the recurring motifs of radical children's books about life in the new Socialist utopia. So too do descriptions of the wonderful recreational facilities available to Soviet children.

Peter and Joy visit a park with a Children's City where they enjoy a parachute jump and discover a series of buildings dedicated to different activities. In the House of Young Technicians they see children doing carpentry, conducting experiments in science laboratories, working with radio and photographic equipment, building model cars, and tinkering with real engines in an automobile shop. The Artists' House caters in the same way for those who want to learn to dance, sing, draw, or paint, and there are equivalents for other skills and disciplines. Peter and Joy are surprised to discover that the children manage all the facilities themselves. When they ask why there are no adults to make sure things are not damaged, their new friend is equally surprised by their question. 'Why should they damage their own property?' she asks. 'They all know that the park and everything in it belongs to them. Only a fool would spoil what is his own' (Trease, 1936 55). This is just one of many times when what the

British children have accepted as common sense is called into question, along with any thoughts they might have had about the relative wealth and superiority of the British way of life. Indeed, the cheerful and invested optimism of the children they meet is deliberately contrasted with their own situations and that of many young people in the Depression-era West. At fourteen Peter has already left school and, like his father, is unemployed, meaning that the family cannot afford for Joy to continue her education, though she wants to. Their prospects are bleak, but the Soviet children they meet are eager to learn because 'we've got something to get on to' (207).

Different amenities especially for children are experienced everywhere the children go. In Kiev there is, among other things, a vast toy library where, a new young friend tells them, 'Thousands of children come here daily.... They have their own restaurant, an open-air stage for concerts, and a special bathing place.... In winter, the park is flooded so that they can slide and skate' (71). They are taken to huge sports stadia just for children, one of the 100 Soviet children's theatres (this one seats 657) where they see a performance of *A Midsummer Night's Dream* adapted for children, and a children's library with 50,000 books in fifty-eight languages. Trease's novel clearly lends support to Pearl Binder's claim that in Soviet Russia, 'only the very best is good enough for the future men and women of the world'. Despite all the wonderful things they see and experience, Peter and Joy cannot help noticing that much remains to be finished and that the Soviet people exercise a kind of double vision which enables them to disregard present circumstances and project themselves into the future, when they believe things will be better. For example, when they ask one of their new friends about the mostly unfinished building work around them, he happily acknowledges that there is much to be done before explaining that it was much worse before and will soon be much better: 'For every bad thing you can tell us, we can tell you a dozen more. But we are doing away with them every month. Have you seen our Metro? Our Park of Culture—which was the city rubbish dump before the Revolution!' (63–4). His vision of the future is so compelling that Joy can 'almost see the city taking shape amid the clouds of cigarette smoke in the café' where they are talking (63–4). As the Soviet cultural historian, Sheila Fitzpatrick, observes, this attitude captures the workings of the doctrine of Socialist realism adopted under Stalin. Fitzpatrick explains how Soviet citizens were trained to see what would become rather than to focus on the material reality of the present (1992 217). She cites Marjorie Fischer's *Palaces on Monday* (1936), another radical children's book from this period, as typifying Socialist realism in action (Figure 2.1). Fitzpatrick (born 1941) read *Palaces on Monday* as a girl growing up in a left-wing

**Figure 2.1.** 'The Children's Train'. Illustration by Richard Floethe for *Palaces on Monday*, 1937. Permission to reproduce the image courtesy of the art estate of Richard Floethe

household in Melbourne and recalls it as, 'A fellow-travelling book about Russia' and 'what fun people seem to have there... how totally unlike anything in Melbourne—that they should share a collective expectation of a better future' (Fitzpatrick, 2010 69–70).

Little is known about Marjorie Fischer, but her book was published simultaneously in the US and UK in 1936 and became a Puffin paperback in 1944 (this was the version the young Sheila Fitzpatrick read), ensuring that it reached a mainstream audience at a time when the Soviets were key allies in the fight against Hitler's Germany. Better told and more satisfying than *Red Comet*, it uses many of the same episodes, settings, and devices to give readers a sense that the Soviet Union was a juvenile utopia where children were living rich and exciting lives. *Palaces on Monday* features another brother and sister, Peter and Judy, who travel to the USSR from New York, where they have been living in increasing penury and anxiety because their engineer-father has been unemployed for two years. When he is offered a job helping to build railways in Russia, the children's parents go on ahead while Peter and Judy finish the school year. This means that the children travel unaccompanied to join their parents. They change ships in the UK, where a family friend takes them sightseeing in London. The city strikes them as stuck in the past and decrepit. As they leave England for Leningrad Judy pointedly sings, 'London bridge is falling down, falling down, falling down' (Fischer, 1944 34).

With Susan, a new friend from Lancashire whose parents are also working in the USSR, they undertake the obligatory river journey, this time along the Volga from Leningrad to Moscow, before travelling by train to Gorky, then on to Stalingrad and beyond. After a journey by air over the Caucasian mountains, they are finally reunited with their parents. As in *Red Comet*, the children's travels are used to give a sense of the scale of the country and its vastly different terrains, climates, ethnicities, and cultures. (While flying across the Soviet landscape Trease's children learn that the USSR covers one sixth of the Earth and has 180 different nationalities speaking 150 languages; later, on board a ship, they see people dancing and sharing music from what were once independent countries in a show of how coming together has enriched the new Soviet culture.) Peter and Judy too go to children's parks and palaces of culture, and learn that children are contributing to the work of modernizing the country, whether by painting a wall in the new Metro system (the Metro features in all three books), repairing a car for an important film director who is making a film to remind the next generation of life before the Revolution, or designing a model glider.

Like Peter and Joy, Peter and Judy are struck by the differences between the socially divided nature of their home country and the comradely behaviour on the many Soviet forms of transport on which they travel. On one boat they meet Ted, a black boy whose parents have emigrated from the US. This forces them to acknowledge and overcome prejudices they did not know they had and which do not exist in Fischer's USSR.[3] Racism is not the only issue they confront: Peter is initially challenged by the fact that girls and women are treated as equals to men and do all the jobs that men do. It is not until he understands that there is more than enough work for everybody that he feels able to acknowledge that the females around him are as capable as the males. As Naomi Mitchison observed when travelling on her own, it was not just outsiders like Peter who struggled with issues around equality: it took time for cultural attitudes to women to change.

One of the principal differences Peter and Judy experience is in attitudes to the future and children's capacity to help bring a new, fulfilling society into being. Like Peter and Joy in *Red Comet*, they have travelled from a country where the future was bleak: with no work Peter and Judy have little prospect of fulfilling their respective ambitions to become an engineer and an actor. Almost as soon as they arrive in the USSR, however, both children have opportunities to use their talents and prove their worth. When he finds himself helping to drive the engine of a miniature train built, maintained and managed by children, Peter proclaims his achievements and delights in the possibilities ahead: 'I'm everything.... I'm a Ford-fixer, and a whistle-blower, and a boy, and an engineer. I'm anything I want to be' (Fischer, 1937 127). The book ends with Peter, Judy, Susan, and Ted spending the summer at Artek, the special camp in the Crimea for those who have made outstanding contributions to Soviet society.[4] This is not just a happy ending but a radical message. After weeks exploring their new country, Peter and Judy are happy, independent, and forward-looking. Their Soviet experiences celebrate the benefits of turning a social vision into a reality. It is tempting to suggest that Geoffrey Trease and Marjorie Fischer were caught up in the Socialist realist gaze; that they saw the future in the present, and presented the vision rather than the reality to their readers. In fact, rather than simply reproducing a Socialist realist state of mind, both *Red Comet* and *Palaces on Monday* subtly encourage readers to think about the difference between a powerful vision of the future and the ability to bring it to fruition.

---

[3] The reality was rather different. Despite the inclusive official rhetoric, in reality those who were not ethnically Russian were widely discriminated against (Kelly, 2007 9).

[4] Holidays feature in all the radical children's books about life in the USSR as a way of ensuring that readers realize that whatever their background or profession, Soviet workers enjoyed a state-sponsored month of fresh air, good simple food, and enjoyable exercise in parts of the country that had previously been the exclusive playgrounds of the wealthy.

## USSR: FACT OR FANTASY?

Marjorie Fischer portrays the USSR as a world in transition with everyone dreaming of what the country will be like when the succession of Five-Year Plans have transformed it into the model society of the future. Everywhere Peter and Judy go they find past, present, and future colliding. One of the first people they meet tells them, 'The future is very close to the present with us . . . . Everything moves fast' (Fischer, 1944 48). The children echo that insight periodically in observations such as: 'Soon and now is all mixed up here' (55) and 'The future is real . . . we're flying right into it' (134). Like *Red Comet*, *Palaces on Monday* is whole-hearted in its enthusiasm for the values and work that characterize Soviet life and aspirations and the idea of planning and building an equitable society freed from the divisions and instabilities of capitalism. The books determinedly avoid mentioning hardships and shortages, and other inconveniences of everyday life in Stalin's Russia. Nonetheless, Fischer and Trease both point to the need to proceed with caution; these are not works that advocate revolution. Trease, writing for a Soviet publisher, only goes so far as to employ the elements of a science fiction framing story in his futuristic Red Comet, suggesting that the Socialist world he describes also belongs to a perhaps distant future. Fischer, however, regularly reminds readers of the magnitude of the task facing the Soviets and any other nation setting up new economic and social systems. The last line of the book, 'Second to the right . . . and straight on till morning' comes from J.M. Barrie's *Peter Pan* which, like Lewis Carroll's *Alice's Adventures in Wonderland*, is a frequently invoked intertext. In combination with the epigraph which gives the book its title (a nursery rhyme about 'An Eastern juggler' who 'Planted plum pips on Sunday, / Which came up palaces on Monday'), *Palaces on Monday* creates a sense of the fantastical about the Soviet Union. The fantasy dimension does not devalue the vision or the determination of the Soviet project, but it does raise questions about whether the dream can be sustained and if not, whether the Soviet people—and all those following their progress—will, like Alice and the Darling children, be returned to the old reality. Not every example of radical children's literature set in the Soviet Union was so circumspect.

In *Russian Families* (1942), which she both wrote and illustrated, Pearl Binder offers a less formulaic and entirely uncritical account of Soviet life. Although she grew up near Manchester, Binder's roots were in the Soviet Union: her father emigrated to Britain from a town on the border between Russia and Ukraine. Born in 1904, her life encompassed that of the USSR (she died in 1990), where she travelled extensively and with which she strongly identified.[5] Her closest friend was a Russian translator who knew Lenin, Kalinin (a one-time revolutionary who served as President of the USSR from 1919–46), and Trotsky, all of whom feature in another of Binder's books about Russia, *Misha and Masha* (1936). A collection of stories about the different kinds of people who helped call the new Soviet Union into being and what happens to them as the state matures, *Misha and Masha* is built around the figure of Masha, a young girl who participates in the 1917 Revolution. The stories show children as equally courageous and capable as adults and in them, as in *Russian Families*, Binder addresses an audience of both children and adults. She does not assume children need simpler stories than adults or that they ought to be protected from knowledge about sex, birth, or death. Nor does she assume that adults are cleverer than children or have ceased to enjoy illustrations. However, despite its grounding in contemporaneous Soviet attitudes to children and its emphasis on the way life for ordinary people improved under the Soviet system, its historical overview means that *Misha and Masha* sits outside the group of stories about everyday life in the USSR.

Pearl Binder's close ties with the Soviet Union make *Russian Families* the most intimate of the books set there and a transition point for moving on to examine books written inside the Soviet Union. Trease's and Fischer's novels feature child characters from Britain and America who are travelling in the USSR, and while this is a useful device for comparing the two countries, it means readers are always looking through the eyes of characters who are outsiders. *Russian Families* is told entirely from the perspective of Russian characters and it is generously illustrated with black-and-white drawings from sketchbooks Binder filled while on visits to the Soviet Union. The story begins by taking readers into a Russian home in a large modern block of apartments such as those Peter and Joy observed from *Red Comet*. It is the eve of a wedding, and friends from many parts of the country have come together to start the celebrations. The guests are introduced in terms of the work they do; no differences are made between the work of men and women, the skilled and the unskilled, the highly educated, and those who are studying after having been denied education in the past. All are equally caught up in the project of building their country, and believe that what they are doing is at the cutting edge of science and technology and will transform not just their world but the whole of this world and possibly even worlds as yet unknown. The young bride, Ludmilla, feels

---

[5] An account of Pearl Binder's life by her children and others who knew her as well as reproductions of some of her drawings and lithographs can be found at the blog, Spitalfields Life: http://spitalfieldslife.com/2010/05/01/pearl-binder-artist-writer/.

sure that her children would live to see great things in the wonderful future
that was literally just around the corner. She felt the world to be on a knife-
edge of scientific developments which would alter the whole pattern of
living... immensely faster communication for instance, the possibility of
interplanetary communication, the conquest of disease and the total aboli-
tion of poverty all over the world.... She had no economic fears for the
future: she felt sure that so long as they played their part fairly in Soviet life
they were secure from want, and their children would be well cared-for,
properly educated and made into worthwhile people. (Binder, 1942 5)

Ludmilla displays the same cheerful confidence in a bright future that is 'just
around the corner' characteristic of Socialist realism, but in this case Binder
strikes no warning note. Ludmilla's optimism is constantly vindicated as, for
instance, when the wedding guests venture out into Moscow and find it a
bustling, cheerful city full of pregnant women; a city where life is steadily
improving (11) (Figure 2.2).

The wedding party is served with copious amounts of rich food, and
though there is no honeymoon for the bride and groom (both must work
the next day), they retire content to a borrowed bedroom: 'They had
work, love, friends. What more could anyone want?' (21). The youngest
wedding guest, a one-year-old who is 'pure Uzbech on his mother's side,
Russian, with some Volga-German and a touch of Napoleonic French on
his father's', is offered as proof that the Soviets are creating a future in
which the best of all the constituent countries are being combined to make
a healthy, attractive, international citizenship.

[The child's] hair was yellow as butter, silky-straight and cut in a tight fringe
over his broad benign forehead. His skin was tawny gold like his mother's
but with rosy cheeks like a European child. His eyes were quite black, with
smoothly hidden Asiatic lids. His lips were full, opulently curved, disclosing
several strong white teeth. (35)

*Russian Families* features all the amenities for children described in *Red
Comet* and *Palaces on Monday* and adds to them facilities for infants and very
young children. Like much in Binder's book, the picture it paints is both
idealized and based on the metropolitan Russian centre rather than representing the reality across the Soviet Union. The one-year-old wedding guest,
for instance, is cared for in an immaculate and well-provisioned crèche with
excellent home-made food. Although this is the kind of facility envisaged in
the 1936 'Mother and Child Decree', the reality for most children was more
limited (Kelly, 2007 404). Since the purpose of *Russian Families* is to
encourage readers to recreate the Soviet model in Britain, no shortcomings
are shown. Instead, Binder resorts to the Socialist realist strategy of treating
the imagined future as if it were the present reality. For instance, the book

**Figure 2.2.** Untitled image by Pearl Binder for *Russian Families*, 1942. Permission to reproduce the image courtesy of Pearl Binder Design Archives, Brighton University. The Bodleian Library, University of Oxford 25614 d.2

does not acknowledge the pressure on women to work that requires the boy to go to the crèche whether or not this is what his family wishes. Instead, it focuses on his mother's achievements: Doctor Gulson-oi Kravchenko stands for all that is best about the new Soviet society. She is not only the head of a gynaecological clinic but a loving mother and a beautiful woman whose 'cropped ebony hair' identifies her beauty as of the androgynous kind suited to an egalitarian society. She is an emblem of the bright future for women in the USSR that makes Ludmilla hope to have a daughter because there is 'so much for girls to do now in Soviet Russia—their lives were so full and fearless, and she could become anything she chose if she was intelligent and worked hard' (6).

The doctor's son is cared for by Ludmilla's mother, 'Mama Pavlova'. This former peasant has been a working woman all her life; now, in her traditional capacity as child-minder, she symbolizes the state's love for its people and the benefits of its investment. Official pronouncements decreed that crèches and nurseries should be places for 'individual development in a family atmosphere' (Kelly, 2007 403) and the crèche where Mama Pavlova works is a place where children of mixed ages, ethnicities, and both sexes play together as if they were indeed one big family. The games they play, the stories they listen to, and the toys provided for them are all designed to foster collaboration and collective problem-solving. As the books that make up the next part of this chapter show, many children growing up in the USSR did find themselves at the centre of state attention and had materials and spaces created for them, but in the case of *Russian Families*—and indeed all the books about the Soviet Union for young British readers—it is important to distinguish between fictional constructions of childhood and the lives of real children. More common than the superb facilities Binder writes about were improvised places for children 'in corridors, kitchens, or the "red corner" of the workers' barracks' (Kirschenbaum, 2001 139) with little equipment, few trained teachers, and low educational content. Quite different insights into life for children in Soviet Russia than Pearl Binder's are found in translated works by Soviet writers of the period.

## LIVING THE DREAM? TRANSLATED STORIES OF SOVIET CHILDHOODS

In his Preface to Nikolai Ognyov's *The Diary of a Communist Undergraduate* (1929), the sequel to a school story discussed below, the book's translator, Alexander Werth, points to the appetite for news about Russia in Britain and the limitations he saw in what was then available.

> 'What's happening in Russia?' is the question that has been and is still being asked even by those who never were in the least interested in Russia *as a country*... almost every week we have some new book by someone who has taken a ten days' trip to Moscow, and who is at last going to tell us 'the truth about Russia.' The fact that the...gentleman doesn't know a word of Russian and has seen no more of Russia than a gala show at the State Opera...doesn't deter him.... As information, these 'last words' are hardly worth the ink with which they are written...in almost every case, the 'last word' could have been written without going to Russia. (in Ognyov, 1929 9)

The extent of publishing activity can be judged by Philip Grierson's *Books on Soviet Russia 1917–1942* (1943), a list of the published sources about the Soviet Union then available. Grierson covers a wide range of publications including scholarly books, reference works, guide-books, periodicals, educational texts, British parliamentary papers, and novels. Of the ninety-five books listed, twelve, so more than a tenth, are for children. Geoffrey Trease's *Red Comet* and Marjorie Fischer's *Palaces on Monday* are two of the nineteen novels Grierson names.

While for the purposes of this study it is significant that Grierson includes children's books, in this area at least his list is not exhaustive.

No mention is made, for instance, of Eileen Squire's excellent *Orphans of St. Petersburg* (1938), which combines a satisfying narrative with a good account of the 1917 Revolution and ensuing years as experienced by a once wealthy young girl and her siblings. After a period of hardship and mental break-down during which she is well cared for by the state, Lydia, the oldest of the children, discovers the whole country has been set to work and decent housing is being provided for all the workers. She and her sister, for example, share 'a large airy room' (Squire, 1938 151) that they furnish with possessions from their grand former home. These have been preserved for them as part of official policy and records about the children's entitlement carefully kept. So impressed is Lydia by the honourable treatment she receives that she becomes a guide for Intourist, showing visitors to Leningrad 'the New Russia—factories, schools, clinics, day-nurseries, collective farms, and all the other countless activities that had been put in hand by the new *régime*' and how 'the Government of the U.S.S.R. are making good all of their promises, since the trying days of the Revolution' (151). Squire's book is also notable for its depiction of Lydia's brother as one of the children who lived wild in post-Revolutionary Russia.

Another book missing from Grierson's list is Lev Kassil's *The Story of Alesha Ryazan and Uncle White Sea* (1935), which also deals with an orphan boy who lives on the streets. The boy, Alesha, runs away when a well-meaning man tries to send him to the State Labour Commune for Waifs. Having grown up in feudal Russia, Alesha fears this will mean a life of harsh servitude, although the man tries to explain that he will be looked after and taught a trade because in Lenin's Republic 'there must be no hapless, homeless waifs, there must be young, happy citizens' (Kassil, 1935 22). The text is not being ironic; this story fully supports the state. Eventually Alesha ends up in a Labour Camp which turns out to be the first step in his becoming a national hero, for he risks his life to save the great dam he is helping to build. Other books missing from Grierson's list are discussed below; while it is not exhaustive, Grierson's map of the extent and range of publishing about the USSR is nonetheless helpful in showing how radical writing for children and young people was fully involved in efforts to report on and evaluate what was happening in that country, not least by getting first-hand information and accounts.

The earliest of the radical children's books originating in Russia that were not written for a British audience is Nikolai Ognyov's *The Diary of a Communist Schoolboy*, published by Victor Gollancz in 1928. This is a fictional diary about events in a single school during one academic year as experienced by schoolboy Kostya Riabtsov. Because the school story was such a well-established genre in Britain, similarities and differences between life for young people under the Bolsheviks and in Britain are readily apparent, obviating the need for the didactic explanations found in some of the translated books from the Soviet Union such as Arkady Gaidar's *Timur and his Comrades* (1940) which is discussed below. For instance, while Young Pioneers rather than sporting captains are the leaders of the school, such things as the rivalries and related pranks between groups of pupils and the separate worlds of teachers and pupils are very familiar from British school stories. Notable differences include the power pupils wield over teachers (teachers are denounced for teaching in pre-Revolutionary ways) and the pervasive atmosphere of surveillance and threat. Early in the new school year, for example, Kostya is warned not to be friends with Lina G because her father is a priest, or a 'servant of the Cult', and the Alliance of Communist Youth (ACY) disapproves of friendships between boys and girls (Ognyov, 1928 11). Ognyov period-ically defuses this atmosphere through humour that for the most part stems from Kostya's naïve pronouncements: at fifteen years and five months he is the Adrian Mole of his day. Typically, after being warned about Lina he writes,

> Lina doesn't exist for me as a woman, but only as a comrade; on the whole I look down on our girls with a certain amount of contempt. They are all interested in clothes and shoes and dancing, and most of all in gossip. If people were put in jail for gossip, not a single girl would remain in our group. (11)

His 'confession' shows him to be callow and sexist although he regards himself as worldly and wise.

One of the most obvious moments when something familiar appears in a strange new guise is found in Kostya's entry about watching a perform-ance of *Red Cinderella* performed by first-grade pupils. As he tells it, the story becomes a comic example of the practice of replacing the royal figures from traditional tales with the new cast of Soviet heroes. The first-graders' *Red Cinderella* features

> two bourgeois sisters and a third one who's a washerwoman; I don't know who wrote it, but I don't believe such a thing is possible, especially with all three living in the same house. Then the two bourgeois sisters go to a dance and Red Cinderella is left behind to wash the dishes. Suddenly a fellow in a red shirt comes in and hands Cinderella a proclamation. She reads it, then puts on one of her sister's dresses and goes out. (88)

All goes more or less according to the traditional tale until the Prince, having found Cinderella and done the slipper test, proposes. At this point 'the agitator in the red shirt appears again and declares that a revolt has broken out, and starts kicking the Prince in the backside' (89). The performance ends with the aristocracy humbled and everyone singing *The Internationale*.

Although he is somewhat bemused by *Red Cinderella* and likes to regard himself as superior to the group of students who were are 'fond of swank' (32) and the first to become Pioneers, Kostya gradually comes to terms with the relationship between school, state, and youth organizations. *The Diary of a Communist Schoolboy* ends with Kostya being accepted as a member of the ACY and charged with setting up a new group of Young Pioneers. For Werth, Kostya's initial ambivalence and the many contradictory and disturbing aspects of life in school during the first decade of Bolshevik rule distinguish Ognyov's school story from the 'last words' of those who, like Naomi Mitchison, were inquiring into and sometimes propagandizing on behalf of the Soviet Union on the basis of short highly orchestrated visits.[6] The importance of the ACY in Ognyov's novel underlines the extent to which the Soviet Union leadership kept children and young people in their sights while they set about making the next generation new in ways that encouraged them to accept and invest in the state. Children were to be 'the vanguard of cultural change' (Kelly, 2007 1) which, as the art historian Arkady Ippolitov observes in an essay on Russian children's books of the 1920s and 1930s, meant children and childhood had to be changed: 'In order that children would mesh with the radiant future being built for them, they themselves had to be rebuilt.... Children had to be not merely new...but radically new' (in Rothenstein and Budashevskaya, 2013 19). Education and books were central to these efforts, but though they were principally intended to form part of children's and young people's political education, the high artistic quality of many of the books testifies to the fact that they were the product of a political culture that saw children as citizens who, like Kostya, were being trained for future roles as workers and leaders.

The potential for children to contribute to Soviet society is central to another of the books listed by Grierson, Mikhail Ilin's *Moscow has a Plan: A Soviet Primer* (1931). Written to explain Stalin's First Five-Year Plan to the children of the Soviet Union, *Moscow has a Plan* was rapidly translated into many languages, enabling children across the world to read about that massive undertaking. Like many of the radical children's books published in the UK, the translation came by way of the US, where it was presented as a book for teachers; in the UK, however, it remained a children's book. *The Young Socialist*'s 'Mr Wiseacre' recommended it as 'a thrilling account

---

[6] After her first trip to the USSR Naomi Mitchison wrote more circumspectly about that country. Her controversial (because it covered abortion, rape, 'free-love', and enslavement) adult novel *We Have Been Warned* (1935) is noticeably darker in its view of the prospects for humanity. Over time Mitchison's hopes for a new world shifted from Soviet Russia to Africa.

of a brave undertaking' and an antidote to the hostility to machines and technology that he feared was holding back Britain's adult population. The 'brave undertaking' is the First Five-Year Plan but, far from being the turgid mixture of political rhetoric and economic data that might suggest, he promises readers that in it they will read about

> great railways being built across deserts of snow and deserts of sand, of mighty dams made to tame the wild waters of the rivers, of oil wells, of iron foundries, of farms where animals and machines work together, and of how even children play their part in the building up of a new Russia out of the ruins of the old. (*The Young Socialist*, 1934 44)

So sure was he of the significance and appeal of Ilin's book that Mr Wiseacre made a copy of *Moscow has a Plan* the 'very good' prize for the competition that always featured at the end of the column in which it features (45).

*Moscow has a Plan* begins with a series of figures—and this is one of the features of his writing that impressed the book's American translators. As they explain in 'A Word to the American Reader', Ilin manages to make complex economic and scientific information and unfamiliar subjects such as social planning not just intelligible to children, but 'literally fascinating' (in Ilin, 1931 vii). In part this is done by engaging storytelling: *Moscow has a Plan* is dramatic, informative, and humorous by turns, and the action is epic: mountains are moved, rivers are created, and prairies are tilled as workers undertake to make the vast landscape of the Soviet Union give up its resources, provide power, and grow crops to feed comrades of all ages. For young readers both inside and outside the USSR, much of the book's appeal lay in the way it highlights the important role they have to play in bringing the new future into being. For example, having followed the work of the scientists and explorers who travelled to remote corners of the republic in pursuit of minerals, sources of power, and areas that can be cultivated, the book turns to the contributions children were making. Just as Kostya and his classmates measure, map, and record the local history of their village in preparation for electrification, so Ilin's readers are charged to undertake tasks that will benefit the state. *Moscow has a Plan* includes a 'Children's Five-Year Plan' with tasks ranging from gathering at least forty pounds of useful 'junk' (rags, ropes, wool, bones, scrap-metal) for use in factories and planting trees, to discovering mineral deposits, helping with crops, and teaching the illiterate to read. These tasks, Ilin assures readers, are not insignificant:

> If children fulfil their Five-Year Plan, they will save from parasites grain worth £400,000.
>
> If children add two good laying hens each to the possessions of each household, they will make a present to the State of five billion eggs, £20,000,000.

From pennies, millions are composed; weak hands, if they be many, can move mountains and plant forests of trees.

Herein lies the power of children. (218)

Ognyov uses fiction to track how Kostya grows into a useful young comrade, but *Moscow has a Plan* belongs to a new Soviet genre: mass-produced and sold at prices affordable by all, 'production books' were designed to explain and celebrate the way science and technology were bringing about the modernization of Soviet society and stabilizing its economy (Rosenfeld, 2009). Such books could have been drearily didactic, but reflecting the high priority children's books were given by Communist Party leaders, the Commissar of Education, Anatoly Lunacharsky, and Lenin's wife, Nadezhda Krupskaya, were given both oversight of their production and the power to commandeer the services of leading artists and writers (Rosenfeld, n.p.). In the hands of skilled writers and artists, production books were often as exciting as fiction. Mikhail Ilin is the pen-name of Ilia Marshak, a young engineer who was also the brother of the renowned Russian writer Samuil Marshak, whose work for children is discussed at the end of this chapter. Ilin too is a fine writer, but his ability to make the material enthralling owes much to his scientific understanding of the technological challenges facing those working to implement the Five-Year Plan and his genuine excitement about the projects in which he has been involved. As Ilin recognized, the sheer scale on which the Soviets were working was intrinsically impressive. This is why he begins *Moscow has a Plan* with a list of numbers: 51 378000 3385 42. Where other books of facts and figures might be tedious, he explains, here the numbers tell an incredible story. The numbers 51 378000 3385 42 represent the 51 blast furnaces, 378 000 tractors, 3385 locomotives, and 42 electric stations that are helping to turn the vision set out in the Five-Year Plan into a reality.

With the advantage of hindsight, it is clear that Ilin's factual approach is as idealized as the Anglo-American stories about life in the Soviet Union. Figures he does not provide include the number of bureaucrats required to oversee the Five-Year Plan, the miles of red tape people encountered, the number of hours they spent queuing for food and clothing, the number of people living in overcrowded apartments, or the number of punishments meted out to 'class enemies' and other new kinds of transgressors. Instead, *Moscow has a Plan* focuses on the vision, telling a tale of giant machines that are assisting the Soviet people to transform their country from a backwards feudal nation of underfed and uneducated peasants into a rich and powerful nation run for the benefit of the people. His narrative is accompanied by photographs and photomontage illustrations by Mikhail Razulevich which match the adventurous spirit of the text: smiling workers driving phalanxes of tractors, diggers, and harvesters are evidently enjoying taking control of their own destinies.[7] The Five-Year Plan seemed to offer a happy ending to a story that began in the bloodshed, chaos, and hardships of revolution and civil war; as those events receded, they provided all the ingredients of the thrilling story Mr Wiseacre had promised, complete with the ousting of despots, the heroism of ordinary people, and the promise of great rewards.

Ilin also tells his young readers about the conditions faced by those living in countries where there is no coordinated economic plan and resources are not in the service of the people. America is made to exemplify capitalist mismanagement, though in this pre-Cold War period, America is not depicted as a bad country, but simply 'A Mad Country', where the illogic of capitalism prevails. In Ilin's America, the greedy businessmen Mr Fox, Mr Pox, Mr Box, and their similarly named fellow entrepreneurs spoil food and manipulate markets to push prices up and wages down, a pattern associated with pre-revolutionary days in the Soviet Union. Radical young readers in Britain were expected to draw their own conclusions from Ilin's portrait of victimized workers and fat-cat businessmen, not to mention the conditions they saw and read about at home.

Although school children were their main audience, the children's books produced in the Soviet Union during the 1920s and 1930s served a secondary purpose in relation to the many adults who were learning to read. The peasant population of the former regime had received little in the way of education, and illiteracy and innumeracy were recognized as significant obstacles to progress. The new children's books, including *Moscow has a Plan* and the many other books written by Mikhail Ilin (those translated into English during this period are listed in the Appendix), were at an appropriate level for new or inexperienced readers and contained basic information in a clear, accessible format. As well as supporting literacy initiatives, the books served propaganda purposes, not least in counteracting the messages contained in earlier forms of children's literature including traditional tales and classics from other countries. The strategy was explained in a 1918 number of *Pravda*: 'In the great arsenal with which the bourgeoisie fought against Socialism', it declared,

> children's books occupied a prominent role. In selecting cannons and weapons, we cannot overlook those that spread poisonous weapons. So focused on

---

[7] Razulevich specialized in montages on similar subjects, some on scales to match the enterprise. His 'The Reality of our Plans is Active People' (1932), now in the Metropolitan Museum of Art in New York, is twenty-one metres long. Created to celebrate the fifteenth anniversary of the October Uprising, it shows a crowd of smiling comrades against a background that the artist created by combining images of several of the major construction projects initiated during Stalin's First Five-Year Plan.

guns and other weapons, we forget about the written word. We must seize
these weapons from enemy hands. (in Rosenfeld, n.p., Rosenfeld's translation)

By the late 1930s, the Soviet people were required to take up actual
weapons again, and children's books began to tell new stories about how
children and young people could serve the state. This is the subject of
Arkady Gaidar's *Timur and his Comrades*. Gaidar, a military term meaning
'scout' in Russian, is the pen-name chosen by Arkady Petrovich Golikov,
who became a war hero in 1918 when, aged sixteen, he commanded a
regiment of the Red Army. Written the year before the Soviet Union
became involved in the 'Great Patriotic War' (the eastern campaign of the
Second World War in which more than 26 million Soviet citizens died),
*Timur and his Comrades* recalls Russian children's contributions during
the First World War and the Revolution, and anticipates the need for the
current generation of young people to help defend and maintain the
Soviet Union in the face of German aggression (Figure 2.3). Written for
Gaidar's son Timur, the book tells of a fictional Timur who organizes a
gang that secretly does good deeds for those whose family members are at
the front or who have been killed. The book, along with the handful of
others Gaidar wrote before he was killed during fighting in 1944, was so
popular and influential in the USSR that it gave rise to the Timur
Movement. According to a note included in the 1982 English-language
version (this was the fourth time the book was translated into English), the
movement had more than 5 million members who

> help war veterans and old people, help prevent youngsters doing damage to
> national property and harming the environment; they see to it that no one
> hurts younger children; they help nursery school teachers, organise play-
> grounds in courtyards and give concerts.... And they donate all the money
> they earn to the World Peace Movement. (n.p.)[8]

Gaidar's story of responsible and capable young people echoes the
'Children's Five-Year Plan' in *Moscow has a Plan*. Evidently it also shaped
the message to Britain's youth conveyed through the 'You Can Help Your
Country' campaign launched by the UK Ministry of Information (MOI)
for the Standing Conference of National Juvenile Organizations in 1940.
In a pamphlet aimed at fourteen to eighteen-year-olds, the MOI pamphlet
about the scheme urged young people to find ways to be useful such as
helping around the neighbourhood, assisting the elderly with heavy work,

---

[8] The reference to world peace reflects the fact that the publishers of this edition, the
Novosti Press Agency, are a state-controlled body founded in 1941 to manage international
news; part of the company's remit at the time was to promote peace and the image of the
USSR as a nation that wanted peace.

**Figure 2.3.** Untitled image of Timur and his comrades by Donia Nachsen, 1943

helping with the harvest, and learning first aid and how to use the telephone efficiently—exactly the kinds of activities featured in *Timur and his Comrades* (Mayall and Morrow, 2011). The similarities are unlikely to be accidental since Gaidar's book featured on a shortlist of Soviet children's books selected and translated by Kathleen Taylor, a senior official in the Russian Division of the MOI (Eve, 2003 79). The translations were originally selected by a small firm called Pilot Press with a view to supporting the work of the United Nations in the belief that knowledge of other cultures would build understanding between children of the world. Pilot

Press was subsumed into Transatlantic Arts, a company directed by Noel Carrington, a publisher who played a key role in introducing Soviet picture-books to British children. During the 1940s radical children's books featuring an idealized Soviet Union rapidly disappeared as children's book makers and publishers began to distance themselves from Stalinist Russia, but the Soviet picturebooks have had a lasting legacy based on their artistic quality. The quality of the books was a direct response to government policy and social vision, and while ultimately the Soviet experiment was widely regarded as a disappointing failure, it is important to remember the conditions and philosophies that called a plenitude of astonishingly vibrant and creative picturebooks into being.

## THE SOVIET LEGACY IN BRITISH CHILDREN'S BOOKS: SOVIET PICTURE BOOKS OF THE 1920s AND 1930s

Once the Soviet's need for children's books had been met at home, attention turned to other audiences. As in the case of *Moscow has a Plan*, the quality and innovation of the Soviet books had started to be noticed outside the USSR, Pearl Binder's article for *Design for Today* being a case in point. To mark the tenth anniversary of the State Publishing Department in Moscow, in 1929 an exhibition of children's books was mounted and subsequently toured throughout the Soviet Union and parts of Europe. In 1931 the exhibition was warmly received in Britain: the *Manchester Guardian*, for instance, praised not just the books, but the exhibition's interactive design which, among other things, encouraged children to reorganize the books to create their own displays ('Russian Children's Books', 1931). The practice of asking children their opinions that Geoffrey Trease had adopted in Yalta was also at work in the exhibition, with children being encouraged to critique everything from the standard of printing to the quality of the prose. The attention focused on the Soviet picturebooks encouraged publishers to produce English translations of some of the less specifically Soviet titles, though this was only a tiny proportion of the total output.[9] In the Soviet Union nearly 10,000 titles by approximately 500 authors were mass-produced and sold at prices affordable to everyone (Pearson, 2010 19). Grierson lists only six of Ilin's picturebooks and Kornei Chukovsky's *Crocodile* (1932). More,

[9] *Inside the Rainbow: Russian Children's Literature 1920–35. Beautiful Books, Terrible Times* contains a detailed picture of the publishing house that was responsible for producing the best and best-known Soviet picturebooks.

including many by Ilin's brother Samuil Marshak (another figure whose books do not appear in Philip Grierson's list), were also available, but nothing like a representative sample. As can be seen by looking at specialist collections, exhibitions, and in the pages of *Inside the Rainbow. Russian Children's Books 1920–35: Beautiful Books, Terrible Times* (2013), most of the books that were translated were aimed at a general audience of modern children rather than targeted at radical readers. Nonetheless, as discussed in the following chapter, with their Russian associations and avant-garde aesthetic the books would have spoken to radical parents and children. They also had a significant influence on British children's publishing, largely through the efforts of Noel Carrington who, as editor of *Design for Today*, was introduced to a range of Russian children's books by Pearl Binder.

Carrington belonged to a circle of commercial publishers who were aesthetically and intellectually interested in innovative design and high-quality printing. He commissioned Binder's article on Russian children's books after publishing a piece by her on 'Posters in Soviet Russia', another area where the Soviets were in the vanguard. Carrington took to heart Binder's message about the importance of producing children's books to the highest possible standards. Over the next decade, working first for the publishers Country Life, then running Transatlantic Arts, and finally launching the influential series of Puffin Picture Books for Allen Lane's burgeoning Penguin paperback enterprise, he commissioned some of the best international writers and artists to produce children's books. He was also involved in publishing Soviet children's books in translation, including those by two of the leading creators of children's books in the Soviet Union: writer Samuil Marshak and illustrator Vladimir Lebedev.[10] Although in the USSR Marshak's and Lebedev's children's books were regarded as successful vehicles for Soviet ideology and, no doubt, radical children and parents in Britain recognized elements of Soviet doctrine and values in them, they are far more than propaganda. Removed from their Soviet context these rich and multi-layered picturebooks can be read as cautionary tales, stories about everyday entertainments, and lessons in good manners. One of their recurring themes, the benefits of progress, was very much in keeping with the message of radical children's literature, though overall Carrington's Soviet imports appealed to a much broader constituency than books such as Gaidar's and Kassil's.

---

[10] The fact that Marshak and Lebedev collaborated on almost fifty titles and Carrington published just three of these underlines how few Soviet picturebooks found their way into British bookshops.

Like his brother Mikhail Ilin, Samuil Marshak was committed to telling children about the grandeur of the Soviet project. His interest in children's literature had begun during a visit to a British progressive school in 1913 when he was a student in London; by 1920 he and some colleagues had established the first arts complex for Soviet children including a library, a theatre, and studios similar to those described in books about child travellers in the Soviet Union. His particular interest in children's books and verse led to his appointment as head of the children's division of the state publishing house, Gosizdat. As this history suggests, Marshak was a firm believer in the Five-Year Plan, and many of his first children's books celebrate its early triumphs in his preferred medium of verse. A typical example for Soviet children that was not published in the UK is 'War with the Dnieper' (1935), a poem about the project to create a hydroelectric station by channelling the waters of the Dnieper river. *Yesterday and Today* (1925), one of his best-known picturebooks in the Soviet Union, compares the old-fashioned way Soviet citizens were living just a short time ago with the new lifestyles achieved under the First Five-Year Plan and suggests the process is just the beginning of the march into a future of achievement, comfort, and modern living.

Marshak's work became known in Britain through a 1943 Transatlantic Arts omnibus of three Marshak-Lebedev picturebooks (reprinted by the Tate Gallery in 2013). One of the stories contains quite obvious traces of its Soviet origins, though it also works as a fairy tale in the tradition of Hans Christian Andersen's *The Emperor's New Clothes. The Ice-Cream Man* tells what happens to an ostentatiously dressed and over-fed businessman who stuffs himself on ice cream. Watched by a group of children who have each eaten only one ice cream, he gulps down all the wares of one seller after another. As each one runs out of ice cream he runs to tell his friends about the insatiable customer and soon the ice cream sellers' chant has changed from 'Lovely ices! Lowest prices!' to 'Lovely ices! Highest prices!' His inability to be satisfied is his undoing; the businessman is gradually transformed into a snowman whose frozen hands can no longer hold his 'well-lined morocco pocket-book' (n.p.). It falls to the ground, signalling a change in his audience. Uninterested in his money, they are delighted by his frozen state which makes it possible to play with snow in the summer. Clearly it is possible to read this as a critique of capitalism and an attack specifically on businessmen who make excessive profits (see, for instance, Pearson, 2010 15). However, Lebedev's bold, geometric images help make this a cautionary tale about the price of greed of any kind.

The *message* of the story might have been familiar, but there was much that was new, exciting, and sophisticated about the artwork and design of these and the other Soviet picturebooks that found their way into the hands of British children in the 1930s and 1940s. The aesthetic qualities of the books and the work of individual illustrators have been explored to a considerable extent in exhibitions and publications and feature more fully in Chapter 3, so for now it suffices to say that, ironically, as the books were introducing artistically radical elements to young readers in Britain, in the Soviet Union the arts were increasingly being required to conform to state controls.[11] Where there had been an affinity between experimental aesthetics and revolutionary ideology, and children's books had been seen as part of the creative fission that was going to blow apart the old world and allow a new one to be remade from the pieces, there was now an insistence on conformity and a return to older artistic forms under the umbrella of Socialist realism. For some time children's writers and illustrators managed to fly beneath the radar of state control, but in 1937 the publishing house where Marshak had headed the children's division was closed and many of its writers and artists arrested for failing to conform sufficiently.

The kind of pressures to which Marshak was subject played an important role in the retreat from the Left on the part of radical British writers, illustrators, and publishers in the second half of the last century. As more was learned about the years of terror under Stalin, it was impossible to continue to construct the Soviet Union as a utopia, and books such as *Red Comet*, *Palaces on Monday*, and *Moscow has a Plan* no longer represented the vision for society that radicals wanted to impart to the rising generation. As later chapters show, throughout the interwar years, radical writers adjusted their ideas about society to speak to British concerns in areas such as the need to improve the health of Britain's youthful population (Chapter 5), its built environment (Chapter 6), its landscape and heritage (Chapter 4), and its vision of the future (Conclusion). Disillusion with the Soviet experiment intensified the British nature of these efforts which in turn contributed to the disappearance and denigration of many of the most radical interwar children's books in the ways described in the Introduction. Nonetheless, as this chapter has shown, while the radical gaze rested on

[11]  A notable and well-explored collection of Soviet picturebooks is held in the University of Chicago Library's special collections (http://www.lib.uchicago.edu/e/webexhibits/sovietchildrensbooks/); recent exhibitions with accompanying catalogues include the 2012 Read Russia exhibition, *The Experimental Art of Russian Children's Books* in New York City. The Museum of Modern Art's 2013 exhibition *The Century of the Child: Growing by Design 1900–2000* and catalogue also featured Soviet picturebooks. Catriona Kelly, (2007); Balina and Rudova (eds), (2008); Rothenstein and Budashevskaya (eds), (2013); and Pankenier Weld (2014) are among the most recent studies.

Moscow, there was an energy, coherence, and internationalism in British children's publishing that has never since been repeated. The encounter with Soviet aesthetic experiments came relatively late to British children's publishing. By then radical writers and publishers had begun to devise their own brand of modernism for children. This is the subject of Chapter 3.

# 3

## Aesthetic Radicalism

### *Avant-Garde and Modernist Books for British Children*

The avant-garde Soviet children's books that found their way to Britain and other parts of the West have received considerable attention.[1] By contrast, the cultural forgetting around British children's publishing between 1910 and 1949 has resulted in the perception that there were no comparable British-made books and publications for children. In fact, during these years an eclectic range of avant-garde texts for children, from Surrealist fantasies to experiments with stream-of-consciousness writing, appeared in the UK. Given the primacy of the British-based Arts and Crafts Movement with its emphasis on total art environments in such avant-garde centres as the Bauhaus, it is striking that these aesthetically radical works have been so thoroughly forgotten.[2] That they have is no doubt partly a problem of perception since children's literature was caught up in a general tendency in interwar Britain to turn away from the most extreme forms of avant-garde activity and the universalizing strategies associated with pure abstraction. British writers and artists tended to favour fusing avant-garde aesthetic philosophies with ancient and vernacular local art forms in ways that look quite different from much European and North American avant-garde activity. As Alexandra Harris documents

---

[1] As well as academic studies such as Marina Balina and Larissa Rudova (eds), *Russian Children's Literature and Culture* (2007) and Sara Pankenier Weld, *Voiceless Vanguard: The Infantilist Aesthetic of the Russian Avant-Garde* (2014), there have been exhibitions including in 2011 *Adventures in the Soviet Imaginary: Children's Books and Graphic Arts*, University of Chicago Library and 'The Experimental Art of Russian Children's Books' as part of the *Read Russia 2012* exhibition in New York City. In 2013 Julian Rothenstein and Olga Budashevskaya (eds) produced a well-received, widely reviewed appreciation of Soviet children's books, *Inside the Rainbow. Russian Children's Literature 1920–35. Beautiful Books, Terrible Times.*

[2] See Olson (2012) on the influence of the Arts and Crafts Movement on the avant-garde.

in *Romantic Moderns: English Writers, Artists and the Imagination from Virginia Woolf to John Piper* (2010), whether drawing on early Celtic carvings, traditional folk arts, or fairgrounds, there was a specifically British response to avant-garde arts and letters in which overthrowing convention and reinvigorating the arts was achieved through re-engaging with tradition and reconnecting with place. In other words, in Britain the 'avant garde promoted a very "English," gradualist vision of social change' (Saler, 1999 9).

In keeping with this context, aesthetically radical children's literature produced in Britain looks different and less challenging than some of the more celebrated examples from the Soviet Union, Germany, and the US but, as this chapter will show, precisely because it was more subtle, more elastic, and calibrated to suit the culture, it went deep. The aesthetically radical works discussed in this and subsequent chapters laid the foundation for some of the most admired writing of the postwar era. Aesthetic radicalism does different but complementary kinds of work in preparing young readers for the future from the kind of writing produced for Socialist Sunday Schools or the Left Book Club. It is specifically concerned with stimulating readers to see and think about the fabric of everyday life: the way things look, feel, and affect individuals, and what happens when conventions for seeing and rendering the world are changed. Children are also positioned differently in aesthetically radical books; works that concentrate on social and political change are inclined to tell readers about the world (though always with a view to instilling the habit of independent thought), while aesthetically radical children's literature generally celebrates activities in which the young are supreme: play and the imagination.

Play and other ways in which the imagination is allowed free rein often involve language, whether in the form of nonsense, riddles, puns, rhymes, or verbal 'magic'—when words are used to set scenes and change reality: 'now you are the mummy/a soldier/a cow/dead'.[3] Juliet Dusinberre has argued that British literary modernists' fascination with how language can be used to capture the way the mind works, how time and memory are experienced, bodily responses to events and emotion, and a host of related phenomena was rooted in childhood reading and particularly that of Lewis Carroll's Alice books, with their intense focus on verbal games and childhood creativity (Dusinberre, 1987 5). The verbal and literary nature of much of the aesthetically radical writing for children produced in the first half of the last century has no doubt contributed to erasing them from

---

[3] For a discussion of children's magical thinking in relation to play, see Jacobus, 2005.

the cultural memory. In other parts of Europe and North America avant-garde publications for children are principally associated with picturebooks and books illustrated with photographs (see, for instance, Higonnet, 2009; op de Beeck, 2010; Reynolds, 2011). Startling images and visual experiments—for example, with typography and design—are more easily recognized as avant-garde than works in which innovation is largely conducted at the level of text; such works are also more effectively displayed and otherwise disseminated than novels and stories. The literary nature of many of the aesthetically radical British publications may explain why *they* have been lost from public memory and overlooked as part of British modernism, but visually experimental works too have also largely failed to be recognized as avant-garde because of their toned-down, romantic modernist style. In fact, as the following examples show, aesthetically radical British children's literature mingles aspects from European avant-garde and romantic modernism to create a recognizably British response to modernist and avant-garde children's literary activities. Like all avant-garde works for children, however, these British stories, novels, and picturebooks are rooted in the belief that childhood is a time of spontaneous, uncensored creativity, invention, and vision with the capacity to overthrow stultifying and compromised traditions. They enlarge the remit of this discussion of radical children's literature in the way they explore ways of representing the world in an attempt to nurture new understandings and values.

## SURREALISM FOR CHILDREN: *THE CITY CURIOUS*

Among the earliest examples of avant-garde publishing for children in Britain are two illustrated novels by the Belgian-born author-illustrator, Jean de Bosschère: *The City Curious* (1920) and *Weird Islands* (1921). When *The City Curious* was published, de Bosschère had been based in London for five years. Although in one sense he was living in exile, having left occupied Belgium in 1915, like many artists and writers at the time, Jean de Bosschère identified more with those who shared his artistic vision than with his birthplace. In 1920 he was living in London and moving in modernist circles that included Ezra Pound and T.S. Eliot. Although he evidently wrote *Weird Islands* in English (no reference is made to a translator), his first novel was 'retold' in English by the writer, illustrator, criminologist, and journalist F. Tennyson Jesse, author of the radical children's novel *Moonraker* (1927).[4]

---

[4] F(ryn), short for Fryniwyd, her own contraction of Wynifried, Tennyson Jesse (1888–1958) was one of the few women reporters to travel to the front line. She wrote

*The City Curious* tells the story of Smaly and Redy, a childless couple who set off on a quest for three daughters to live in the three empty bedrooms in the beautiful home they have created. Although the basic plot has much in common with traditional quest and fairy tales (between 1917 and 1918 de Bosschère illustrated two volumes of folk tales from Flanders so was well versed in such stories), the book is in fact a vehicle for exploring aspects of Surrealism. Indeed, *The City Curious*, with its child-like characters and close connection to the activities of play and day-dreaming, anticipates the call in the first Surrealist Manifesto of 1924 for artists to return to the unrepressed condition of childhood, 'the most fertile [condition] that exists' (Breton, 1924 n.p.). Both the writing and the illustrations make use of a wide range of Surrealist devices at the levels of imagination, illustration, and the modes of telling. For example, the narrative develops in a largely associative and spontaneous rather than logical manner, leaping from one set of events to another in ways that resemble dreams and automatic writing, while the relationships and events it describes and depicts are often bizarre, mysterious, and occasionally violent.

*The City Curious* was immediately recognized as an example of avant-garde writing for children. It was reviewed in *The Little Review*, one of the foremost English-language periodicals for publishing and reviewing experimental writing (the same volume in which *The City Curious* was reviewed reports on the arrest of the magazine's publisher and ensuing court case following serialization of James Joyce's *Ulysses*). The review of de Bosschère's novel was written by John Rodker, a British modernist poet, writer, and publisher of modernist work. Rodker refers to it appreciatively as a 'sinister little story' with 'equally sinister decorations', referring to the many illustrations drawn and painted by the author (Rodker, 1920 67). What Rodker means by 'sinister' soon becomes apparent. Smaly's and Redy's travels comprise a series of strange episodes including having their mouths replaced by beaks and meeting a crow who wears black spectacles so that he is forced to look on his inner self rather than out at the world. At the same time, the crow wears a third eye on a chain around his neck which he uses to show his house-bound mother events in the world. The eye is hers, and because he uses only one eye, she sees only one side of things which, in de Bosschère's drawings, results in the kind of two-dimensional, fragmented images associated with Cubism (Figure 3.1). At one point, Smaly sees that his wife's hands are wet and

about the invasion of Belgium for *Collier's Magazine* among others. It is possible that she and de Bosschère met while she was in Belgium.

**Figure 3.1.** 'She sees only one side of men, birds, and things' from Jean de Bosschère's *The City Curious*, 1920. Permission to reproduce the image courtesy of Alain Bilot. The Bodleian Library, University of Oxford FIC. 27526 d. 21

for no obvious reason assumes that they are covered in blood. He then realizes that 'poor Redy's hands were crying with fright' (7). The disturbing and dreamlike quality of this incident is typical of *The City Curious*. Although there is a discernible narrative arc—the couple's quest is completed and they return home with three little girls to fill their home—the story develops through a disjointed series of uncanny and absurd episodes. Fish fly through the air, objects that are normally inanimate are alive and bizarrely endowed with legs, eyes, and the ability to speak, while characters are liable to melt or morph into unexpected forms.

One of the most violent incidents in the story concerns a prisoner whose three daughters eventually become the girls that Smaly and Redy take home. In a scene reminiscent of Heinrich Hoffman's *Struwwelpeter*, the prisoner has his head cut off by an executioner wielding a huge pair of scissors. The prisoner then carries his own head to a magician's house where, in a macabre but comic scene, it is re-attached. Having suffered and survived his punishment he is not, as might be expected, set free, but re-imprisoned. Like a character from Kafka, the prisoner is tattooed with epigrams that say more about him than he does himself; indeed, he rarely speaks, though his story is told by others. Much of the prisoner's back story is told by an old crow. In an elaborate moment of the kind of diegetic embedding often found in modernist writing, she tells Smaly and Redy the prisoner's story up to the point when he arrives in the land where he is imprisoned. When she reaches that moment she is automatically and involuntarily silenced because his presence is part of her country's history and only the official Historian can tell it. Such arbitrary laws and an underlying military menace convey a distrust of government that pervades avant-garde writing between the wars.

*Weird Islands*, the story of Carpenter, who joins a group of strangely dressed individuals on a voyage to a cluster of islands where birds speak and creatures and objects inexplicably change size and adopt new shapes, is equally invested in Surrealism as well as other areas of avant-garde activity. It makes use of many of the same modernist storytelling techniques found in *The City Curious*, including temporal shifts, abrupt changes in narrative modes, characters that are made from found objects, illustrations and descriptions that reference Cubism, and comments about the arbitrary nature of existence. To these it adds an avant-garde theatre performance and a high degree of nonsense and word-play that gives it a Dadaist quality.

De Bosschère uses children's literature as a space in which to develop his own creativity and explore the world of the unconscious. The same can be said of Mervyn Peake's *Captain Slaughterboard Drops Anchor* (1939) which, despite being a comparatively short picturebook, has much in common with *Weird Islands*. Peake's story too takes readers into uncharted territories: 'Far beyond the jungles and the burning deserts lay the bright blue ocean that stretched for ever in all directions.' In modernist terms travelling to distant islands and encountering strangely attractive others brings to mind Gaugin and the artist's quest for the primitive. Metaphorically, the islands in Peake's story may represent aspects of the self, and in the same way, when they finally reach land, the creatures moving in the undergrowth can be understood as external-ized aspects of Captain Slaughterboard's unconscious desires (Armstrong, 2012). There is a discernable homoerotic dimension to the relationships between Captain Slaughterboard (who has an un-piratical penchant for pink) and his grotesquely rendered crew (disproportionate, missing body parts, hairy, and over-endowed with knives, pistols, bottles, and telescopes). Like repressed thoughts, the pirates pop up in all kinds of places until at last Captain Slaughterboard finds the 'creature as bright as butter' he has seen in the jungle and who becomes his companion for life. The creature 'does the cooking and can make the most exciting things out of practically nothing'; one of the final images shows the pair cuddling together under a tree (n.p.).

By 1939, aspects of Freudian psychoanalysis would have been familiar to someone from Peake's background and education, and *Captain Slaughterboard* may be a playful way of exploring some of its theories. It is not possible to know how far Mervyn Peake was conscious of incorporating influences from psychoanalysis; an illustrator who claimed he had done so unintentionally is Edward Bawden. At the same time that Peake was working on *Captain Slaughterboard Drops Anchor*, Bawden created a series of 'free-flowing and bizarre enough to be called surreal' (Yorke, 2007 87) illustrations that at his request were turned into a children's story by his friend, the poet and artist Thomas Hennell. The illustrations were responses to games of Consequences based on three invented characters (Lady Filmy Fern, Mr Virgin Cork, and the Welsh Polypod) played by Bawden, the artist Eric Ravillious, their wives, and their friend Gwyneth Lloyd Thomas, a Cambridge don. Before a publisher was found Bawden had become part of the War Artists' Commission and the project was forgotten for decades. Upon re-discovering the manuscript of *Lady Filmy Fern or The Voyage of the Window Box* (1980) in 1979, Bawden was acutely conscious of the revealing nature of the collective fantasy in this story about the beautiful socialite Lady Filmy Fern who longs to be creative and so retreats to the sea where she is pursued by a spider-paparazzo (the Welsh Polypod) and rescued by Mr Virgin Cork, an environmentalist carpenter (Yorke 87). The (unmarried) couple set off on a bohemian voyage around the world, reading poetry and painting, pursued but never caught by the unlucky photographer.

De Bosschère, Peake, and Bawden all produced rather disturbing children's books that deal with modernist themes and preoccupations but seem more interested in how children's literature can provide a vehicle for exploring the adult unconscious than in appealing to children. A more child-centred modernism is found in Enid Bagnold's *Alice and Thomas and Jane* (1930), a lengthy and episodic illustrated work that is interested in dreaming, play, and child art, and which incorporates a number of modernist literary devices.

# CHILD ART AND CHILDREN'S LITERATURE IN BRITAIN

As a young woman Enid Bagnold studied drawing with Walter Sickert and was briefly part of the bohemian scene: she was a journalist, friendly with notable literary figures including Katherine Mansfield, Vita Sackville-West, and Rebecca West, and was sculpted by Henri Gaudier-Brzeska. When she married into money and the establishment, Bagnold moved to Sussex where she continued to mix in artistic circles including the Bloomsbury set, several of whom had relocated to Sussex during the First World War where they were frequently visited by a wide range of artists and writers, including Roger Fry. Fry's influence in particular can be seen in *Alice and Thomas and Jane*, which stands out among radical publications for the way it incorporates real children's art and imaginations. Outside Britain, a pantheon of avant-garde artists including Dubuffet, Kandinsky, Klee, Matisse, and Miro collected artwork by children and sometimes exhibited children's drawings and paintings alongside their own.[5] (Many also created children's books, notable examples being El Lissitzky's *About Two Squares, a Suprematist Tale* (1922) and Dadaist Kurt Schwitters's *The Scarecrow* (1925).[6]) Children's art was given a showcase in Britain by Roger Fry, who began writing about children as natural artists akin to 'primitives' in his 1909 *Essay in Aesthetics*, and mounted a widely publicized exhibition of children's drawings at his Omega Workshop in 1917.[7] Despite Fry's efforts to generate interest in children's art, British artists and writers rarely acknowledged children as artists or returned the favour by creating artworks for them. Bagnold was highly unusual in having a child, her nine-year-old daughter Laurian Jones, help illustrate a children's book and then modelling her own illustrations for the book on the nine drawings provided by her daughter.[8]

*Alice and Thomas and Jane* features the adventures of the three eponymous siblings who are growing up in Rottingdean, East Sussex (where

---

[5] Marina Warner traces artists' debt to child art in *Only Make Believe* (2005).

[6] Margaret Higonnet (2009) discusses the relationship between modernism and children's books including those by El Lissitzky and Schwitters.

[7] Kümmerling-Meibauer (2013) discusses a series of earlier European exhibitions that feature both children's art and art for children. Richard Shiff (1998) provides a detailed discussion of Fry's interest in and writing about children's art.

[8] Laurian went on to illustrate Bagnold's most successful book, *National Velvet* (1935). Another book that involves a collaboration between progressive parents and artistic children is *In and Out of Doors* (1937) by Susan Williams-Ellis with the help of her siblings, Charlotte and Christopher, and her parents, Amabel and Clough, who feature in other chapters of this book. The book was attractively presented in a style reminiscent of Bloomsbury; Susan Williams-Ellis became a notable ceramic artist and designer.

Bagnold herself lived and raised three children). These are not the kind of children who tend to feature in socially radical children's literature: they have a large, comfortable home, a cook, a governess, and a nursery maid. Their parents, however, have much in common with some of the well-to-do, liberal figures who wrote and published radical children's literature. They are affluent, cosmopolitan, opposed to corporal punishment, and genially interested in how their children engage with the world—which they are given free rein to do. Some of the children's 'adventures' are relatively mundane: trying to raise money by drawing pictures on the pavement, for instance. Others are considerably more intrepid: they blackmail some local shopkeepers who they have caught smuggling into taking them out to tea in the countryside, and Thomas sneaks onto a ferry to Dieppe. At points it is difficult to tell what is real and what is make-believe: does five-year-old Alice really get towed behind the smugglers' boat in the middle of the night and lose her clothing in the process?

One reason that it is difficult to distinguish between the real and the imaginary is because the stories, like the illustrations, are largely told from the children's point of view; they are action-packed and capture the intensity of make-believe. For the children, everything they do is real at the time they do it, and in the stories extended collective fantasies and everyday reality are often fused.[9] The same kind of fusion brings together visual and verbal aspects of the storytelling: words and images coincide and overlap as they do in avant-garde collages and films. Breaking down barriers between artistic media and modes is a hallmark of avant-garde activity; so too is the mixing of registers and the use of multiple perspectives. In *Alice and Thomas and Jane*, the mingling of visual, verbal, and stylistic modes is particularly cunning since it combines innocent and knowing perspectives and incorporates central and peripheral characters in ways that are simultaneously comically confused and destabilizing. The children's perspective and inner worlds are prioritized, but occasionally other centres of consciousness briefly intrude into the narrative. When this happens it is done without the use of inquit tags or other overt cues to establish who is speaking or thinking. For example, at the end of an eventful day when the children are in their beds the text reads:

> They each had their slates and their slate pencils and their slate sponges by their beds ready to draw in the morning while they were waiting to be wakened, and they each had a glass of water, and a handkerchief under their pillows. So they were done for the night... (Bagnold, 1930 60)

[9] Here Bagnold's observation of children's play captures insights into the nature of play that were subsequently explored formally in Johan Huizinga's *Homo Ludens* (1938).

Until the final sentence, this could be the thoughts of the children: a kind of collective omniscient overview of their own sense of having been put to bed. 'So they were done for the night' establishes it as a moment of free indirect speech which allows a glimpse into their governess's mind; it is really *she* who is done for the night.

Some passages are almost impossible to attribute. For example: 'The sun was being murdered in his bed, and was sending up streams of blood like a squashed octopus all over the sky. The village was shining like a ruby, and all the cobbles were red' (45). This is presented as third-person narration, but the imagery and vocabulary are childish, suggesting that Laurian (and her siblings?) may have contributed to the storytelling as well as to the pictures. The book's frame supports such a reading. It begins with a Preface in which the narrating persona seems to be closely identified with Bagnold, a view supported by the fact that the illustration that accompanies it is by her rather than Laurian. The first-person Preface explains that the book is based on stories told to three children and that 'during the time Alice and Thomas and Jane ran about the house and rushed about the village and did all the things my children would like to have done', the three [Bagnold] children for once 'sat still' (n.p.).

Pictures contribute both to the storytelling and characterization: images enter into characters' thoughts and feelings and often employ a kind of visual form of free indirect speech. For instance, when the children confess to having raided the larder in the middle of the night to the fury of Cook, the accompanying illustration does not show the children but a diminutive, disempowered image of their mother standing cowed and anxious before an enormous, angry Cook. The mother-Cook image is another of Bagnold's drawings (her entwined initials are clearly visible in the top right-hand corner) though, as in the description of the sun as a squashed octopus, it is not clear whose point of view is being given. Readers are left wondering whether this insight into the relationship between Cook and her employer is meant to be the children's, their mother's, or a joke between the narrator and a knowing reader.

Alice and Thomas and Jane are often confounded by and slightly contemptuous of their parents—and, indeed, all the other adults they encounter. In their eyes, grown-ups tend to be tediously predictable, interested in the wrong things, and unaware of what is happening around them. When Alice has slipped out early in the morning to stow away in an aircraft parked near the family's house and is eventually returned by two airmen to the bosom of her family (who have not realized that she is missing), she notes, 'Father was in his Jaeger dressing gown, because it was only half past eight' (21). When taken to the beach by a maid rather than their usual governess they know they can escape because, 'The school-room maid always came on the beach with high heels' (27). On one of the many occasions when he has been troublesome, Thomas dives past the maid into the bathroom and tunes out the sound of her scolding by turning the bath on 'and then he could only see her lips moving' (46). As already seen in the incident with Cook, their mother too is well understood by the children. When they are in disgrace and know they ought to be having lunch upstairs in the nursery, the text reports, 'they had lunch downstairs... [because] mother hated punishments that punished herself. And she liked lunch downstairs' (84).

As well as incorporating a child's drawings, *Alice and Thomas and Jane* experiments with combining words and images in ways that reference children's play. Arguably, all the children's adventures are in fact shared games, stories, and fantasies used to pass time in their highly predictable lives where Monday is 'baked-egg day' and the eggs are always 'baked in little dishes with handles' and followed by 'a boiled suet pudding, with treacle separate' and 'They always had some sort of home affair at eleven o'clock, like milk and biscuits. And they had early workmen's tea at four' (47). The secret world of the children's games, by contrast, does away with such monotony, and a wholly different hierarchy prevails from the one the adults believe they are managing. As the children see it, Thomas is truly in charge of the nursery and the children only appear biddable to deflect the adult gaze. Meanwhile, their play provides them with good opportunities for observing (and sometimes misinterpreting) the world around them, as when they accept what they have obviously been told—that Father is poor—although all the evidence of the text shows that they live very comfortably. Playing off the discrepancies between how children and adults view the world is not, however, one of the avant-garde features of the book, but a well-established device in children's literature, used to particularly good effect in *fin de siècle* and early twentieth-century works such as Kenneth Grahame's *The Golden Age* (1895), the children's novels of E. Nesbit, and the William stories of Richmal Crompton.

Laurian's drawings constitute an original and less duplicitous way of injecting an authentic child's version of scenes and events into the narrative. It is also the illustrations that enable Bagnold to incorporate in a book for children such avant-garde concerns as multiple perspectives and renderings of the subjective nature of time. The picture of 'Mummy having a baby' (Figure 3.2), for instance, captures a moment when several things are happening at once, and characters are experiencing events in different ways: Thomas is being scolded at the same time that the nurse is bringing Mummy the baby and Alice is watching. The sense of simultaneous action is achieved through the characteristically childish simplification and literal rendering in the drawing that so intrigued Roger Fry (Shiff, 1998 174). Although there is an attempt at perspective in the placement of a picture and fireplace on what is meant to be the back wall, in fact the figures are

**Figure 3.2.** 'Mummy having a baby' by Laurian Jones from Enid Bagnold's *Alice and Thomas and Jane*, 1930. Image reproduced with the kind permission of Laurian d'Harcourt

clearly on the same two-dimensional picture plane, which makes every action equivalent and implies each is happening in the same moment. This effect is enhanced by labelling which mingles text and image.

Bagnold borrows and adapts Laurian's visual storytelling techniques to bring different temporal moments together in a single picture. For instance, on the morning when the airmen return stowaway Alice, Bagnold's illustration for the scene incorporates an image of Thomas on his way to the airplane *after* it has already taken off in a picture primarily about Alice hiding in the airplane and thinking lovely thoughts *before* it leaves the ground.

As these examples show, *Alice and Thomas and Jane* makes use of the naïve, unreasoned, spontaneous, and exuberant attributes of childhood imagination, play, and art associated with the 'infantilist aesthetic' that had become a defining feature of some key areas of Soviet and European avant-garde arts and letters (Pankenier, 2014). Bagnold, however, is clearly working in the romantic modern tradition: the book is irreverent rather than iconoclastic, and in its use of established genres such as the family and adventure story it also reaches an accommodation between tradition and innovation. Enid Bagnold was unusual in making a child a co-creator of a children's book but she clearly believed it was necessary to have an adult's experienced hand shape the material.

A figure who had a much lighter touch in presenting the work of child artists and writers to a juvenile audience was Stephen King-Hall. A Commander in the Royal Navy who became an established presenter on the BBC radio programme *Children's Hour*, King-Hall wrote regular articles for children for the London *Evening Standard*, and founded and edited the magazine *MINE: A Magazine for all who are Young* (1935–6). Despite his naval background King-Hall's writing for children was radical in its efforts to explain taxation, the importance of the League of Nations, and the need for a large-scale house-building programme as well as on its stress on the importance of peace, its efforts to make the relatively affluent children of the Home Counties understand the hardships of those who lived in the north of England, and its support for workers' right to strike. It was in his capacity as editor of *MINE* that King-Hall was sent the stories and drawings by children that, with the addition of some drawings provided by the Royal Drawing Society, make up the pages of *Young Authors and Artists of 1935* (1935).[10]

---

[10] Founded in 1888, the Royal Drawing Society took the idea of children as artists seriously, running competitions that attracted as many as 15,000 entries from which annual publications were made. However, the approach taken by the Society, which sought to train children to draw well, was at odds with the philosophies of Roger Fry and the avant-garde,

The respect the volume accords to children as authors and artists chimes with contemporaneous modernist interest in children and childhood that had four years previously seen Leonard and Virginia Woolf publish the first of two collections of poems by the teenage poet Joan Easdale on the grounds that 'children and their writing had something valuable to contribute to modernism' (James, 2012 279).[11] Woolf undoubtedly valued childhood, but on the basis of her two children's stories, *The Widow and The Parrot* (1923) and *Nurse Lugton's Golden Thimble* (1923–4), she did not regard children as a suitable audience for modernist writing.[12] Both stories are rather conventional in form and substance and it was left to others to introduce young readers to the modes and matters of modernism. Before looking at an example of literary modernism for young readers, however, it is important to consider some works in which interest in child art resulted in aesthetically radical books for children as in the picturebooks of the author-illustrator known as 'Klara' (1910–89).

Born in Poszony (modern Bratislava), Klara Szántó was educated at the School of Graphic Art and Design in Budapest. After moving to England in the 1930s she produced a series of highly inventive picturebooks for William Collins and Sons. Two are of particular interest to this discussion, the first being *Paul and Mary* (1941). This short picturebook features young brother and sister, Paul and Mary, whose status as artists is validated when the Highways and Railways Department of Paris chooses a picture they have made for a poster to advertise the beauty spots of France. Before this happy ending the children, who with their need of money, anxiety, and lack of adult protection bring to mind the many similarly unaccompanied and distressed children who were moving around Europe at the time, travel alone across Paris to find the Department's offices. In rendering their journey, Klara references many modernist themes and interests: the city is a place of speed, energy, and noise that creates a somatic reaction in the children whose 'little hearts [are] beating faster and faster' (n.p.) as they walk the streets of Paris. Perspectives from high vantage

which appreciated precisely the untrained and so fresh, direct, and emotionally expressive qualities of children's drawings and paintings.

[11] Emily James (2012) gives the background to the publications and discusses Virginia Woolf's interest in children as writers.

[12] Neither work was intended for publication. Woolf's nephew Quentin Bell notes in his introduction to the 1988 Hogarth Press edition of *The Widow and the Parrot* that it was sent in response to his and his brother's request for a story for their family newspaper *The Charleston Bulletin*. Woolf supplied—presumably with her tongue in her cheek—not the comic piece they hoped for but an improving story modelled on the Victorian past. *Nurse Lugton's Golden Thimble* was written for her niece, Anna Stephenson, some time in 1923–4 when Woolf was writing *Mrs. Dalloway* and first published with illustrations by Duncan Grant in 1966 (Reynolds, 2007 25).

points, human forms reduced to hurrying stick figures, and onomatopoetic words for the sounds of the city create a modernist portrait of the city that draws on children's simplified ways of representing the world (Figure 3.3). An additional radical dimension is added in the final pages of the book which explain how Paul and Mary's poster is eventually reproduced using lithographic printing. The detailed explanation and illustrations mean that readers get both facts and fiction in a single work.

The second of Klara's radical picturebooks, *7 Jolly Days* (1942), mixes genres and formats more creatively by incorporating letters (and their envelopes), drawings, posters, signs, newspapers, and rebuses into the story. *7 Jolly Days* is highly self-referential and interactive: it begins immediately—there is no title page—with a schoolgirl, also called Klara, standing on a stage before an audience of children whose backs are to the reader, implicitly positioning readers in the audience. Klara asks if they

People rush to their offices.   Cars hoot constantly.   Who would notice those two little ones ?   Could anybody hear their little hearts beating faster and faster ?

**Figure 3.3.** From 'Klara's' *Paul and Mary*, 1941. Image courtesy of the National Library of Scotland

want to know 'how Klara spent 7 days at Broom Hill? Yes? Just turn the page then.'[13] This frame is completed on the inside back cover, which shows Klara on the stage again, this time bidding farewell to a waving audience, while on the back cover she has popped her head through the curtain to watch the audience depart. This is, then, the performance of a story; the story of how Klara spends the Easter holidays with her cousins in the Lake District, which is told in a variety of modes.

Like *Alice and Thomas and Jane*, the illustrations in *7 Jolly Days* incorporate labels and other features of children's art, though in more self-conscious and controlled ways than in Laurian Jones's drawings. Readers are frequently addressed directly, thereby breaking the illusion of being in the world of the book. A typical example comes at the beginning of the book: Klara's aunt has asked Klara to write and tell her what time her train will arrive. Upon receiving no reply, the aunt writes to Klara's Head Mistress, at which point the narrator comments, '(Klara *did* write that letter, I can tell you that, for I saw her doing so)' (7). Other aspects of this picturebook also emphasize such modernist themes and preoccupations as speed, machines, and transport though here, unlike in *Paul and Mary*, the hectic pace of Klara's life is seen as creative and enriching. She rushes here, dashes there, and speeds off in an impressive red automobile to catch the trains that will take her from the world of school to her cousins' large house in the country and back again (Figure 3.4). The fact that no time is spent on the journey makes travel seem instantaneous and globe-shrinking, in keeping with the modernist preoccupation with the way modern transport speeds up movement and compresses space and time (Trotter, 2012).

Like *Alice and Thomas and Jane*, *7 Jolly Days* is set in a large family home where, from the children's perspective, the things they do are all-important. Their games are absorbing and creative: they mount an exhibition, put on a circus show with clowns, 'Red Indians', and magicians, and create a zoo from local animals and pets. To publicize their events they create elaborate posters and a newspaper complete with advertisements; all of these are reproduced in the book. These texts-within-a-text show an awareness of print and mass media, another way in which Klara references the concerns of modernist arts; they also highlight the constructed nature of the 'reality' of the book's storyworld. The inclusion of print matter within a printed book makes *7 Jolly Days* a kind of three-dimensional collage

---

[13] There is a strong autobiographical element to this book. After moving to England Klara taught at Whitcliff Grange School, a private girls' school in Richmond, Yorkshire. The school in *7 Jolly Days* is called 'Whitecliffe Grange School'. Just like Klara in the story, Klara Szántó stayed with friends in the Lake District. (Information provided by Klara's son, Pete Biller, in private correspondence.)

**Figure 3.4.** From 'Klara's' *7 Jolly Days*, 1942. Image courtesy of the National Library of Scotland

with moving parts (covers and pages) all based around children's play and artwork. Despite its clear avant-garde themes and stylistic features, the story exemplifies the hybrid (traditional and experimental) nature of the British avant-garde in the way it makes a middle-class home in the English countryside the place where children can be their most spontaneous and creative. Moreover, since the goal of the entertainments Klara and her cousins mount is to raise money for charity (they send five shillings and six pence to Dr Barnardo's Homes at the end of the vacation), it harks back to the Victorian 'ministering children' tradition of British children's literature. *7 Jolly Days*, then, shows an émigré author-illustrator, using the persona of a creative child, accommodating her European avant-garde influences to the taste and dictates of romantic modernism in a picturebook that captures modernist concerns and idioms. When it came to longer fiction, however, it was two British-born writers, Edith Saunders and P (ercy) H(oward) Newby, who produced the quintessential examples of literary modernism for children.

## MODERNISM IN MINIATURE

*Fanny Penquite* is the only children's book by Edith Saunders, a minor translator and historical novelist of the 1940s. Reflecting its modernist character, Oxford University Press commissioned a cover for the volume from illustrator Lynton Lamb. Lamb's design is a fine example of the way British artists were reinterpreting traditional art forms and vernacular culture to create an 'energetic style that was both national and modernist' (Pearson, 2010 133). In this case a stylized use of forms and shadows cuts across traditional expectations of wood-engraved scenes of rural life to create a disturbing, menacing image largely derived from the square-shouldered rider and the powerful horse. The figure of the girl, whose back is to the viewer, prepares readers to experience events through her eyes (Figure 3.5).

The seven much less accomplished internal illustrations were done by Edith Saunders herself. Although rather crude in execution, they match the story well. In keeping with this tale about death and resurrection in a small village, Saunders's watercolour paintings take their cue from the work of her contemporary, Stanley Spencer. Spencer's *Resurrection, Cookham* (1926) was described by *The Times* in 1927 in terms that highlight the mingling of old and new approaches to art typical of romantic modernism; it was, the reviewer said, the work of a Pre-Raphaelite shaking hands with a Cubist as well as 'the most important picture painted by any English artist in the present century' (in Chilvers, 1999 597). Spencer's painting, in common with all his images of Cookham, combines sex and religion, love and dirt, the heavenly and the ordinary (Hauser, 2001). Like Spencer, Saunders shows figures rising joyfully from the local churchyard on the Day of Judgement, and though her images feature figures in pure white, especially in combination with her text, they are made of the same potent mixture (Figure 3.6).

*Fanny Penquite* (1932) tells the story of the last minutes in an adolescent girl's life (calculating the passage of time is complex as the events start as a minute-by-minute account of Fanny's walk through the village, traverse a century in a sentence, and then shift from human time to eternity). The book is largely focalized through Fanny, who moves through her village rather like Leopold Blume walking around Dublin or Clarissa Dalloway moving through London. She sees and is seen. Her sensibilities are heightened; the language is saturated, and everything she

**Figure 3.5.** Lynton Lamb's cover for *Fanny Penquite*, 1932. By permission of Oxford University Press

sees and hears is shot through with an intensity of feeling. Even insentient things like the bridge that she crosses at the start of her walk are imbued with value: 'The bridge was clear and static; each stone stood out with equal emphasis' (3). As this sentence illustrates, the sense is in the sounds and feelings as much as any literal meaning.

**Figure 3.6.** Edith Saunders's illustration of the Day of Judgement in *Fanny Penquite*. By permission of Oxford University Press

In keeping with much modernist literature, focalization as it relates to Fanny is coenesthetic and somatic: she experiences her world largely through sensory impressions and the body is regarded as the site of truthful emotion. When the text pulls away from Fanny's inner world it is to offer vignettes that add information about her and display that she is just one of many centres of consciousness into which the narrator can enter at any given time. So, when Fanny passes Mrs Samuel's house, Mrs Samuel sees her and thinks, in a passage highly reminiscent of Woolf:

> She [referring to Fanny] was fourteen years old, and tall and thin and active and had not dreamed of love; and Mrs. Samuel heated her teapot, her Sunday teapot adorned with a picture of the Good Prince Consort, and continued to think of Mrs. Tremeer. (Saunders, 1932 4)

At several points the text mentions that Fanny has not yet dreamed of love, but it protests too much. She is fascinated by a voluptuous figurehead and an attractive classmate who is not as good as she should be according to village thinking. Fanny's mother prophesies that, 'That girl will come to a bad end, sure enough' and her words give Fanny's 'strained thoughts' some relief (12). The strained thoughts are associated with an uncomfortable, unfamiliar tension in her body that clearly would have been transformed into erotic desire if it had had the chance: as she looks at William Tremeer's home, 'Fanny's prosaic mind was suspended by an unfamiliar emotion that swept on to her, fixing her where she stood as though entranced' (18).

A somatic crisis is reached when Fanny becomes aware of her own heart beating to the sound of horses' hooves as the handsome local Squire amorously pursues the lovely Miss Anna de Lacey. The horse startles, tramples Fanny to death, and 'All the world looked on, but Fanny Penquite was no longer of it' (21). The memorial on her grave proclaims that she 'leaves a whole village bereaved. UNTIL THE TRUMP SHALL SOUND', signalling an interlude under the ground where Fanny lies buried next to relatives and other figures from the village. Like the Sleeping Beauty she wakes after a hundred years, and with all the dead in the churchyard she is resurrected. Before she ascends to Paradise there is a form of pageant in which past, present, and future mingle as do figures great and small, old and young, human and mythic. Like Stanley Spencer's *Resurrection, Cookham*, Saunders's short story offers a generous, democratic, and optimistic version of the end of time.

As Fanny observes those around her it seems that her interrupted pubescence is shaping her experience of Paradise: she watches as the still-handsome Squire and the perpetually beautiful Miss de Lacey are united in a kiss of 'subdued and sanctified joy' (40). A great deal of kissing goes on in Fanny's Paradise, and though it is erotically charged, it is repeatedly referred to as pure and sexless, making eternity rather dull for some of the more passionate figures who find themselves among the Good. The book ends with Fanny having a fleeting recollection of 'an unfamiliar and intense emotion that had come and then passed away she could not remember how' before she is left to 'long hours of eternity passed in unchanging pleasure' (43).

Edith Saunders's book is clearly a rebuttal of Puritan and Victorian stories of children who die young and in which to die young and sinless is regarded as a blessing; Fanny's is a life unfulfilled, and her heaven reeks of missed opportunities and sexual frustration. In style and references—but perhaps particularly in its acknowledgement of erotic desire in the young and its ambivalent attitude to provincial life—*Fanny Penquite* constitutes a fully modernist British text for children.

A novel that is committed to both social and aesthetic radicalism is P.H. Newby's *The Spirit of Jem* (1947), boldly illustrated by Keith Vaughan.[14] Like *Fanny Penquite*, *The Spirit of Jem* is dark, strange, and dreamlike; indeed, it begins with a scene in which a boy and a man in a bowler hat, both of whom have lost their memories, meet in a strange landscape and believe they are in a dream. It transpires that they and the population of wherever they are (it appears to be but is never identified as England) have had their memories wiped by a drug put in the water supply by a young revolutionary named Jem. Before Jem's role in their plight is revealed, however, he seems to be their friend and accepted leader. Jem is mustering an army of the memory-less to fight what he refers to as the oppressive mechanisms of law and order. He explains the situation as a kind of Marxist-socialist parable in which the past, which the boy remembers as Edenic-like, is exposed as an illusion, and their supposed happiness a product of what he calls 'the system'. As the story unfolds, dream and reality, truth and lies, good and bad, past and present constantly shift and readers are as disoriented as the characters as the plot twists and turns in unexpected ways. Keith Vaughan's dark, expressionist illustrations capture the book's mood of urgency and uncertainty (Figure 3.7). Although it is the work of two British men, *The Spirit of Jem* is far removed from romantic modernism. By contrast, as seen in the work of Klara, many of the émigré writers and illustrators who settled in London in the 1930s and 1940s found ways to adjust their avant-garde interests to British tastes and sensibilities along romantic modernist lines.

## IMPORTED MODERNISM

The Polish partners Jan Le Witt and George Him, who usually published under the name Lewitt-Him, were particularly adept at finding effective

---

[14] Newby, both an award-winning novelist and a Managing Director of the BBC, wrote two children's stories. At the time, Keith Vaughan was an emerging artist; he subsequently became a notable painter who worked out ways to reconcile figuration and abstraction.

**Figure 3.7.** One of Keith Vaughan's illustrations for P.H. Newby's *The Spirit of Jem*, 1947. © The Estate of Keith Vaughan. All rights reserved, DACS

ways to incorporate avant-garde elements in radical British picturebooks. For instance, at one level *The Football's Revolt* (1939) is a politically pointed, highly topical parable about the responsibilities and abuses of power supported by illustrations that clearly draw on avant-garde movements from Cubism to the Absurd. At another level it is a rather traditional moral tale about the consequences of failing to treat others well that employs such familiar features as children who are wiser than adults and a victory for the weak over the strong, all in a friendly community setting (Figure 3.8).

*The Football's Revolt* tells the story of a football match from the ball's point of view; this football is tired of being kicked around by twenty-two strong men just because 'he was nothing but a football, who could not even talk English' (n.p.). When it is kicked high into the air, the football finds a berth on a comfortable cloud and refuses to come down. He is joined by all the other objects the players throw at him to try to knock him down until the air is filled with a bizarre range of items. Eventually the grown-ups retire defeated, and the children invade the pitch and speak nicely to the football, who agrees to join in their game. It is a well-told

**Figure 3.8.** Lewitt-Him illustration from *The Football's Revolt*, 1939. The Bodleian Library, University of Oxford, 252 d.2246, p.11. With permission of the Jan Le Witt and George Him estates

story that makes clever use of carnivalesque reversal and anthropomorphism, but what makes this story radical is the way images and design employ a wide range of avant-garde techniques including distorted figures, emphasis on pattern, and calling attention to the two-dimensional nature of the painted surface. The illustrations also display expressive use of colour, experiments with rendering dynamic motion on the page, and incorporation of collage effects, unusual perspectives, and a delight in excess. Throughout, the book's images and design are characterized by a tendency towards abstraction that sets it apart from mainstream British children's books; at the same time, the use of wit, humour, and some established children's literature components brought *The Football's Revolt* into a sufficiently familiar ambit to prevent it from alienating British audiences (specifically the adult gatekeepers who generally publish, purchase, and introduce books to children). It is a kind of modernism by stealth; Lewitt-Him use humour and a predominantly figurative version of modernism as a way of introducing aspects of avant-garde thinking and art to the rising generation and their parents.

A similar approach is used in *Blue Peter* (1943), a story about a puppy who is persecuted for being the wrong colour, thus serving as a topical allegory of the victimization of minorities in Europe at the time. Stylistically it is expressionistic; the images are scratchy and distorted for emotional effect, and colour is used symbolically: Peter is blue, the colour of sadness and the blues, with all its connotations of oppression. The Blue Peter is also the international signal that a ship is about to leave port, and one of the radical dimensions to this story comes when Peter and his friend Sailor Jeff sail away from persecution and discover a friendly new land full of blue dogs. Peter saves his new friends from disaster, becomes a hero, and brings together his old and new worlds, allowing the traditional happy ending expected in children's books.

The most fully modernist of the Lewitt-Him picturebooks are *Locomotive* (1939) and *The Birds' Broadcast* (1939), published in an omnibus edition with text by the avant-garde Polish poet, Julian Tuwim. *Locomotive* celebrates machinery in the form of the powerful locomotive engine, 'black, stupendous, / Dripping with oil, its heat tremendous'. Tuwim creates a sound portrait of the massive engine, which dwarfs the humans who tend it and travel on it, and contains goods and travellers from all parts of the world:

> Here goes the whistle with a sudden scream,
> And now the engine gets up steam
> As the wheels turn and the axels creak
> With a slow, thin, grinding shriek...
> Crash! As the wagons are jerked into motion,
> Then rumble slowly out of the station.
> But, gathering speed, it starts to race,
> And dashes ahead at a furious pace,
> With the noise of a hundred singing fountains.

*Locomotive*'s modernist emphasis on speed, energy, time, machinery, internationalism, and transportation is matched by its geometric, highly patterned, brilliantly coloured illustrations. As its title suggests, *The Birds'*

*Broadcast* switches focus to communication media and the corporate nature of mass culture. The illustrations show a boardroom meeting with birds speaking into microphones as they complain about the quality of the transmission of their songs.

Lewitt-Him were experimental, but as graphic artists they always worked with paints and drawing materials. Another émigré artist, the pioneer photographer Zoltan Wegner, worked with Gilbert Cousland, another experimental photographer, to produce books comprising photo-collages and dioramas made up of found objects from the nursery, garden, and beach. Using a mixture of lighting effects borrowed from the cinema and games with perspective facilitated by cameras, their images make even the most mundane objects seem strangely new and interesting. The assemblages photographed by Wegner to illustrate stories such as Hans Christian Andersen's *The Emperor's New Clothes* and *The Little Mermaid* go further in the way they draw on avant-garde set designs and experiments with puppets. Wegner injects unsettling, multi-perspectival effects through the use of shadows, mirrors, and other reflecting surfaces. As seen in the cover image for *The Emperor's New Clothes* (1945), the reflections allow several views of the central figure to be seen simultaneously (back, front and profile, above and below, real and reflection). The appearance is realistic, but it also plays with time and point of view in ways similar to Cubist art and, particularly, the experimental photographic images created by Alvin Langdon Coburn, an American associated with the British Vorticists. Coburn's portraits of influential figures use multiple exposures to create a single image composed of a succession of photographs. Although they are in fact static, the images create a sense of movement, including movement through time, which equates to the multiple times and vantage points featured in Cubist artworks. Superficially Wegner's compositions look simple, but as viewers take note of the interactions between the reflecting surfaces, the effect has much in common with a Coburn or Cubist portrait.

The range of forgotten work by émigré writers is wide. It includes, for instance, Franciszka Themerson's *My First Nursery Book* (1947), with its stylized, simplified figures in anti-naturalistic colours, dynamic use of typography, and design that defies the top-to-bottom, left-to-right conventions for reading texts and images in books.[15] Also among the Europeans who enriched the avant-garde dimension of radical children's literature were the writers and illustrators published by another migrant, David Gottlieb, who, in 1943, set up a publishing company specializing in

---

[15] With her husband Stefan Themerson, another Pole living in exile, in 1948 she founded the Gaberbocchus Press which specialized in high-quality printing of avant-garde works.

children's books that employed many authors and artists who had been working in what became occupied countries. The history of his enterprise has been documented by Peter Main (2012 and 2013); here it suffices to say that Gottlieb had a good eye for fine artists and many of those who illustrated his books went on to become distinguished in their fields. In the five years during which Peter Lunn was active, the company created a space in which avant-garde as well as more mainstream figures could earn their livings as children's writers and artists.[16] Among the modernist-influenced books published by Peter Lunn was R(olf) A. Brandt's and Stephen MacFarlane's (pseudonym of the Scottish writer John Kier Cross) *The Story of a Tree* (1946). Rolf Brandt was German by birth and studied at the Bauhaus with Kandinsky and Klee before relocating to London. His style was Surrealist and abstract; in *The Story of a Tree* his leanings towards Dada and Surrealism are apparent in the use of shadows to convey states of mind and information, the highly stylized and geo-metric nature of the artwork, and the way the trees take on the forms of what they will become—furniture, toys, and other everyday items. Brandt was well matched with Scottish writer Stephen MacFarlane, whose story is highly metatextual, referring to itself and beginning where it ends in a complicated *mise-en-abyme*. The last page reads:

> If you look at the picture on the page before this, you will see that we have got back to the point where we started this book. There is Ian's Nursery exactly as it was described to you on the pages called *The story of this story* . . . . And it is right that we should come back to the beginning in this way. For really and truly this story *has* no ending . . . . I think the little Mouse should begin his story with the words:—'Once upon any time you like, there *is* a very big tree . . . .' (n.p.)

As this quote indicates, the book is also interested in the nature of time—real time, story time, historical time, cyclical time—but it introduces questions about time through the familiar refrain of 'once upon a time', again fusing traditional tales and modernist preoccupations.

*The Story of a Tree* is a deeply optimistic book about human ingenuity and the possibility of harmonizing craftsmanship and mechanization. It also offers a reassuring message about sustainability and cycles of life. The old world of witches turning children into frogs has been banished for one in which humans turn trees into furniture and pencils, and when the wood is finished with it is burned and returned to the ground in the form of ashes where it is absorbed by new seeds to make new trees, and so life goes

---

[16] Peter Main (2012 and 2013) provides a detailed history of the company, its founder, and many of the artists and writers he employed.

on. Brandt, like most of those published by Peter Lunn, knew at first hand the horrors of the recent past and would have been well aware of the potential threat to the future posed by atomic weapons. Like all Lunn's émigré authors and illustrators—and all makers of Britain's radical children's literature—he chose to use the medium of children's books to prepare readers to move forward, learning from the past and thinking about how the world could be different and better.

In the 1940s, the modified and gradualist approach to modernism adopted in Britain offered a way to heal the rifts between past and present, generations, and peoples caused by two world wars and the economic and social upheavals associated with them. What is often called the second 'golden age' of children's publishing, with its interest in time, memory, and childhood imagination, is traditionally seen as a break with what came before. Recovering these early aesthetically radical works shows that writers such as Lucy Boston, Alan Garner, Penelope Lively, Mary Norton, and Philippa Pearce are in fact indebted to these precursors. There is a difference, however; where second golden age books tend towards the lyrical, the reflective, and the nostalgic, and tell readers what childhood should be like from a position of adult knowledge, early avant-garde/ modernist children's books are part of a two-way exchange in which writers and artists refreshed their own creativity by 'opening themselves up to children's perceptual universe' while at the same time aiming to 'release youthful energy and imagination, and thereby shape the society of the future' (Kinchin and O'Connor, 2010 59). They address children as re-makers of the future, celebrate them as artists, introduce them to ideas of interiority and subjectivity, encourage them to embrace modernity, and provide them with insights into contemporary ways of understanding and representing the world. As the following chapters show, the significance of seeing the world in new ways was central to radical children's literature in which social transformation and aesthetic innovation were closely allied.

# 4

## Radical Ruralism

### *The Transformative Power of the Landscape*

In radical children's literature, excitement over the changes brought about by revolution in Russia was matched by efforts to ensure that British children understood their own radical past. Publications such as *The Revolution, Martin's Annual,* and *The Young Socialist* regularly carried features celebrating the many rebellions through which civil liberties were won and a democratic tradition established; e.g. the Peasants' Revolt, the campaigns of the Diggers and Levellers, and the protests of the group who became known as the Tolpuddle martyrs. As this list makes clear, Britain had a long history in which struggles for social and political reform were fomented in rural areas. These associations injected a political charge to radical children's literature set in the countryside, especially at a time of frequent—often fierce—struggles between landowners and walkers demanding open access to the land. In the interwar years the right to roam freely was an area where the concerns of the radical parts of the population entered the mainstream: walking in the country had featured prominently in the recreational life of the British Left from the late nineteenth century, but by the 1930s enthusiasm for rambling was 'a national craze' (Samuel, 1998 141). Militant walkers, such as those who took part in the mass trespass on Kinder Scout in the Peak District in April 1932, were the extreme face of a wider movement to gain free access to the countryside.

From the perspective of the Left, walkers' confrontations with landowners reprised earlier protests against the enclosure of common land. This sentiment underpins Geoffrey Trease's 1937 *Mystery on the Moors*, in which young campers are outraged when they are forced to leave their chosen site by an aggressive gamekeeper, but Trease is unusual in directly featuring children who experience at first hand the power and hostility of private landowners (Sheeky, 2012 102–3). As seen in the texts discussed in this chapter, more often radical children's literature took a broader and often a symbolic approach to demonstrating the significance of the relationship between ordinary people and the land. Doing so created opportunities for social and aesthetic radicalism to intersect. Whether they address poor children who are confined to cities, feature better-off children who hike and camp in remote parts of Britain, or look at those who have been sent to the countryside for their health or safety, radical stories and illustrations construct the countryside as a site of individual and social transformation.


## THE BATTLE OVER MERRIE ENGLAND

Many of the ideas about the countryside that find their way into radical children's literature stem from the work of two early British Socialists, Edward Carpenter and William Morris. Both men were critical of the effects of industrialization and mechanization on workers and society and argued that life for the masses could be improved by reviving ways of working and living from the time when Britain's economy was founded on agriculture. Their view of pre-industrial life as a time before class, hier-archy, and money was highly romanticized; as J.B. Priestley observed, rural life in the past could not have been all that enjoyable or people would not have rushed from it to 'work in a factory for twelve hours a day for about eighteen-pence' (Priestley, 1934 400). Nevertheless Carpenter's and Morris's ideas were widely taken up by those on the Left who sought to rebuild the health of the nation by reversing the migration from the country to the city brought about by industrialization. Employing more people on the land was also seen as a way of reactivating a sense of community that was widely perceived to have atrophied under urban conditions.[1] By 1913 these aims had been policy in the Independent Labour Party's 'Rural Programme', which advocated nationalizing the land, establishing small holdings to enable more people to work on the land, and setting a min-imum wage for agricultural workers (Howkins, 1986 67). Many of those involved in setting up and running Britain's progressive schools were equally convinced of the value of spending time in the countryside, as seen in their preference for rural locations and their emphasis on students growing food, learning traditional manual skills, and taking part in outdoor pursuits such as hiking and camping (Bonnett, 2010 8; Samuel, 1998 135).

---

[1] In fact, Michael Young and Peter Willmott's *Family and Kinship in East London* (1957), based on research conducted between 1945 and 1951, revealed that in the first half of the twentieth century the urban working class was underpinned by strong social relationships.

Because they looked to the rural past for solutions to some of the problems of modernity, in *Left in the Past: Radicalism and the Politics of Nostalgia* (2010) Alistair Bonnett places Morris and Carpenter in the portion of the Left he refers to as 'radical nostalgics'. Radical nostalgics were not opposed to modernity; rather, they wanted to fuse the best of past and present to make a better future for the masses. Their views need to be distinguished from the attitudes to the past propagated by what might be called 'conservative nostalgics', those who considered modernity to be the antithesis of progress, something to be endured until it could be corrected. Differences between the two as well as points of congruence quickly become apparent through a comparison of the attitudes of radical and conservative nostalgics to the phenomenon of 'Merrie Englandism' and the way these were expressed in writing and illustration for the young.

For both Left and Right the image of the past known as Merrie England grew from the belief that the 'true England' was found in the rural spaces of earlier times: the shepherd's pasture, the greenwood, the hay field, the village green, and the squire's manor. Conservative-nostalgic books about Merrie England constitute an extreme example of what, in *Culture and Environment* (1933), F.R. Leavis and Denys Thompson argue is a central task of literary tradition in the modern age: to preserve the past and minimize the disruptions of modern life (Leavis and Thompson, 1964 1). Although they do not discuss writing for the young, Leavis and Thompson capture the sense of anxiety about the fast pace and mechanized nature of modern life that gave rise to the retreatism usually associated with the interwar years in children's literature. The conservative-nostalgic evocation of Merrie England is extreme because it does not so much preserve tradition as invent and mythologize it. A typical example is F(rank) L(eonard) Stevens's *Through Merrie England: The Pageantry and Pastimes of the Village and the Town*, an attractively produced, generously illustrated children's book of 1928.

Stevens's Merrie England is a romantic fantasy in which the past, whether in the form of houses, fashions, games, village greens, festivals of misrule, the City of London, or that icon of Merrie England 'Gloriana', is made to look picturesque, playful, and harmonious. The opening lines refer to Merrie England as a dream; it is a vision of the world as conservative nostalgics thought it should be:

> The dream of Merrie England is a tapestried thing of colour and gaiety. There is laughter in the air. The ploughman salutes the lord of the manor as he rides by; across the fields adjoining the village comes the sound of the bell; its echoes return from the depths of the great forest. Even harsh winter is the occasion for happy singing. (Stevens, 1928 1)

In this version of Merrie England, modernity is the culmination of centuries of decline and degeneration. Stevens illustrates the theme using the example of houses: in the past, he explains, houses were built of soft woods—willow, plum, elm—and oak was reserved for churches, religious houses, and princes' palaces. Now oak is used to build the homes of common folk, a symptom of misplaced values and decadence: 'When our houses were built of willow, then we had oaken men' (7–8). Although conservative-nostalgic works such as *Through Merrie England* create a longing for the past, they do not suggest that readers must work to restore it. The only hope of a return to Merrie England was found in myths such as those that promise King Arthur will return and lead Britain to a new golden age. Such fatalism was anathema to those on the Left: Marxism, Socialism, and Communism were all committed to the belief that people could bring about positive change. The fact remained, however, that Merrie England was a deep-seated phenomenon which shaped the popular imagination and so it needed to be managed, not least in radical children's literature.

One strategy the Left used to deal with Merrie England was to confront it directly and strip it of its appeal. This is the approach taken by Geoffrey Trease in *Bows Against the Barons* (1934). Realizing that his own boyhood imagination had been fired by the Robin Hood cycle, with its deep roots in the conservative-nostalgic world of Merrie England, and that he had had to educate himself away from it, Trease determined to write a novel that exposed 'the falsity of the Merrie England image' (GT/05/01 180). To this end, *Bows Against the Barons* repeatedly draws attention to the sufferings, brutality, and degradation experienced by the majority of the people in medieval England. Life, it shows, was not better in the past if you were poor. His *Comrades for the Charter* (1934) does a similar job of ensuring that readers understood the hardships and exploitation experienced by workers in earlier ages. Although they are paid a wage, it is meagre, and the miners in Trease's story are hardly better off than the serfs in *Bows Against the Barons* since they are in thrall to company-owned stores and housing with prices and rents set at levels that keep workers in debt.

Other radical writers followed Carpenter and Morris, believing that much about ways of working and living in the past had been good but, instead of lamenting the passing of a golden age, they urged readers to make England merrie again by taking action in the present. This is the line taken by F.J. Gould in *This England, and Other Things of Beauty* (1930), a collection of short essays that introduces radical-nostalgic ways of thinking about the countryside to children, many of whom had extremely limited if any access to it. Gould, a committed pacifist, Socialist, secular-humanist, and teacher, was much admired by the editorial team of *The Young Socialist*. A review of his *Pages for Young Socialists* (1913), for instance, describes it as 'the work of a rare and discerning genius' (1913 220), and the magazine included a profile of Gould in a series about such notable figures as Vladimir Lenin, Edward Carpenter, and William Morris. Born into a comfortable middle-class family, Gould spent many years teaching poor children in London and he knew well the cramped, dark, and unsanitary conditions in which many of them lived and the polluted air they breathed. Many of the essays that make up *This England* extol the beneficial effects of contact with the countryside, which is figured as a repository for the values and traditions that had been squeezed out of urban life. The opening essay 'This England' pays tribute to the work of those from the past who 'built up the strength of our dear England by their farm labour, their cattle-breeding, their wood-cutting, their toil in quarry' (5). 'This work', he continues, 'was the secret of England's greatness' (5).

As a radical-nostalgic writer, however, Gould does not just celebrate past accomplishments. He explains that work is being undertaken that will reunite working people with the countryside and reports on the projects, plans, and organizations that will make this a reality: the Council for the Preservation of Rural England (formed 1926), the National Parks movement (begun in 1931), the National Trust (founded in 1894, the Trust gained momentum in the 1920s and 1930s), and the creation of garden cities (Britain's second garden city was started in 1920). People, he explains, are banding together 'to build up a new civilization that shall have those elements of order, pleasantness and seemliness which distinguished England in the past' (v).

*This England* makes no obvious use of enscripting strategies, but it clearly assumes that readers will join the band of those who are working to protect and preserve the countryside and the right of public access that had recently been gained. The activities Gould lists are closely linked to the work of Robert Blatchford, editor of the influential Socialist weekly paper *The Clarion* and author of *Merrie England* (1893), a pamphlet that reworked Merrie Englandism to serve Socialist ends and in doing so, offered many ways for readers to both develop and perform their commitment to Socialism in the countryside. *Merrie England* sets out a vision of a reformed, Socialist Britain organized to promote the health and happiness of body and mind for all. According to *Merrie England*, the key to realizing this vision was renewing people's connection to the land and rural traditions. Blatchford did not write for children, but *Merrie England* was recommended for readers aged fifteen and up by the *Young Socialist* Education Bureau,[2] and with total sales of nearly a million copies

---

[2] The reference appears in Chapter 8 of *Socialist Sunday Schools: A Manual* (1923). The chapter contains lists of recommended reading by age.

over a number of years, *Merrie England*'s influence was considerable (Waters, 1982 20). In combination with the many long-lasting societies for all ages that grew up around *The Clarion* (young members of a Clarion Cycling Club, for instance, attended the Sheffield Peace Congress discussed in Chapter 1), Blatchford's views influenced the generations of those on the Left who were parents, grandparents, and educationalists between 1910 and 1949 and so were choosing and recommending books and activities for their children. His views were also propounded by radical children's publications such as *The Red Corner Book*, which contains features on 'Tramping' and 'The Do's and Don'ts in Swimming' ('Swimming is healthy.... Swim, therefore, as often as you can. You must be strong and healthy, for in the fight for freedom a strong and healthy fighter is of more use than a weak one' (49)). *The Young Socialist* regularly recommended hiking as a way of promoting health and creating activists as in this extract from an article on 'Developing Your Body':

> the value of such open air trips cannot be overestimated. Not only because of the bodily exhilaration which they ensure, but because the new environment clears the mind, rests the overworked brain, refreshes tired eyes and over-wrought senses. It takes the young person far away from the everyday humdrum of life, and infuses new courage, new vigour, new fervour into his spirit. It will change him from a mentally dulled and physically exhausted slave into a fighter for our cause. (1913 189)

Some children from radical households, among them the Marxist historian Raphael Samuel, had regular access to the countryside. As a boy, Samuel (born 1934) spent weekends on walks organized by groups such as the Workers' Musical Association and holidays camping with members of the Young Communist League and the Woodcraft Folk (Samuel, 1998 142). In line with Blatchford's teachings, Samuel and his companions considered time spent in the countryside 'not so much a relaxation as a way of strengthening body and soul' (139). Instead of the gentle arcadia of conservative-nostalgic Merrie England, they sought out landscapes that were as unlike the prettified home counties as possible: 'bold scenery, rugged coastlines, grey granite and crags.... We preferred the mountain peaks to the valleys, the rocky cliffs to the golden sands. We had... no taste at all for the drowsy or the lush' (133). In such landscapes they found a 'spirit of place' (146).

'Spirit of place' is a phrase particularly associated with Paul Nash, one of Britain's first modernist painters. Nash used it to refer to the spiritually revitalizing but disquieting sensations he associated with terrain that is unmarked by industrialization but bears the traces of ancient culture such as burial mounds, megaliths, or cairns (Holt, 2002). These elements find their way into radical children's literature about the countryside where, for readers like Raphael Samuel and his peers, they worked to sustain the connection to the land and the natural world they had found while walking, cycling, and camping. (Raised in a liberal, intellectual household, a pupil at two progressive schools and a teenage member of the Communist Party, Samuel is typical of one kind of child for whom radical children's literature was produced and on which many of its characters are modelled.) Of course, not all readers of radical children's literature had regular access to the countryside; engendering a connection with the landscape that evoked the spirit of place is one of the tasks undertaken by radical children's writers and illustrators. This is what inspired David Unwin to begin writing for children: 'I had an urge to proselytise, to sing the praises of the English countryside, to reach out to children—and there were enormous numbers of them—locked away in big cities and unable to escape' (Unwin, 1982 95). Writing under the pen-name David Severn, Unwin's 'Crusoe' books are quintessential examples of radical children's novels about the countryside.

## AESTHETIC RADICALISM AND THE SPIRIT OF PLACE IN DAVID SEVERN'S 'CRUSOE' SERIES

Son of the publisher Stanley Unwin and brother of the illustrator Nora Spicer Unwin, whose work is discussed below, David, born in 1918, was the ninth Unwin boy and the third generation of the family to attend Abbotsholme School. The school's emphasis on learning by doing in nature clearly shaped his writing. The five 'Crusoe' books he published between 1942 and 1946 introduce Derek and Diana Longmore who, at the start of the series, are holidaying on the farm where twins Brian and Pamela Sanville live. Superficially the books look like mainstream examples of 'camping and tramping' fiction, but from the outset there are clues that these are radical stories. The first clue relates to clothing. Brian Sanville wears shorts and an open-necked shirt of precisely the kind worn by Unwin and Raphael Samuel (and their teachers) at their progressive schools. Loose, minimal clothing was considered to be beneficial to health, especially if it exposed large parts of the body to the sun (Samuel, 1998 135; Unwin, 1982 37). Brian explains this is how he dresses at school, prompting Derek to compare his own 'pale and freckly' arms with those of the twins (Pamela evidently dresses like her brother—such unisex clothing was also favoured by walkers). 'Real, deep sunburn', Derek muses, 'was a marvellous colour; why [the twins'] limbs looked almost velvety, almost as if they had a bloom on their skin, like the bloom on those big, dark bunches of grapes you saw in shops in the town' (159). The extended, almost lyrical description reflects the fact that, like hiking, tanning was a general craze between the wars, but only progressive schools adjusted pupils' clothing to promote it. References to the children's tanned skin recur throughout Severn's series and as discussed below, in *Hermit in the Hills* the sun is associated with key moments of changed perception.

Another clue that these are examples of radical children's literature is found in the title of the first book in the series, *Rick Afire!* (1942). The words associate the story with the Swing riots of the 1830s, when agricultural workers burned ricks to protest against the introduction of the threshing machines that were threatening their livelihoods. The most overtly radical character in the series is Bill Robinson, a young man who the children befriend and call 'Crusoe'. Crusoe works in an office, but once a year he escapes to the country where he camps and attempts to write. For Crusoe, retreating to the country is not just about breaking with routine and escaping from the pollution and pressure of the city; it gives him liberty of mind and body. In the countryside he is freed from confining clothing, office hierarchies, and restrictions on what he can think and say.[3] Through Crusoe the countryside is established as an energizing space where it is possible to rethink who you are and how life should be lived. While camping he writes a book about country ways that gives him the means to establish a simple, bohemian life on the land. This is radical Merrie Englandism two generations on from Blatchford.

In book two, *A Cabin for Crusoe* (1943), Crusoe and the children plan to repair a derelict cabin so he can live in it, but a dispute between some gypsies, who claim the land on which the cabin sits, and a farmer, who legally owns it, makes that impossible. Instead, Crusoe buys an old gypsy caravan and spends the holidays roaming country lanes, accompanied by Derek, Diana, Pamela, and Brian. They make friends with some local gypsies and learn much about the life and lore of the different Romany clans whose deep connection with their cultural history is contrasted with the loss of continuity experienced by urban dwellers like Crusoe. The detailed information about gypsy life and the mutual respect and friendship that grow between Crusoe, the children, and the gypsies contribute to the radical ethos of the series in other ways, too. In the manner of D.H. Lawrence and some of his modernist contemporaries who were drawn to what they saw as less repressed and habituated (not to mention more affordable) peasant and primitive cultures, Crusoe finds that there is something about the gypsies 'that never failed to stir deep-seated longings...a "something" that seemed to conjure up all those little

---

[3] Sheeky (2012) explores the theme of liberty in Severn's series in relation to American transcendentalism.

wants and urges never allowed to come to the surface in the ordinary way' (Severn, 1943 50). He speculates about whether this arises from instinctive or aesthetic responses to 'their brown faces . . . the colours of the clothes they wore and the bright paint on their caravans' or 'their life in the open; a life full of movement and changes of scenery . . . days lived with the sun and wind and rain, out on the open heath or in the shelter of the hedgerow' (50). The gypsies are connected to the spirit of place in a way that modernity obstructs, and so is the eponymous hermit Crusoe and the children meet in the penultimate book in the series, *Hermit in the Hills* (1945). This is also the book in which an interest in aesthetic radicalism in the form of modernism, a persistent but until now minor aspect of the series, comes to the fore.

The modernist elements in the earliest Crusoe books consist of brief musings on time, memory, dreams, and the unconscious that together reflect an interest in the bohemian strand of British modernism. Initially this is developed around the figure of Crusoe who, with his interest in literature and the arts, travels in a caravan, friendship with gypsies, and ability to interpret his dreams, brings to mind the members of the Bloomsbury circle. It is possible that Crusoe is modelled on Augustus John, who also had a gypsy caravan and was surrounded by children (he had at least ten of his own with various partners). References to modernist arts and bohemia become stronger as the series evolves; especially when the group begin to travel with the Crosbies, a family of holiday walkers whose father is a painter. By *Hermit in the Hills*, which is about a holiday in the gypsy caravan in the hills near Wales, painting, primitivism, abstraction, folk culture, experiments with rendering time, and the importance of being out in the natural landscape to the process of purifying and enlarging perception have become dominant themes. The opening scene, for instance, has the children climb a high hill from which the landscape stretches below them. In mainstream children's books such a scene would have been about power and colonization as in the children's game 'King of the Castle'. This is how Arthur Ransome uses a similar perspective in *Swallows and Amazons* (1930); when the Walker children have a picnic on a promontory overlooking the lake where they are staying, Titty names it 'Darien', referring to the peak on which Cortez stood as he began the work of claiming land in what is now Mexico for Spain.[4]

---

[4] Ransome uses the lines about 'stout Cortez . . . with eagle eyes' staring at the Pacific '[s]ilent upon a peak in Darien' as the epigraph to Chapter 1 of *Swallows and Amazons*. Aishwarya Subramanian (forthcoming) offers a postcolonial reading of such views in British children's literature between the wars.

In *Hermit in the Hills*, however, the first precipitous view over a landscape begins the process of teaching the children to look at the world around them with new eyes. They are not conquerors but artists, and far from aggrandizing human achievement, the spectacle below them makes people appear as 'small and puny, insignificant as ants on a pathway' (Severn, 1945 141). Similar perspectives are used in several of Joan Kiddell-Monroe's powerful scraperboard illustrations for the book; the fact that they show largely uninhabited terrain, devoid of modern buildings, endows them with the spirit of place. The scraperboard illustrations give the appearance of wood engraving and this, together with the rural scene, is striking since at the time it was more usual to find such perspectives in Futurist paintings inspired by views from airplanes ('aeropittura') and modernist photographs taken from skyscrapers.

The spirit of place is also created by the organic connection between the ancient stone buildings and the landscape. For example, as he surveys the countryside from his high vantage point, Crusoe thinks the buildings are 'stronger and more vigorously beautiful than anything he had seen before' (12). Seeing is the leitmotif of *Hermit in the Hills* and changed perception is implicitly credited to the working of the spirit of place. The members of the group have set off with the intention of becoming better at writing, drawing, and painting. In one of the opening discussions of the subject Mr Crosbie tells the children that 'People don't use their eyes enough' and warns them about the difficulties faced by those who see things in new ways. For the children, being in the countryside heightens their ability to look closely and to render experience in new ways. Each begins to explore the difference between rendering things realistically and rendering them truthfully. The process is accelerated when they encounter the hermit of the title; a self-taught artist who has instinctively developed a form of primitive abstraction that Mr Crosbie immediately recognizes is superior to his own attempts to break with realism.

The hermit's vision is grounded in the landscape and the natural world; this point is driven home when the group visit his 'gallery'. This is one of the moments when the sun becomes an agent in the children's development. The hermit's work is displayed in a cave lit only by sunlight in the few minutes of sunrise when light shines through the cave's opening. This moment of collective witnessing is the culmination of the individual transformations that have been taking place during the holiday. Mr Crosbie's paintings, for instance, have become simplified and more vital, while Pamela, who wants to be a writer, has experienced a spiritual epiphany giving her to understand that this world is 'only a shell and that another, altogether stranger, world encircled them' (134). Michael, one of the Crosbie children, creates a map of their journey that dispenses with topographical accuracy and renders the area subjectively. Places of personal importance are given prominence, for instance, and distances indicate how long it took the hikers to reach destinations rather than how far they actually travelled. Created at the end of the trip, the map merges time and space to create a document based on impressions and memories.

As the holiday draws to a close, the travellers leave even the caravan behind, hiking deeper into the hills to the hermit's territory where 'they shed the last of their old ideas and expectations and, as moths emerge at twilight, spread wings in a dream-like world where they felt that anything might happen' (175). While 'Compared with the hermit', who lives his whole life in the deepest parts of the hills, 'they might be looking through dusty windows', the children understand that they have been changed in ways unavailable to 'people, crowded together in the towns out and away beyond the hills' (203). The extent of the change is signalled in another scene in which the sun plays a prominent role. Far into hermit-country Diana wakes before the others and climbs to the top of a hill to watch the sunrise. When the sun touches Diana's cheek she ceases to be a spectator and becomes part of the scene because she has seen it properly (Figure 4.1):

> '*This is the most wonderful thing I've ever seen.*' Diana whispered the words to herself. . . . She knew she was part of this sunrise; yes, really a part, for she had *seen* it. . . . A sunrise like this kindled your whole body to flame. You burned and were ten times as alive and a thousand times as happy as you had ever been before. (196, original emphases)

The effect on her vision is given form in Kiddell-Monroe's accompanying illustration: the clouds which Severn describes as a 'misty sea' are abstracted to form rhythmic patterns enveloped by the sculptural shape that represents the ridge where Diana stands, seeing the world as she never has before.

On this trip Severn's children have gone more deeply into the countryside than ever before, and the transformative effect of the spirit of place has been commensurately greater. *Hermit in the Hills* is the epitome of a radical children's book about the importance of connection with the landscape and ancient ways of seeing to the work of rebirthing the rising generation, making them ready to remake and differently inhabit Britain.

## REGENERATION, RE-EDUCATION, AND RECONNECTION IN THE COUNTRY SIDE

Severn's characters are middle class, making the point that while in real life figures such as Carpenter, Morris, and Blatchford were advocating contact with rural life for the masses, in radical children's fiction it is not only the

**Figure 4.1.** Joan Kiddell-Monroe illustration of Diana and the sunrise from David Severn's *Hermit in the Hills*, 1945

poor who are shown as benefitting from transformative contact with the landscape and time spent in the natural world. Several radical children's books show country interludes as instrumental to breaking down middle-class prejudices and the tendency to stereotype. For example, M(arion) Frow's *Four Stowaways and Anna* (1920) uses a journey across the country to raise questions about fear of foreigners and gender stereotypes. The story follows three middle-class children who set off for what is intended to be a holiday in the Welsh countryside. Their father, who works for British Intelligence, has been called away and his wife decides to travel with him, leaving the children to make their way independently to the family's summer house. Their mother forgets to leave them their rail tickets and through a series of misunderstandings the children do not receive the money their father has sent for them to purchase replacements. Supposing their new maid, Flossie to be a spy and believing that they must look after an important confidential letter for their father, the children flee their home and are required to find ways to support and feed themselves as they cross the countryside. They live like tramps, sleeping in various makeshift kinds of accommodation, including a military airplane they discover parked on a small landing strip. The plane is one of several ways in which *Four Stowaways and Anna*, published shortly after the end of the First World War, offers insights into the impact of that war on the national psyche. Others include the children's suspicions about Flossie the maid, their mother's tense state at living in 'this new world of worry and suspicion' (Frow, 1920 21), and the siblings' belief that they are being followed by enemy spies who are trying to intercept their father's letter.

Their situation requires them to confront not only the uncertainties experienced by those without money (exigency finds them seeking out pawnshops and selling suspect goods door-to-door), but also the way people are categorized by class, nationality, and gender. To fool the 'spies' (these turn out to be government officials attempting to give them the money their father has sent for train tickets) the children change their appearance: the girls dress as boys and the oldest boy pretends to be an effeminate French student. When they finally reach the safety of the cottage in Wales all the mysteries are resolved and their anxieties prove unfounded: Flossie is only bad-tempered, and the letter contains the money for their tickets. Nevertheless, their time in the countryside has taught them a great deal about how other people live, though, in common with most radical children's books, not about everyday life in the countryside. Despite the tendency to celebrate ways of working and communal lifestyles among country-folk on the part of the Left, and interest in farm work and manual labour in progressive schools, radical writing pays little attention to how actual country people live and work. These books are not intent on making a nation of farmers but of using the symbolic power of the countryside to promote change.

A similar pattern pertained two decades on. Barbara Euphan Todd and Esther Boumphrey's *The House that Ran Behind* (1943) has a similar plot: a group of middle-class siblings who are exploring the New Forest in a caravan find themselves under pressure when they mislay the ten pounds they have been given to cover their expenses. Without money and beyond the urban world they know so well, the children lack security for the first time in their lives and quickly learn the difficulties faced by those who live on the economic margins of society. Tony and Bridget, the oldest siblings, seek work to earn enough to feed them all, and though they are still well dressed and speak in the kind of accents that in mainstream children's books would command respect and aid whatever their circumstances, here the fact that they have no money or references means that they are mistrusted and exploited. Tony and Bridget are shocked by the way they are treated, and the illustrations by Nora S. Unwin underline the book's message that the hardships endured by the poor often have nothing to do with what kind of people they are. The drawing of Tony and Bridget tramping in the rain to find work clearly references photographs of the hunger marchers and the 'Jarrow Crusade' of the previous decade (Figure 4.2). The disproportionate relationship between the effort they put in and their wages soon has Tony talking of unions, though as Bridget points out, to little purpose since they don't belong to one.

Another group of middle-class siblings who unexpectedly have to learn to survive in the countryside are the five Dunnett children in Eleanor Graham's *The Children Who Lived in a Barn* (1938). The children, aged between seven and thirteen, are required to look after themselves when their parents, who have been called away to look after a sick relative, fail to return and the children are told their plane has crashed. Without an income the young Dunnetts are evicted from their comfortable home in a small village and find themselves living in a primitive barn offered to them by a farmer who is almost the only friendly and supportive person around them. With just a cold tap, no heating, and, presumably, no indoor lavatory facilities, their new home is not unlike the cottages/hovels in which many agricultural workers lived at the time. Sue, the oldest at age thirteen, becomes the principal carer. Her efforts are constantly undermined by the District Nurse, who is vigilant only with a view to separating the family and putting them into orphanages. The Dunnetts learn to forage and cook using old country ways (clay for baking rabbits, hay-boxes for slow cooking), and by the time their parents return, having survived the plane crash, they have been made stronger, more independent, and more resilient by their months in the country.

**Figure 4.2.** Great Depression 1929–36. Jarrow March of unemployed miners and shipbuilders from North East England set out on 5 October. © World History Archive / Alamy Stock Photo

Although the Dunnett children find inner resources and learn new skills in the countryside, *The Children Who Lived in a Barn* directs readers to think about the inadequacies of official provision for the poor and the need for modern social housing. The upheaval, displacement, and caring responsibilities experienced by the Dunnett children also anticipate the experiences of the generation of child evacuees during the Blitz, the situation explored in another book about transformation in the countryside, Kitty Barne's *Visitors from London* (1940).

*Visitors from London*, the story of seventeen evacuees from London who are billeted in a farmhouse in Sussex, was celebrated in its day, winning the Carnegie Medal for 1940. Kitty Barne wrote fourteen children's novels during the 1930s and 1940s, several of which can be classified as examples of radical children's literature for their concern with topics including war, children as artists, and class society. In *Visitors from London*, time spent in the countryside brings about social change and personal growth of various kinds, starting with class relations. Barne also uses the opportunity to bring city and country together to make a subtle dig at conservative-nostalgic Merrie Englandism. This takes the form of a comic episode in which Mrs Meredith-Smith, a well-intentioned, middle-class volunteer, attempts to teach the streetwise young Londoners how to play old country games. The games she chooses are of the kind that had been on the verge of disappearing before they were rediscovered (and sometimes reinvented) during the folklore revival of the early twentieth century. The episode exposes what very different Englands the two groups inhabit, and gently mocks some aspects of the fashion for folk customs and past lifestyles.

> She had now assembled all the children she could and was trying to instruct them as to how to enjoy these recreations. Joe Jacobson, small for nearly eleven, a sinewy, wiry person with black hair and gleaming black eyes that missed nothing, was listening with a furrowed brow.
> 'You throws the ball. I 'its it with that tiling. Then wot do I do?'
> 'You run, dear.'
> 'Where to?'
> 'From there to there to there.'
> Mrs Meredith-Smith waved the curious-looking bat gracefully in all directions, and added: 'See, dear?'
> Joe didn't see. . . . (Barne, 1940 79–80)

The first game, stoolball, proving unsuccessful, the well-meaning volunteer tries to interest them in a game with bean bags, but the children take command and launch a game of cricket by adapting the bean bags and stoolball bats. As she joins in, Mrs Meredith-Smith thinks, 'The national game. Quite right of the dear children to play it, of course. And what fun it was!' (80). Faux heritage loses out to the robust present: some things from the past, the scene suggests, have been forgotten for a reason; they belong to their time and place and change has been an improvement. The class politics of the incident implicitly suggest that the Mrs Meredith-Smiths of the world may soon themselves be obsolete since the working-class city children are shown to be more effective and resourceful than their social 'superior'.

Barne pokes fun at earnest middle-class attempts to recover and perform rural working-class culture, but *Visitors from London* treats those who are genuinely from the country and whose knowledge has been acquired over generations with considerable respect. This treatment is very much in line with the attitudes of Carpenter, Morris, and Blatchford, but there are also points of connection and crossover with conservative texts. In the conservative-nostalgic version of Merrie England, for instance, genuine country-folk are regarded as descendants of the 'men of oak', but a similar construction is used by radical writers since both radicals and conservatives employed the discourses of genetics and eugenics in which genuine country-folk were equated with pure stock, uncontaminated by either degenerate racial or class blood or the false values of metropolitan life (Howkins, 1986 69). There is, however, a pronounced tendency in mainstream children's books to treat those from the country, along with foreigners, gypsies, and members of the working-class, as imbeciles or villains. In *Visitors from London*, by contrast, the venerable shepherd, Old Tolhurst, belongs indisputably to the men of oak; his wisdom is held to extend beyond his flock and the weather. For instance, the shepherd's opinion about the likelihood of war is held in higher regard than that of politicians and reporters because 'Shepherds see most of the game' (38).

Josephine Elder's *Exile for Annis* (1938) strikes a similar balance between acknowledging the potential absurdity of some aspects of the fashion for folk culture and valuing true country lore. Like Barne, Elder (pen-name of Olive Gwendoline Potter, a doctor as well as a writer for children and adults)[5] infused a traditional genre with radical content. All ten of the children's books she produced between 1924 and 1940 were variations on the school story; *Exile for Annis* is the first of a trio of books about the Farm School, a progressive school in the countryside. Annis is sent to the Farm School to recover from a long illness while her parents are travelling. Shortly after she arrives the whole of the school, which is not much larger than a big family, goes on a picnic. After they have eaten, a violin is produced and folk-dancing suggested. City-girl Annis is dismayed:

> She had watched a folk-dancing demonstration on Hampstead Heath not long ago, performed by the most astonishing set of freaks she had ever seen. She remembered her mother's comments on it—'Hideous! A lot of elderly spinsters and a sprinkling of weedy young men, and they all dressed up most unsuitably in white, and tied belled garters below their knees and leaped! Most ungainly. The worst sort of cranks!' (Elder, 1938 36)

Her fears prove unfounded. When done by knowledgeable young people in the genuine countryside, Annis discovers, there is nothing freakish or embarrassing about folk-dancing. Far from being a clumsy pastiche, it is a simple way to connect with tradition. Learning to appreciate country pursuits such as folk-dancing is one step in the process of making Annis

---

[5] Potter was one of a small group of women allowed to train at the London Hospital between 1919 and 1922 owing to a shortage of doctors at the end of the First World War.

a healthier, happier, more productive child and future citizen. Like the Dunnett parents, Annis' mother and father find her much improved on their return. As discussed in more detail in Chapter 5, Annis's time in the country has restored her to full health, corrected her social prejudices, and made her more competent. Improving the health and social relations of all children was a central concern of radical children's literature. Chapter 5 considers how children were encouraged to learn about, care for, and liberate their bodies as part of this process.

# 5

# Making Better Britons

## *Health, Fitness, and Sex Education*

The desire to improve the lives and living conditions of the masses is a defining feature of radical children's literature. Whether writing about war, economics, education, or social experiments, the radical works so far discussed have focused on social and cultural factors that affected children's lifestyles, opportunities, and world views. Here attention shifts to how radical writing for children positioned children's and young people's bodies in the drive for social improvement. Improving the nation's health and fitness was a topic of national interest, and from the late 1920s mainstream children's publications regularly carried articles and stories that enthused about the pleasures and benefits of outdoor activities and exercise regimes. They also gave instruction in sports, prioritizing those such as swimming, tennis, and cricket that could be done using public facilities and with others. From the 1920s through the 1940s the covers of popular annuals such as *Blackie's Boys'/Girls' Annual* and *Warne's Pleasure Books for Boys/Girls* regularly showed attractively toned youthful bodies engaged in a variety of outdoor activities: riding, sailing, playing tennis, and, particular favourites, sunbathing or diving gracefully into one of the open-air swimming pools or lidos that became fashionable during the 1930s (Figure 5.1). At the time, images of healthy young bodies engaging in recreational sports implicitly identified the subjects as middle or upper class, pointing to one of the key differences between radical and mainstream publications' treatment of youthful bodies.

Almost without exception, mainstream books from this period feature children who represent a physical ideal. Like Arthur Ransome's Swallows and Amazons, they have plenty of nutritious food to eat, clean comfortable homes, suitable clothing for every occasion, and regular access to the countryside. Viewed from the perspective of the new science of eugenics, the strong, well-formed bodies and freedom from chronic illnesses or congenital weaknesses indicate that these youngsters come from good 'racial stock'. The middle-class children in these stories spend their leisure time out of doors hiking, camping, in boats, bathing in cold streams, and

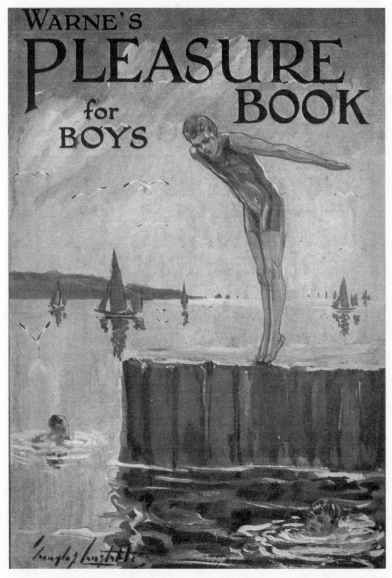

**Figure 5.1.** 1929 cover for a *Warne's Pleasure Book for Boys*

otherwise engaged in health-promoting activities that are punctuated by adventures and mysteries. The unstated message in such texts is that the nation needs as many of these children as possible; they are the model and the measure of good Britons. By contrast, in these same texts the children of the poor are nearly always either absent or associated with a toxic set of traits that establish them as dysgenic. The term had recently been coined in response to new genetic knowledge, but the characterization of the poor as contaminated and inferior was deeply rooted in British culture.[1]

In the course of the previous century poor children, many of whom used the streets as playgrounds, places of work, and in some cases as alternatives to homes, came to be seen as a threat to society. Often dirty, ragged, and unruly, as Anna Davin points out in *Growing Up Poor, 1870–1914*, they tended to be lumped together and given pejorative labels: 'arabs, urchins, scaramouches, guttersnipes; "a wild race", "nomadic", "a multitude of untutored savages", even "English Kaffirs" and "Hottentots"' (Davin, 1996 162). Such characterizations were compounded and intensified as poor girls and boys matured. Working-class girls were often assumed to be sexually active and carriers of sexually transmitted disease and, since precocious sexual experience was held to be symptomatic of promiscuity, they were also deemed to be morally degenerate (Overy, 2010 149). The inadequate bodies of poor boys came to attention when worrying numbers of young men were deemed unfit for military service in the Boer War. The damaged, often diseased bodies of working-class children, then, were regarded as a threat to Britain's imperial prowess and efficiency, meaning that their absence in mainstream children's books needs to be understood in the context of public debates about the desirability of removing them from the British gene pool (Overy, 2010 96). This is not to say that such books were consciously supporting some of the proposals put forward by eugenicists to 'save the world' and 'solve the problem of decay of civilizations' through programmes of officially controlled breeding.[2] Nonetheless, where the waif novels of the Victorian/ Edwardian era had deliberately brought such children to the fore as a way of urging readers to sympathize with and provide for them, in the years after the First World War they were conspicuously absent from most writing for children.

Radical children's literature, by contrast, introduces poor child characters to refute claims that such children are intrinsically inferior to those who are well-off and that the poor are responsible for their unhealthy and

---

[1] The term 'dysgenic' was coined to talk about the negative genetic impact on the population of war; being deemed unfit for military service preserved the lives of those who were not physically robust while those who were fit were enlisted and died in large numbers (Overy, 2010 108).

[2] These are the words of, first, Caleb Saleeby, one of the founders of the British eugenic movement speaking in 1909, followed by Cambridge geneticist Ronald Fisher speaking in 1926. Both are quoted in Chapter 3 of Richard Overy's *The Morbid Age*, which focuses on perceptions that Britain's 'racial body' was diseased and scientific theories for addressing the problem (Overy, 2010 101).

grim lifestyles. Many radical texts also present mass poverty as economically wasteful, morally degrading (not least to those who permit it), and capable of being rectified through better pay for parents, government investment, legislation, and education. Foremost among those producing stories and articles along these lines was Margaret McMillan. McMillan was a Socialist propagandist and champion of Britain's poor city children. Through publications, projects, and political activities she was instrumental in developing the Left's interest in children and childhood. As well as addressing the general public and politicians (she was on the Independent Labour Party national executive board), Margaret McMillan wrote fiction and journalism for children in which she explained or dramatized key Socialist ideas and urged readers to fight against the unfairness of a society sharply divided between haves and have nots. In the course of writing three studies about childhood and the education of socially disadvantaged children—*Early Childhood* (1900), *Education Through the Imagination* (1904), and *Labour and Childhood* (1907)— McMillan became convinced of the importance of children's physical bodies and material wellbeing to their intellectual and social development. These ideas are distilled in 'The Child of the Future' (1913), one of the more than forty contributions she made to *The Young Socialist* (Steedman, 1990 175).[3]

## WASHING AWAY THE STAINS: PHYSICAL TRANSFORMATION THROUGH SOCIAL REGENERATION

'The Child of the Future' imagines a time when 'every sign of disease, every trace of impurity, has been washed away' from all poor children (*The Young Socialist*, 1913 36). The piece introduces readers to one of the most important of the many projects to improve the conditions of Britain's slum children that McMillan and her sister Rachel initiated: the Deptford Camp School. A nursery school by day and a camp where children over eight could wash and sleep in safety by night, the Camp School shared many of the principles and practices of the open-air school movement that had recently been imported from Germany to combat the spread of tuberculosis: fresh air, sunlight, a nourishing diet, rest, and medical

---

[3] Margaret McMillan and her sister Rachel, with whom she worked closely, were also involved in Keir Hardie's The Crusaders campaign (1893), a fellowship for those under sixteen and the roots of the Socialist Sunday School movement (Jane Rosen correspondence, 30 May 2013; Sumpter 2006).

treatment, all in a hygienic setting. In 'The Child of the Future' McMillan describes the 'first fruits of the new order' (36) and prophesies that, if done on a grand scale, this regime could reverse the decline in the health and efficiency of Britain's population. The problem stems, she argues, not from defective genes but poverty and inequality.

'The Child of the Future' mingles fact and fiction; it begins by locating events in the Camp School: 'Yesterday a wonderful thing happened. It was at the Evelyn Street Home, a humble little house where ambitious projects are entertained' (36). Evelyn Street in Deptford was the address of the part of the School where the girls were based (boys stayed in nearby Albury Street). Other details, such as the size of the rooms and the costumes the girls have made, indicate first-hand knowledge:

[The girls] are dressed in cotton bodies with embroidered turn-down collars, and in serge knickers and shoulder skirts, and each wears a cardinal sash of coarse braid. Each girl has made her own costume and paid for the material in instalments. The costumes entire do not come to more than 2/- to 3/-. (36)

The 'wonderful thing' is an exhibition of drill performed by girls aged nine to thirteen, each of whom, readers are informed, initially arrived at the Camp School with her 'beauty trampled under and hidden by the stains of disease and poverty' (36). In the course of a single year the girls have been so transformed by good diet, comfortable, sanitary conditions, and education that for the McMillan persona who witnesses the performance, it is as if she has 'never seen them before'. There is Lily, brought in as a 'cripple' but whose limbs are now 'straight and strong'; and Alice, with 'every mark of high race', and 'trooping behind [Alice], and on either side, other girl-forms, almost as beautiful, almost as instinct [sic] with what is precious in our race' (36). After describing the exhibition, the piece proclaims, 'Deptford! Yes, this is Deptford—with the stains wiped away' (36).

The optimism of the account is undercut as it draws to a close, however; the vision that had seemed so concrete and so quickly and economically achieved is revealed to be a dream of how things could be. The focus at this point shifts from celebrating the changes in the Camp School girls to lamenting the fact that the benefits are limited to the small number of children who can be accommodated in a single house in a single city in a single country. It ends by acknowledging that if the future is to be different, versions of the Deptford Camp School need to be rolled out across the globe so that the 36 million children living in poverty can, like Lily and Alice and the other girls in the story, be transformed into 36 million happy, healthy, productive 'aristocrats' (37).

Although it ends with a global vision, 'The Child of the Future' is principally concerned with conditions in Britain and, as can be seen in her use of the word 'aristocrats', in it McMillan confronts a range of national attitudes that restrict the lives of the poor. She starts by setting the Camp's insistence on the need for children to bathe regularly against G.K. Chesterton's quip that 'only Pharisees and English aristocrats go in for washing' (37). From his privileged position, McMillan suggests, Chesterton may take bathing lightly, but for those living in cramped, often squalid conditions, it is both nearly impossible and essential to health and social acceptance. The comparison takes her argument beyond the ameliorating effects of good diet and regular baths, however, and reveals the design in McMillan's lexical choices. Words such as 'race' and 'instinct', for example, are drawn from scientific discourses arising from evolution, genetics, and anthropology, and suggest that the children's new-found beauty and grace are innate. The vocabulary underpins the message that there is nothing unique about these children; the qualities that have emerged in the conditions at the Camp School have been there all along, but were obscured and distorted by dirt, disease, and diet. By extension, there is nothing special about those who are officially recognized as aristocrats; they are not by nature superior to others, but simply better nurtured, better educated, and better endowed materially. 'The Child of the Future' identifies child poverty, wherever it occurs, to be a waste of lives and human resources that undermines the future progress and security of the nation. The glance into the future it offers underscores this message and the logic associated with it: caring for children's bodies improves children's health and with it their ability to learn and work thereby changing society for the better. However, it also serves as a warning that unless the situation is rectified, the processes of decline and degeneration will continue and the child of the future will be even more stunted and dependent than the child of the present.

Other radical texts make similar points about the benefits of caring for rather than eliminating the nation's poor children. For instance, Aubrey de Sélincourt's *Micky* (1948) tells of the discovery of working-class orphan Micky by a group of middle-class children who closely resemble the Swallows and Amazons in their backgrounds and interests. Micky has fallen asleep in their island campsite after running away from a local farm where he has been abused by the family in whose care he has been placed. The children take him home and eventually their family adopt him, but this rather easy happy ending does not detract from a sensitively told story that conveys the effects of abuse on Micky's mental state. De Sélincourt's text and the illustrations by his brother Guy (who also illustrated some of their brother-in-law A.A. Milne's books) place a child at its centre who, at the time, would normally have been outside the purview of children's fiction. Micky is not an innocent, instantly recuperated Oliver-Twist figure. When the children bring him home, he has difficulty adjusting and everyone has to work to repair the damage that has been done to him. Because *Micky* is a longer, more complicated work than 'The Child of the Future', de Sélincourt is able to show that, as well as having his physical needs attended to, Micky requires emotional support, education, and security. Like McMillan's girls in Deptford, however, ultimately he *is* healed and becomes healthy, happy, loved, and loving. He is given a new start and in his own way becomes a child of the future.

There is a considerable degree of middle-class do-gooding in de Sélincourt's text, and the same is true of Norman Dale's books featuring Sidney Parr, another working-class orphan who is taken up by a middle-class household. Dale (pen-name of Norman George Denny) wrote three books in which Sidney and his friend Tim, a middle-class boy who is also an orphan, have adventures. The pair meet in *Exciting Journey* (1947) when Tim discovers Sidney 'roving the countryside, alone and half-starved' having run away from the institution where he has been placed (Dale, 1948 10). In *Mystery Christmas* (1948), the second book in the trilogy, Sidney is rewarded for having returned to the institution and applied himself to his lessons with an invitation to spend the Christmas holidays with Tim and his uncle. Dale's use of two orphans makes the point that the kind of people children become depends more on the sector of society into which they are born than on their genes. Without a wealthy uncle to take him in, Tim could have ended up in the same position as Sidney; when dressed in one of Tim's school blazers Sidney looks 'much like any other boy' (57)—looking middle class being the default norm in this story. Although the two-orphan device is to some extent equalizing, *Mystery Christmas* does not skirt over the tensions arising from the clash of class experiences when a boy who has been 'dragged up in a London slum' (10) enters a middle-class household. The housekeeper mistrusts Sidney, he doesn't have the right clothes, and at first he doesn't fit in with Tim's friends, who have set up a club in an empty old house that once belonged to a mysterious miser. Things improve when the boys stumble upon clues to where a treasure is buried. At this point the adventure-mystery aspect of the plot overwhelms any social commentary and the group of boys become an effective team in which Sidney plays a full part in thwarting some villains who have planned to steal the treasure that rightfully belongs to the miser's son. When they are given £100 for capturing the crooks, the boys decide to give it to Sidney so he can set up a savings account. This action is presumably intended to set a good example and show the middle-class characters in a favourable light, but it strikes an unfortunately patronizing note on which to end a book that has attempted to break down class barriers.

As *Mystery Christmas* shows, the politics of class and poverty are complex, and writers of radical children's stories often make similarly inept assumptions predicated on middle-class experiences, tastes, and aspirations. Both Micky and Sidney benefit from middle-class interventions that extricate them from poverty, but this also entails leaving their class behind. Since both boys have already been cut off from their communities by being orphaned and uprooted, in the context of these stories this is not a major issue, but it does raise questions about how some well-intentioned radical writers represented the working classes. A book that, in its day, was hailed as a welcome and successful representation of working-class life is Eve Garnett's *The Family from One End Street* (1937), about dustman Jo and washerwoman Rosie Ruggles and their seven children. Garnett was motivated to write the book when she noticed that the waifs, orphans, and children of the poor that had featured in her own childhood reading of Victorian children's literature were absent in the children's literature of the time. Her characters are based on first-hand observation of real children and families conducted when she was commissioned to illustrate Evelyn Sharp's *The London Child* (1927), which involved her spending time studying the lives and behaviour of London's poor children. Winner of the Carnegie Medal and taken up by Puffin, *The Family from One End Street* was never forgotten as the other books discussed in this chapter were, though towards the end of the twentieth century it was frequently criticized for displaying a patronizing attitude to the working class (e.g. Townsend, 1974 187). That criticism has been contested (the book was a World Book Day recommended read in 2011), and when it comes to the care of the children it is certainly undeserved. Jo and Rosie are loving parents and their children are thriving (Figure 5.2). One daughter wins a scholarship to attend secondary school, and the baby wins his category in the local baby contest.

No doubt one reason why Garnett's book has been remembered is that it stands out among those from this period that represent working-class children for the way it shows the Ruggles family as happy with their place in the social scheme, comfortable in their class culture, and benefitting from a nascent welfare state without becoming dependent on it (as well as Kate's scholarship it is mentioned that the family once received state support when Jo broke his leg). This makes comfortable reading for the conservative parts of society, but significantly, in many ways the Ruggles children, with their access to the Sussex countryside, ability to wash, regular meals, and even enough money for family outings, embody the vision of a thriving working class Margaret McMillan conjured up a quarter of a century earlier. Garnett's book sets out a vision that can be shared by both radicals and conservatives. Importantly, the success of

**Figure 5.2.** 'His brothers and sisters crowded round' from Eve Garnett's *The Family from One End Street*, 1937. Image courtesy of Penguin Books

Garnett's book meant that this image of working-class children was not just reflected back to those who already shared this view as was the case with *The Young Socialist*. Winning the Carnegie Medal and being offered as a Puffin paperback from 1942 (it is now a 'Puffin Modern Classic') took *The Family from One End Street* into middle-class homes and provided a corrective to the perception that poor children came from degenerate stock and were unfit for the nation's needs.

As the examples here show, when it comes to depicting poor children, the degree of radicalism in radical children's books varies with intended audience and genre. Where Margaret McMillan is preaching to the converted and so can quickly map out her plan to transform the lives of all the poor, de Sélincourt and Dale use mainstream genres (holiday and mystery-adventure stories) to show how individual acts of kindness can be transformative. While de Sélincourt and Dale show poor children being assimilated into the middle class, Garnett presents a fully functional working-class family. Their approaches are different, but all four writers put children who are usually marginalized or criminalized at the centre of stories in which they become known and valued. Each contributes to the effort to make child poverty an issue for young British readers. They do this by showing working-class child characters as worth the investment: they are educable, responsive, and so can be expected to become useful members of the work force. It was not until the late 1960s, when debates about racism, sexism, and classism began to dominate children's book publishing and criticism, that the work of pioneer radicals in validating the lives and roles of the working class was developed in a sustained way across the sector.

## CHILD HEALTH, CHILDREN'S BOOKS, AND PROGRESSIVE SCHOOLS

The crisis in child health in early twentieth-century Britain was focused on children of the poor, but not all better-off children were the perfect specimens featured in adventure and camping fiction. From the beginning of the century and throughout the interwar period, raising overall levels of health and fitness was a national project; a government White Paper (1937) gave rise to the Physical Training and Recreation Act and begat the National Fitness Council which provided grants for the kinds of facilities— swimming pools, sports clubs, playing fields, and youth hostels—that featured in popular publications for children (Gardiner, 2011 516). Fears about the unhealthy lifestyles of the poor were seen as well founded following a 1935 report that indicated that 91 per cent of boys aged fourteen to eighteen never engaged in any form of physical activity (2011 515) and Britain's undistinguished performance at the 1936 Olympics (twelfth out of thirty-two competing nations).

Children's literature—both mainstream and radical—had been involved in various attempts to improve the health and childhoods of British children from the beginning of the last century. Mention has already been made of the way popular stories, magazines, and other texts encouraged readers to take part in sports and games in the open air, but children's books and authors promoted ideas about health and fitness in a variety of other ways. Children's literature, for example, featured among the displays of toys, clothing, health-promoting exercises, and lectures on caring for children at the two Children's Welfare Exhibitions held at London's Olympia in 1912–13 and 1914. Jenny Bavidge notes that in the absence of other recognized authorities, children's books and their authors were brought in to speak 'by those concerned with the lives of Edwardian children, and [they] helped to define categories of childhood around welfare issues' (2009 125). Bavidge looks in detail at the example of E. Nesbit, who as a founder-member of the Fabian Society, feminist, and campaigner for rational dress was certainly on the radical spectrum. Nesbit was enlisted to support the work of the exhibitions in stimulating debate and disseminating up-to-date knowledge around childhood and child welfare on the basis that to write for children she must understand their minds and imaginations (126–7). Children's literature had a long history of depicting children from all backgrounds who suffered from real and hysterical diseases. The early twentieth century saw such children being cured through regimes of activity in the fresh country air and good diets: the epitome of sickly child characters who are restored to health in this way is found in Frances Hodgson Burnett's *The Secret Garden* (1911). Mary Lennox arrives in Yorkshire as a sickly and sulky orphan of the Empire (her parents having died in an outbreak of cholera in India). From a lethargic, self-centred child accustomed to picking at rich and exotic foods and being waited on, she is transformed into a vigorous, capable girl by quantities of plain food and gardening. Using the same method, Mary in turn cures her cousin Colin, who imagines he has a congenital deformity in his spine.

Mary's regime is undertaken on the advice of a local country woman, Susan Sowerby, a rare instance in children's literature from this period of the working classes advising the well-to-do. Links between the enthusiasm for the countryside and the wisdom of country folk discussed in Chapter 4 can readily be made here. Susan Sowerby's advice for building up Mary's body and character also reflects the kinds of programmes of health and fitness popular with the liberal-leaning parents and in place at many progressive schools, with their organic gardens where pupils were required to work, emphasis on open-air sports, and concern with children's diets (several headmasters of progressive schools advocated, though they did not enforce, vegetarianism).

In the light of evidence gathered and disseminated by nutritionists, psychologists, doctors, and experts in physical culture, hygiene, and child development, in terms of children's health and wellbeing much of what at the beginning of the century had been dismissed as eccentric came to be accepted as good practice and common sense during the interwar years. This was especially true among the left-leaning liberal intelligentsia who helped create, and whose children were among the main consumers of radical children's literature. Many of the children from this part of society also attended progressive schools which, as Virginia Nicholson explains in *Among the Bohemians* (2002), offered palatable alternatives to adults (mostly men) who had suffered in their own school days from the rigidity and militarism of public schools.[4] Radical writers capitalized on the more receptive environment for new ideas about children's health to reinforce and spread the progressive schools' message. For example, Chapter 4 shows how David Severn incorporated aspects of the Abbotsholme philosophy into his children's fiction, and between 1916 and 1939 A.S. Neill, founder and Headmaster of Summerhill School, published six books for children that in various ways reflect his developing philosophy and pedagogic practice. More influential in this regard, however, were works that took the popular school story format into progressive school settings. By encouraging readers to imagine themselves in experimental schools, they introduced radical ideas about the curriculum and teaching methods to child readers. In life and in fiction the major departures from traditional schools related to children's bodies and discipline: their freedom from corporal punishments and constrictive uniforms; days organized around spending time in the outdoors; flexible attitudes to teaching schedules; self-governance; and cultivation of an uninhibited attitude to bodies and bodily functions. These differences all feature in radical school stories such as Josephine Elder's *Exile for Annis* (1938), which was briefly discussed in Chapter 4 in relation to the folk culture revival.

When Annis Best learns that her parents have enrolled her in the Farm School to help her complete her recovery from whooping cough while they are travelling in connection with her father's work, she is appalled. Her illness has left her weak, but Annis is otherwise a typical example of the middle-class child characters found in most holiday-adventure stories: she is sporty, happy, and popular. Her dismayed reaction to her parents' announcement stems from the fact that Annis has assimilated her selective High School's scorn for 'cranky schools of all sorts, whether they were fashionable, artistic, co-educational, or, in fact, anything other than a High School or one of the big public boarding schools' (Elder, 1938 14). As the tone of this quote signals it will do, the story sets about dismantling this prejudice. It also raises questions about how healthy life is for children even in the suburbs of Britain's cities since Annis's doctor says she needs country air to complete her recovery. The doctor's prescription is also an indication of how widely the general ethos of the open-air movement that the McMillan sisters helped to found had become established by the 1930s.

---

[4] Chapter 3, 'Children of Light', looks at several aspects of bohemian childhood, including children's experiences at some of Britain's progressive schools, among them the Beacon School, Bedales, Gresham's School, King Alfred's School, St Christopher's School in Letchworth Garden City, and Summerhill. Nicholson takes a dim view of the schools but notes that many lasting friendships and marriages were formed in them: 'The homogeneity of tastes, of ethical ideals and social codes experienced at an impressionable age created a kind of freemasonry that . . . was to last a lifetime' (2003 900–1).

At first Annis sees the school as exactly the 'batty institution' she expected, with children playing instruments in the meadows and no school bells, punishments, or other obvious systems for managing pupils, but she soon begins to enjoy the new environment and to be impressed at the quiet competence of the students, their success in exams, and the general excellence of the teachers and their methods. The Farm School is co-educational and has very small classes where each child is treated as an individual; most classes take place in the open air. As in most real-life progressive schools, the Farm School curriculum involves manual labour such as gardening, looking after poultry, working in the dairy, and learning to ride and care for ponies.[5]

The success of the Farm School's methods is evident when Annis's parents return from their travels and are impressed by 'the amount she had grown and filled out, and at the redness of her cheeks and the size of her appetite' as well as all her other accomplishments: 'I can ride and drive and milk, and look after chickens and pack fruit for Covent Garden—and pick it, of course—and we've made a boat and I can paddle that and sail, *and* manage a proper canoe and a punt as well' (222). The changes in Annis's body are matched by those in her mind; Annis shows her parents that she has learned to think independently and objectively and become more self-controlled. Asked whether she wants to return to the High School, she acknowledges the benefits of some of what she learned there but concludes that the Farm School 'makes better people' (223). Making better people is the chief goal of radical children's literature. In *Exile for Annis*, making better people means developing children's bodies and self-esteem as much as intellects.

As ideas drawn from progressive schools began to impact on general teacher training, even writers who are usually regarded as highly conventional became advocates for progressive education, notably Enid Blyton, whose series of Naughtiest Girl books (1940–52) bears a striking resemblance to Elder's novels about the Farm School. Like Annis, Elizabeth Allen, the eponymous 'naughtiest girl', arrives at Whyteleaf School determined to dislike it but is gradually converted to its philosophies and lifestyle. Whyteleafe School is co-educational, pupils work in the school's gardens and stables, and a jury of twelve pupils manages punishments and privileges. The most significant difference between Blyton's school and Elder's is the emphasis placed on understanding and addressing children's

---

[5] J.H. Badley, founder and Headmaster of Bedales, explained the place of manual labour in progressive school life in one of his regular addresses to pupils. It served, he said, as a corrective to too much mental work, and it helped pupils not to assume one kind of work was superior to another. It taught the dignity of working for others and through it pupils learned how much things cost in effort and materials so they valued them more (Badley, 1920 87).

psychological rather than physical needs. Although the school's healthy outdoor lifestyle is clearly beneficial, emphasis is given to how its ways of treating pupils bring about Elizabeth's mental and emotional transformation from an unhappy and badly behaved child to a happy, well-adjusted one.

A writer who, though certainly not in the radical vanguard, nonetheless produced a book in praise of progressive schools' ability to heal troubled children is 'Carol Forrest', the pen-name of Margaret Tennyson, a long-term advocate of open-air activities through her work for the Girl Guides. In *Caravan School* (1946), three siblings, Jocelyn, Bobbin, and Steve, have returned to England after having been evacuated to the US for three years during the Blitz. They are struggling to readjust to life in England and particularly to the rigidity of traditional schools so, unbeknownst to them, an aunt (one they have never met) decides to help them discover an alternative. The aunt's plan is used to weave together several themes and motifs of radical children's literature: the children acquire practical skills by fixing up the caravan in which they will travel; they spend time in the countryside where they learn about country crafts; and during their travels stereotypical gender roles are dismantled. For instance, jobs are shared between the three children irrespective of sex, and the eldest boy is required to take his turn cooking even though at first he fears it will make him look a 'sissy'.

Once the caravan has been restored, they set off on what Jocelyn, Bobbin, and Steve think is a holiday in the company of the woman they know as 'Miss England'; she is, of course, their aunt. Miss England has mapped out a route that introduces the children to a number of rural landscapes and craftspeople before culminating near Quarry Foot, a progressive school where pupils learn a range of traditional crafts and study because they are motivated to do so, not because they have to. Exactly as their aunt has hoped, the three children recognize that they will thrive at Quarry Foot and ask to join the school. It is not just the teaching methods of Quarry Foot that are valued in *Caravan School*. Their aunt's goal is to provide them with an education that will inspire them to want to change the world and see it as their responsibility to prepare to manage the world they make. It is clear that this aspect of her plan has also been achieved when Jocelyn announces: 'The way I see it is—we've all got to think, 'cos it's up to us who bosses the world—really. If we aren't interested that way—then we haven't any right to complain when we don't get things the way we want them' (133).

Each of these books is an ambassador for progressive education; together they show progressive schools as enjoyable, healthy, and enabling places. This positive attitude to progressive education was reflected in an increase of provision that prompted publications such as L.B. Perkin's introduction to *Progressive Schools* (1934), which was enthusiastically reviewed in *Out of Bounds* (1934, 3 36) by a pupil from Wellington. Victor Gollancz responded to interest in progressive schools by commissioning a guide on the subject. Gollancz's *The Modern Schools Handbook*, edited by Trevor Blewitt, appeared in 1934 with an introduction by Amabel Williams-Ellis. Amabel Williams-Ellis is another of the interlocking figures in the world of radical children's literature: she was the sister of John Strachey who helped Victor Gollancz found the Left Book Club; cousin of Lytton and James Strachey, members of the Bloomsbury set (Lytton also attended and later helped manage Abbotsholme); wife of the influential left-leaning architect Clough Williams-Ellis; and on the board of *Left Review*. The *Handbook*, she explains, is 'as widely representative as possible of all types of progressive *private* schools, the numbers and variety of which are so bewildering to parents' (Foreword n.p., original italics). That it is representative rather than comprehensive is, according to Williams-Ellis, a consequence of the fact that there were by then so many progressive schools. For the purposes of the *Handbook* she defines these as schools that reject aspects of the conventional public schools system, insist on the needs of the individual child, and believe in a changing world (Foreword, n.p.).

The 1920s and 1930s were the hey-day of progressive schools; nevertheless Williams-Ellis's comment on the size of the sector needs some qualification. The *Handbook* provides descriptions by their Heads of seventeen progressive schools that catered for children aged two to nineteen as well as a section on progressive junior and preparatory schools. Some, like Abbotsholme (founded 1889), Bedales (founded 1893), and Leighton Park (founded 1890), were well established; others, like Bertrand and Dora Russell's Beacon School (founded 1927), had been running for only a few years. Given that at the time there were some 34 300 elementary schools and 969 secondary schools in England, Wales, and Scotland, even allowing for the fact that this is a sample rather than a comprehensive list of all progressive schools, it is clear that while the numbers were growing, they were still very much in the minority (Bolton, 2012 3).[6]

Although they were attended by a tiny proportion of Britain's children, by the 1930s many ideas and practices usually associated with progressive schools had been incorporated in teacher training and the curricula of state schools, and education was a key aspect of the drive for Britain to become a socially progressive society. One area of the progressive curriculum that was rarely included in state education before the 1930s—and one

[6] These figures are based on provision across England, Scotland, and Wales in 1900, the most recent year for which reliable statistics were found. *A Modern School's Handbook* looks only at provision in England in 1933.

on which children's stories about fictional progressive schools are noticeably silent—is sex education. This was a topic that put the child's body in
the midst of radical debates about eugenics and birth control from a
perspective that differed in some important ways from Margaret McMillan's. Since writing about sex implicitly challenged religious teaching,
social convention, and legislation on blasphemy and decency, it was also
one of the most contentious areas of radical publishing for children.

## SEX EDUCATION, PROGRESSIVE PEDAGOGY, AND RADICAL TEXTS

Each progressive school approached sex education in its own way, but all
encouraged children to regard their bodies and sexual feelings as normal
and natural. The range of approaches is reflected in radical children's
publications about sex. For example, at the Russells' Beacon School there
were no sex education classes, but children were encouraged to ask
questions and initiate discussions when they were curious about anything
to do with sex. In his entry for *The Modern Schools Handbook* Bertrand
Russell explains,

> We make no secrets in regard to any kind of knowledge. We answer sex
> questions, and we do not impose taboos on nakedness. We do not find it
> necessary to give special sex instruction, as this always comes into the biology
> work, and when any new child shows ignorance, then explanations are given.
> (Russell in Blewitt, 1934 39)

A similar approach is taken by Amabel Williams-Ellis in *How You Began*
(1928), a book for younger children which ends with a chapter of
questions from real children. *How You Began* is more concerned with
embryology than reproduction, but it holds to the principle that it is
important to answer children's questions fully and honestly. The questions establish that children are naturally curious about bodies. Using real
children's questions allows Williams-Ellis to expose the potential for
misunderstandings—and the risky behaviour this could lead to—in the
absence of accurate information, one of the key justifications put forward
by those who favoured teaching children about sex.

At Summerhill A.S. Neill took a more direct and controlling approach
with both children and parents than the Russells or Williams-Ellis:

> Every child is oriented about sex, not vaguely by talks about bees and pollen,
> but bluntly about the whole business. The parents are asked to co-operate

with the school in contradicting any lies that have been told to the child about sex and religion. (A.S. Neill in Blewitt 121)

However sex education was managed in individual progressive schools, it involved becoming familiar with the human body, inside and out. Most schools and publications took the approach that physiologically reproduction was a bodily function like any other. Children needed to know how their bodies worked in this respect as much as they needed to know about nutrition, waste, breathing, and the circulation of blood. Progressive boys' schools (no similar evidence has been located for girls' schools) developed an ideology in which the healthy naked body epitomized a series of virtues: humans are born naked so to be naked is our natural condition; clothing marked Adam and Eve's expulsion from Eden so nakedness connotes innocence; the ancient Greeks extolled the symmetry and proportion of the human body which can only be appreciated when naked, and so on. All of these are ways of combating embarrassment, guilt, shame, and other negative responses to bodies and are the motivation for the examples of radical children's publications about sex and bodies discussed below (Figure 5.3).[7]

The determination to combat thinking that constructed the naked body as a source of shame owed much to the teachings of Sigmund Freud and his followers such as Wilhelm Reich (a powerful influence on A.S. Neill), who argued that sexual repression was a cause of personal and social illness, not least as manifested in the rise of fascism in the interwar years.[8] This view was shared across the Left-liberal spectrum and permeated modernist writing, although more generally it was feared that 'the uninhibited sexuality implicit in Freudian thinking would provoke a moral crisis that might threaten social order and civilized behaviour' (Overy, 2010 149). As early as 1913 *The Young Socialist* carried a review-article about 'Books on Delicate Subjects' which similarly pointed to the personal and social consequences of ignorance and repression:

the books deal with subjects which, vitally important though they are to the needs of childhood, are yet persistently neglected by present-day teaching authorities. Sex subjects, for growing people, need to be handled carefully and delicately, but they need to be handled. Until such matters are dealt with

[7] Havelock Ellis includes a chapter on 'Nakedness and Education' in volume six of *Studies in the Psychology of Sex* (1927). The list of justifications for pupils to be naked in front of one another comes from that chapter.

[8] Turner (2011) maps the influence of Freud and his set on the early twentieth century and looks in some detail at the relationship between A.S. Neill and Wilhelm Reich. The belief that at least some of society's ills could be cured by being open about sex from childhood and teaching children the facts of life was not confined to supporters of Freud. Cyril Burt, who was highly critical of Freud, connected sexual repression and juvenile delinquency (Overy, 2010 153).

**Figure 5.3.** Natural nakedness; boys bathing at Abbotsholme School circa 1920. Image courtesy of Abbotsholme School

openly, in sympathetic and intelligent fashion, we may expect nothing but unhappiness to come as a result in years after.... Prudery and calculated ignorance are responsible for a thousand evils in our land. There is no room for either of them in the socialist movement. Lessons on sex and kindred subjects should have a more prominent place in our schools [Socialist Sunday Schools] than they have at present. (1913 220–1)

As detailed below, the most concerted Socialist effort to publish instructional literature about sex for the young fell foul of the censors. Progressive schools were more successful.

The importance placed by progressive educationalists on providing young people with reliable information about their bodies and reproduction is evident from a 1935 conference and companion publication, *Experiments in Sex Education*, led by J.H. Badley of Bedales for the Federation of Progressive Societies and Individuals. The aim was not so much to induct teachers into how to introduce children and young people to the mechanics of sex as to reform attitudes to it starting with the school system. Participants wanted schools to help the British public recognize sex as 'one of the great and beautiful bases of a well-evolved life, a thing to be understood scientifically ... and to be felt with joy and power' (Badley, 1935 4). As the examples discussed below show, these were the messages that progressive schools imparted to their pupils and which find their way into radical children's books about young people as sexual beings. It is important to say at this point that for all their desire to liberate children from sex-guilt, and unlike most other areas of radical writing, radical books did not encourage readers to act immediately on the knowledge they were given. The aim was to eradicate ignorance and guilt, not to launch children into sexual activity and especially not on school grounds where teachers were expected to be *in loco parentis*. Striking the right balance between providing information and encouraging experimentation was difficult, but the conviction that a healthy, enjoyable sex life was good for individuals and the nation was strong. Feeding this belief was new scientific knowledge about bodies, instincts, and minds particularly associated with the work of Havelock Ellis, whose six-volume *Studies in the Psychology of Sex* was completed in 1927. In it Ellis argued that healthy sexual relationships were just as important in the creation of a successful, civilized, modern society as good genes.

## SEXUAL PLEASURE AND SOCIAL HEALTH

Havelock Ellis was a founder-member of the Fabian Society, a eugenicist, and a pioneering sexologist. His views on the importance of sex education, controlled breeding, and cultivating guilt-free and shame-free attitudes to the human body are hallmarks of both radical writing for children and the progressive schools with which many radical writers and readers were associated. Ellis's work also informed the thinking, behaviour, and political actions as well as the literary work of radical writers working outside the educational sphere. Naomi Mitchison, for instance, campaigned for and disseminated information about birth control, and her novels for both adults and children follow Ellis in their matter-of-fact and unjudgemental attitudes to all forms of sexuality (Ellis's *Sexual Inversion* (1897) was the first comprehensive, objective, and sympathetic study of homosexuality and the first to question traditional ideas about sexual deviance).[9] *Cloud Cuckoo Land* (1925), for example, includes a conversation between two Spartan boys in which one unselfconsciously remarks that he and an older boy have been 'lovers ever since I was quite small and he was captain of my class' (Mitchison, 1925 25–6). It is clear from the way the relationship between the two is portrayed that this is not to be regarded as an abusive or an unnatural relationship. Neither is the homosexual nature of the relationship treated as problematic. When, as part of the same conversation,

---

[9] Originally published in German in 1896, an English translation appeared the following year and was soon condemned by the formula for identifying obscene publications as 'lewd, wicked, bawdy, scandalous libel' in the British courts. In 1898 copies were withdrawn from sale (Green and Karolides, 2009).

the other boy confesses that he is also in love, he remarks on the fact that it is a girl he loves, but there is no emphasis or significance attributed to this. The exchange is matter of fact, and both kinds of love and desires are treated as normal in the young as well as in adults.

Today Havelock Ellis's emphasis on controlled breeding sits uneasily alongside the arguments of campaigners such as Margaret McMillan who were working to show that the perceived deficiencies and pejorative labels associated with the poor (feeble-minded, feckless, improvident, incompetent, degenerate, dependent) were not congenital but the products of economic circumstance. Theories about racial purity were certainly adopted by right-wing and fascist groups, but there was much in the science of eugenics that also spoke to the theories and plans of many on the liberal left for creating a new world and new people to inhabit it. Eugenics was not the only science expected to help create a generation of British 'supermen': nutrition, sanitation, psychology, and physical education were all to play their parts, but as evident in 'The Child of the Future', public concern over the nation's gene pool and who should and should not breed could not be ignored in any discussion of how to improve the population. With the advantage of hindsight it is easy to see unconscious elitism and problematic ethics at work in these debates, but they were for the most part well intentioned: even in relation to the physical culture movement and National Fitness Campaign, in Britain the fascist overtones associated with attempts to build a race of Nietzschean 'supermen' failed to take root (Zweiniger-Bargielowska, 2006 609). As a consequence of competing ideologies, multiple agendas, and some unexamined (because unrecognized) ethical issues, in the areas of sexual knowledge and activity, radical writing can be contradictory and politically conflicted. This is apparent in individual books examined below. On the whole, however, in Britain radical writers tended to concentrate on positive action to promote the health of the existing population and to ignore or gloss over the arguments for negative eugenics based on improving the racial stock through controlling reproduction.

Rather than focusing on issues to do with racial stock, radical children's writing emphasizes the view espoused in progressive schools that decontaminating attitudes to sex, sexuality, and the human body will benefit the physical and psychological health of the nation, starting with its children. Again Ellis's work informs this approach, but many of his views were anticipated by feminist campaigners for birth control and women's right to sexual pleasure. Notable among these were Stella Browne (1915) and Marie Stopes (1920), both of whom maintained that there was a correlation between sexual pleasure and the quality of offspring, making it in the interests of the nation's health for women to enjoy satisfying sex (Robb,

1997 67). In this context it is not surprising that, like Naomi Mitchison and Amabel Williams-Ellis, most women who wrote radical children's books regarded themselves as beneficiaries of a new sexually enlightened age and proselytized for both sexual liberation and women's reproductive rights. During the years covered by this book, however, even writers for adults were likely to be prosecuted for obscenity if their work included descriptions of sexual activities between characters, so the number of books that provide information of various kinds about sex for children and young people is surprising. Writing in 1927, Havelock Ellis observed,

> The number of little books and pamphlets dealing with the question of sexual enlightenment of the young—whether intended to be read by the young or offering guidance to mothers and teachers in the task of imparting knowledge—has become very large during recent years.... (Ellis, 1927 67)[10]

For radical children's writers, determining how to package the information so that it would not rouse the censors or alienate the gatekeepers who vetted young people's reading (parents, librarians, critics, teachers, and clerics) was paramount; especially since radical writers were loath to resort to euphemism, metaphor, analogy, or the kind of coy (and so usually confusing) devices frequently found in mainstream books for children about sex. A typical example of the models these authors set themselves against is *Life How it Comes: A Child's Books of Elementary Biology* (1921) by vicar's wife L. Dorothy Parsons, writing under the name of Stephen Reid-Heyman. Although it appears to take a scientific approach and begins by looking at reproduction in organisms, starting with the amoeba and working up to humans, the discussion is indirect, obscure, and overlaid with a heavy Christian message. Readers are warned against 'abusing the great gift of reproduction', though they are never told what that entails—or indeed how humans reproduce. They are also given lengthy warnings about the consequences of self-abuse culminating in the threat:

> unless [young people] keep their bodies clean and their hearts pure, and never allow themselves even to dream of indulging their sense of reproduction outside of marriage, then they can never find that sleeping beauty of pure love. They will become, instead, evil and unclean and diseased and degraded. (Reid-Heyman, 1921 167)

---

[10] Ellis refers to five books for younger children and five designed for boys and girls who have reached puberty, particularly recommending *Almost Fourteen* by American teacher M.A. Warren, dating back to 1892. The others listed are Ellice Hopkins's *The Story of Life* (1914), Arthur Trewby's *Healthy Boyhood* (1909), and Edward Bruce Kirk's *A Talk with Boys About Themselves* (1904) and, with Mrs Bramwell Booth, *A Talk with Girls About Themselves* (1905).

Radical books take a more genuinely scientific approach, which also justified more detailed and wide-ranging discussions of bodies and functions than could readily be incorporated in fictional accounts of sex. Keeping science to the fore was crucial to the viability of any publication for or even about young people and sex. The consequence of failing to fly beneath the radar monitoring taste and decency is illustrated by the case of radical Marxist Tom Anderson's *Proletcult*. The fourth of Anderson's left-wing periodicals for children, from March to May 1923 *Proletcult* carried a series on 'Sex Knowledge' by 'Margaret Dobson' (one of Anderson's many pseudonyms). The controversy around the series was such that it was withdrawn, though with the promise that similar material would be made available in pamphlet form. The pamphlet duly appeared, though its title was changed to *Sex Knowledge for Parents* (1924). Despite the (putative?) change in audience, the pamphlet was confiscated after Anderson's activities were denounced in the House of Lords in a debate on the 'Seditious and Blasphemous Teaching to Children Bill' ( J. Rosen, 2012 14). The Duke of Atholl read out one example, the rest of the content, he claimed, being unfit for the ears of those in the House as 'for downright filth I do not think I have ever read anything that came anywhere near the publications [on sex] contained in that paper, which was a magazine for boys and girls'.[11] The example he chose was an announcement in *Proletcult*: 'A special class on sex knowledge is held on the last Sunday of each month.... Everyone should purchase the booklet on sex knowledge, and a copy of the Proletcult each month, so as to get the child's lesson and song' (Hansard, n.p.).

The first two of Anderson/Dobson's articles on 'sex knowledge' are in fact little different from the other examples discussed. They explain the sex drive as an inherited instinct, begin the discussion with an analogy between how humans reproduce and how other organisms reproduce (the example here is a plant seed that grows into a flower), and justify the lesson on the ground that it is natural for children to be curious and risky to deprive them of basic biological knowledge since ignorant children become ignorant, potentially diseased, adults.

> Nearly everyone who objects to the children being told these things say it is hurtful as it lets the children know too much. The very reverse is the case. We have all in our beings a primordial inheritance, which acts for us unknown to ourselves, and the more we learn of ourselves the purer we become. There is not a man or woman in the world who has a true knowledge of their sexual nature that ever abuses them. (April 1923)

[11] The full transcript of the debate can be read at http://hansard.millbanksystems.com/lords/1924/jul/03/seditious-and-blasphemous-teaching-to.

The 'two million syphilitic men and women in our country to-day', the piece continues, 'are the result of gross ignorance and superstition regarding sexual matters. There are millions of men to-day lower than the beasts. Go to any garrison town if you want to see an inferno, and if you go with your eyes open you will be astounded' (April 1923). In the third article in May 1923, the discussion becomes more contentious as it acknowledges that children are autoerotic and likely to experience wet dreams and experiment with masturbation. Other books and articles also recognize these tendencies but 'Sex Knowledge' writes somewhat more directly about them. It is at this point that the articles were discontinued.

As the reaction to Anderson's series and pamphlet indicate, even when directed at minority audiences in educational contexts (*Proletcult* was the magazine for Anderson's Proletarian Colleges), publications dealing with sex were always potentially inflammatory. Nevertheless, by employing a variety of strategems, radical writers produced a range of works that together provided information about the sexual organs, sexual drives, and the sexual act from biological, psychological, and emotional perspectives. Readers of these works were offered the chance to have a completely different relationship with their sexual selves than any generation in living memory. Sex, they were told, was natural, important, and enjoyable for those who were well informed and responsible in their actions. This was the task with which the radical writers who heeded Havelock Ellis's declaration of 'the absolute necessity of taking deliberate and active part in [young people's] sexual initiation' (1927 n.p.) charged themselves. As the examples below demonstrate, radical books were one means by which progressive adults introduced children and young people to themselves as sexual beings and provided them with reliable information.

## FICTION, FACTS, AND EMOTIONAL FREEDOMS

The climate might have been receptive to discussions about sex education, but at a time when *Ulysses* and *Lady Chatterley's Lover* were regarded as obscene, imaginative fiction for children could not afford to be pioneering in this area (with a very few exceptions this remained the case to the end of the last century as evidenced by the number of Judy Blume's books that were banned by school and public libraries). Even the most obviously progressive British children's stories, poems, and novels of the period avoid referring explicitly to children's and young people's sexual desires and behaviours. One writer who tried to break with tradition by exploring adolescent sexuality openly was the German playwright, Frank Wedekind, whose *Spring Awakening*, first performed in Germany in 1906, deals with a group of young teenagers who are tormented by their sexual feelings because they cannot understand them. Wedekind's young characters show the consequences of generations of repression and misinformation. None experiences happy, healthy sex, and none becomes a happy, healthy adult: one commits suicide, another is raped and dies when her mother (who has not explained to the girl that she is pregnant) organizes an illegal abortion, and the one boy who tries to spread knowledge and relieve guilt is expelled from school as a pervert. Although not published in English in the UK until the middle of the last century, with their interest in sex education, regular exchanges between German and English progressive schools, and the publicity around both the 1906 German production and the 1914 production in New York (closed as obscene after its opening night) it is likely that heads of progressive schools and radical publishers in the UK would have been aware of the hostility to *Spring Awakening* and so pitched their own material about sex and young people accordingly. Fiction, which could not fall back on a pedagogic justification, needed to be handled with particular care.

A few works that pushed at accepted limits did succeed in being published. For example, Edith Saunders's *Fanny Penquite* (1932; discussed in Chapter 3) is clearly concerned with a young girl's sexual awakening and explores desire in some stylistically interesting ways, but apart from some unspecified observations about Fanny's rival and the wooden figurehead, chaste kissing in heaven is the closest the book comes to acknowledging that it is about sexual feelings. As has already been mentioned, in her historical novels for children Naomi Mitchison accepted both that the young are sexually aware and active and that there are multiple sexualities, but her work is always carefully set in antiquity when it was accepted that ideas about both sex and childhood were different. Both Saunders and Mitchison set their stories in some version of the real world. Ralph Fox, communist, Russophile, and *Daily Worker* columnist, set *Captain Youth: A Romantic Comedy for All Socialist Children* (1922) in an alternative world. The play opens with a scene in which two children, Dick and Phyl, are kissing and talking about making love in an extremely uninformed way. Phyl complains that boys and girls are not allowed to make love after dark (though she has presumably done it because she says she enjoys it more than doing it in the day). When she asks Dick to kiss her again he asks 'You are sure it is quite safe? We shan't have a baby or anything?' To which she replies, 'Of course not, silly. You know very well that they come in those ugly black bags doctors carry. Kiss me at once' (Fox, 1922 11). To modern eyes this level of ignorance might seem exaggerated—almost as if Fox is laughing at those who think children do not know about sex—but Phyl and Dick are no more ignorant than the teenagers in *Spring Awakening*. The remainder of the play has nothing to do with sex, so the opening scene, with its exposure of youthful ignorance and acknowledgement of sexual exploration among the young, is notable only because it does not mark the children as sinful or depraved. More important than what they do is the level of ignorance Phyl and Dick display about where babies come from. They are clearly the kind of young readers radical writers about sex and reproduction hoped to reach.

A more developed and practically helpful example of radical writing about sex is F.J. Gould's *On the Threshold of Sex: A Book for Readers Aged 14 to 21*. Published in 1909, it falls just outside the time frame for this book, but since so many of Gould's books feature in other chapters it seems appropriate to include it. As always, Gould's implied readers are working-class Socialist children and young people. Clearly he and his publishers regarded the topic as potentially problematic, for they include an introduction and recommendation by a medical doctor who vouches for the accuracy of the material and the importance of providing young people with reliable information. The author also inserts a note that, 'Three ladies and three medical men have read and approved this book before publication' (in Gould, 1909 5). Similar strategies for reassuring adult purchasers that books covering sex education are sensitively managed and will do no harm to young readers are employed in every book from this period, radical or conservative, that takes sex as its subject.

Gould's book was published in association with the London-based Eugenics Education Society, an organization concerned with 'responsible reproduction'. 'Responsible reproduction' requires managing the 'racial instinct', meaning the urge to have sex. According to *On the Threshold of Sex*, such management can only be achieved by ceasing to regard sex as shameful and bestial since that results in the kind of ignorance that leads to instinct driving behaviour rather human reason taking charge. The book argues that it is not sufficient, and is indeed harmful, merely to advise young people to exercise self-control; the whole way of thinking about sex and reproduction needs to be changed. Gould proposes that attitudes to sex would be healthier and more responsibly managed if parenthood were made an 'honoured condition' for which a person must be well prepared (9–10). The sex act would then become something planned, purposeful, valued, and even sacred—as well as something to be enjoyed, though only under the right conditions. Explaining what the right conditions are is one of the main aims of the book.

Despite Gould's determination to teach the biological basics of reproduction, *On the Threshold of Sex* begins in a rather oblique and literary way by telling two stories. The first sets up role models in the form of 'two comely young people' who, though tempted and given opportunity, do not give in to desire. In this way they begin to understand the nature of their bodies 'and how the powers of sex are prepared for the honour of motherhood and fatherhood' (18). The second story relates the temptation of and consequences for Paolo and Francesca as a warning to readers not to go to the 'beyond of sex' before they are ready. Here Gould carefully distinguishes between restraint and repression, explaining that it is manly to be controlled and responsible, but this does not mean denying one's feelings. Although control is urged on boys, the book is not exclusively or even primarily addressed to males. His advice is the same to both boys and girls:

> The time will come for going beyond, and you can go in either of two ways.
>
> You can love as knight and lady, all in the open air, and under the blue of the sky, and in the sight of the men and the women who are your friends; and they will bless you in their joy of heart, and wish you all happiness.
>
> Or you can turn love to poison, and the green vesture [worn by the comely couple] will hide a serpent of disgust and disease, so that you will hate yourself, and the eye that sees you will pity and scorn you. (23)

Part three of *On the Threshold of Sex* introduces the physical aspects of sex education, beginning with a discussion of the changes that happen to boys' bodies and the making of semen. This section includes a 'just say no' message, suggesting that semen in boys is not 'ready'; that it needs plenty of fresh air, cold baths, and exercise to mature. This may not sound very progressive, but taken as a whole, *On the Threshold of Sex* is informative and accepting of young people's bodies. It contains none of the fear, threats, and confusing euphemisms encountered by the young people in *Spring Awakening*. In fact, following some limited but useful advice about contraception, labour, and breast-feeding, the book ends on a surprisingly light-hearted note. Gould advises readers not to become obsessed with self-control. Mistakes will be made, he says, but '"there is not a just man on earth that doeth good and sinneth not." Courage! The sky is blue above, and your heart is brave' (48). Contradictory and oblique as it sometimes is, young readers who found themselves in possession of Gould's book would have had more information than earlier generations and were no doubt grateful for it. The desire for young people for information about themselves as sexual beings is expressed by 'P.D.', a reviewer in *Out of Bounds* who, in discussing L.B. Perkin's book about progressive schools, praises the book's support for co-education and its enlightened attitude to sex which causes him to lament 'how much one has missed through an "orthodox" education' (1934, 3 36).

Amabel Williams-Ellis's *How You Began* (1928) was for younger readers. Like Mitchison, Amabel Williams-Ellis was a left-wing activist and writer with a strong interest in women's rights. Her books for adults include strikingly direct accounts of the female body that clearly show awareness of both Ellis's work and Freud's (her cousin, James Strachey, was Freud's first English translator). *Noah's Ark; Or, The Love Story of a Respectable Young Couple* (1925), for instance, explores the problems arising from the strength of the sex drive and the pressure to marry. It goes on to describe in detail the central character's physical and psychological reactions to pregnancy, birth, and breast-feeding. Williams-Ellis shared Mitchison's belief that the young were entitled to benefit from the knowledge women like them had gained. *How You Began* provides the biological basics of evolution and cell development. Williams-Ellis draws on the then-popular Recapitulation Theory: the belief that in developing from embryo to adult humans go through stages that correspond to the development of the species. Her scientific approach and knowledge are praised in the book's testimonial, which was provided by J.B.S. Haldane, a highly respected scientist at the University of Cambridge and popularizer of science in forums such as the *Daily Worker* (he was also the brother of Naomi Mitchison and a contributor to *An Outline for Boys and Girls and Their Parents*, providing another example of the close-knit nature of left-wing and progressive publishing circles during this period). Haldane praises the book's account of evolution, and points to the importance for later life of providing children with good information about conception and gestation.

> All girls and boys should know how they grew. I did not know this when I was quite young. Now I wish I had. But there was no book like this then . . . I have to teach people who are going to be doctors. I should find it much easier if they had read a book like this when they were children. (In Williams-Ellis, 1928 inside front cover)

The most comprehensive discussion of the body and reproduction addressed to young people is found in Naomi Mitchison's and Victor Gollancz's *An Outline for Boys and Girls and Their Parents* (1932). It was the material on reproduction that led to one of the chief accusations against the volume: that it was 'smattered with Socialism and Sex' (Lynd, 1936 11). In fact, it carefully eschews discussion of repression and other psychological and emotional aspects of sex, concentrating instead on imparting biological information about reproduction and the science of genetics. In Section I: Science, readers learn about how plants, insects, and other animals reproduce as well as how humans do. There are detailed explanations of growth, respiration, digestion, death, instincts, cell division and genetics, and much more. The information is more detailed and at a higher level than in other publications and its tone is studiously detached and scientific. This prevents it from being in any sense titillating, though it does venture briefly into the area of pleasure through a comparison with eating:

in the higher animals the act of transferring the sperms gives a great pleasure to both, which can be compared to the pleasure of eating. If eating were not in the slightest degree pleasant, a dog would not eat, and he would starve. If the transferring of sperms were not pleasant, he would fail to reproduce himself, and his race would die out. (1932 188)

The book's coverage of sex and reproduction is informative, not salacious or an example of campaigning for sexual liberation. Mitchison does not let her personal commitment to sexual pleasure (she had an open marriage and many partners) skew the text, evidence that the campaign against *An Outline* gave a distorted view of its project and contents.

As this account of radical writing about sex has shown, when teaching children and young people about their bodies, writers attempted to overthrow centuries of convention and concealment by providing up-to-date scientific information and evidence on which to form opinions and guide behaviour. They gave children and young people information that had previously been the preserve of adults and which readers could verify by referring to their own bodies. In doing so they encouraged readers to resist automatically accepting the status quo and gave them the knowledge they needed to make decisions about managing their own bodies. Radical writing about sex, then, inevitably raised questions about many long-standing attitudes and the social bodies and mechanisms that regulated behaviour. Of course, how far readers could act on the information they were given depended to some extent on their economic and material circumstances, but the publications open up aspects of behaviour that had long been secret and which were central to tackling the challenges of population, disease, women's health, and family finances that affected the whole population. These books also offered insights that their authors hoped would make future generations happier, more creative, and less aggressive. In tenor, appearance, and factual content they have dated more than most of the material covered in this study, but in their efforts to liberate thinking, change behaviour, and prepare for a future when people of all backgrounds could live more healthily and freely, they are benchmarks of radical children's literature.

Nothing is closer to children than their own bodies, but the next chapter looks at another area with which all children also had some experience: buildings, and especially homes.

# 6

# Rebuilding Britain through Radical
# Children's Books

Britain entered the twentieth century with an acute housing shortage. In cities some of the nation's poorest families lived in 'one or two rooms... sleeping three and four to a bed with never enough chairs (or boxes) all to sit down at once'.[1] Poor children in the countryside fared no better. In *This England and Other Things of Beauty* (1930), a book of essays for children, F.J. Gould directed readers' attention to the squalor and privations of rural poverty where children were growing up in

> houses with no gardens; houses with no proper water supply and no proper drains; houses with wet walls; houses that were so built on a slope of earth that rain soaked down the hill into the building; houses built close together all along a dull straight street; houses with no paving at the door, and so open to the entry of filthy boots; and houses containing rooms that had no fireplace. (Gould, 1930 166)[2]

Images of home in mainstream children's literature produced between 1910 and 1949 range from cosy cottages as pictured by Beatrix Potter and Ernest Shepard to the large town houses of the kind lived in by the Banks children in P.L. Travers' *Mary Poppins* (1934). In real life, home was not always clean and spacious and safe. From the 1930s, radical children's books began a sustained effort to focus readers' attention on the urgent need for new housing and to involve children in the debate about what houses, villages, towns, and cities should look like. By the end of the Second World War, the effects of bombing and the large number of stately homes that had become unviable in a world of high taxes and fewer servants meant that the plans to rebuild Britain were affecting all parts of

---

[1] These were the conditions recorded by members of the Fabian Women's Group in a 1913 report on living conditions among stable working-class families in Lambeth, *Round About a Pound a Week* (in Jones, 2012 190).

[2] *This England* is one of Gould's many titles for children. In this case the book reads as if it were for use in school assemblies and Socialist Sunday School classes rather than something to be enjoyed by individual child readers.

the population. Radical children's books presented the need for a nation-wide building programme as an opportunity for planned development that could improve life for the many and make Britain more efficient and less class-riven. This was a consciously positive response to a situation that alarmed such left-leaning cultural commentators as George Orwell. Orwell feared that the opportunity to improve the conditions in which people lived and how they worked would be lost as, between them, government and opportunists supplied unimaginative, poor-value housing for the masses while traditionalists insisted on restoring rather than rebuilding the nation.[3] He suspected that their combined efforts would result in reproducing the pre-war problems of inadequate housing, exploitation of the vulnerable, social divisions, and an infrastructure that was not fit for twentieth-century needs. In an unprecedented campaign to capture the youthful imagination for the side of change, professional architects and radical writers produced a quantity of books that showed how up-to-date and integrated infrastructure together with new materials, new ways of thinking about communal housing, and new designs that emphasized healthy lifestyles (light airy rooms, glass designed to maximize the beneficial rays from sunlight, modern hygienic bathrooms, integrated exercise areas) held out the promise that building, and especially home-building, could be instrumental in positive social change.

## ARCHITECTURE FOR CHILDREN

One of the first to write about the importance of good building and urban planning for an audience of children was F.J. Gould. *This England and Other Things of Beauty* (1930) makes connections between how well a society enables its people to live, the values it holds, and its productivity. In it Gould explores the way spatial and aesthetic aspects of housing affect the social relationships and behaviours of those who inhabit them, and explains why he is an enthusiast for the Garden City Movement.

Garden cities sought to provide affordable mass-produced housing grouped in carefully planned settlements. They were the brainchild of Ebenezer Howard who, in *Garden Cities of Tomorrow* (1902), maintained that bringing different social groups together to live and invest in the same

---

[3] George Orwell tackled this problem in 'A home of their own' in his 'As I Please' column for the *Tribune* in February 1944. Pointing out that 'English houses are for the most part very badly built', he champions the use of high-quality prefabricated buildings and insists on the need for the public to overcome its dislike of flats to improve the standard of accommodation and defeat the vested interests of those in the building trade and rent racketeers. In Peter Davison (ed.), 2001 280–1.

community could reduce tensions between the classes. (The logic is reminiscent of the housing schemes seen by the child visitors to the Soviet Union discussed in Chapter 2.) As well as addressing social problems around class, garden cities began the work of correcting the historic lack of city planning. In the UK, where most cities had grown up willy-nilly over centuries, inadequate infrastructure was adversely affecting Britain's industries and meant long, tiring journeys for workers. Gould argued that for Britain to succeed in the future, the work of rebuilding had to look at all the aspects of modern life that are connected to housing. *Garden Cities of Tomorrow* provides detailed plans in which housing, places of work, social services, recreational facilities, and transport all feature as part of complete and sustainable communities. Gould invites his young readers to join him in visualizing the splendours of a Britain made up of the kind of 'handsome houses, good roads, trees, gardens and clean bright factories' he had seen in Welwyn Garden City, the second of the two garden cities to be built (Gould, 1930 164).

A more wide-ranging approach to getting children to think about the importance of the built environment was taken by the architect Clough Williams-Ellis in 'Architecture, or Using the Pattern', his contribution to *An Outline for Boys and Girls and Their Parents* (1932). Williams-Ellis is best known for building Portmeirion, a curious assemblage of a hotel and fifteen Italian-inspired buildings intended to conjure up Italy in North Wales. His chapter begins with an illustrated history of the principles of architectural design. Clough Williams-Ellis was largely self-taught and, possibly reflecting this, his way of writing is both quirky and accessible. For instance, he tackles the vexed problem of how to manage the relationship between new buildings and the existing housing stock by referring to clothing. He uses the analogy to illustrate the infelicitous nature of pastiche and the taste for incorporating random references to buildings of the past in in popular contemporary architecture (how far he heeded his own advice in the case of Portmeirion is debatable):

> you yourself would look rather foolish if you stood in the street dressed in a top hat, a steel breast-plate, and a pair of shorts. The clothes all belong to different times and different kinds of living; they do not make a very happy or comfortable mixture; they are certainly not convenient, and no one... would think you beautiful. Yet plenty of buildings stand along our streets got up just as absurdly in odds and ends out of the architectural 'dressing up' cupboard, and nobody seems to notice how silly they really are or to laugh at them as they deserve. (in Mitchison, 1932 815)

The piece enjoins readers to learn to admire and understand great buildings from the past, but its central concern is with the importance of building for the present and future. Williams-Ellis criticizes Britain for being slower than other countries to adopt modern design, choosing instead to live in the 'muddle ages': the illustrations that accompany the piece show examples of 'truly' modern buildings from Germany, Russia, and the USA, but none from Britain (Figure 6.1). The best contemporary buildings, it claims, are 'lovely and exciting' because they are built to modern tastes and needs, from modern materials using modern methods (819). Because such buildings are 'not mere copies... because they are bold and adventurous, honest and straightforward, and because they meet our needs', Williams-Ellis predicts they, not such confused faux-historical styles as the 'Tudorbethan' houses that were in vogue at the time, would be the twentieth century's architectural legacy. Despite this optimistic claim, 'Architecture, or Using the Pattern' concludes with a warning that the obvious reluctance on the part of the population to accept modern architecture and design was depriving the nation of the benefits they could bring. It identifies the problem as so important that professionals like him felt compelled to reach beyond recalcitrant adults to appeal to the more open-minded young (819).

The number of children's books by high-profile architects and designers that appear in the years leading up to and during the Second World War supports Williams-Ellis's claim. There is, for instance, Jane Drew Fry and Maxwell Fry's *Architecture for Children* (1944). Both the Frys were among the few home-grown modernist architects (Jane Drew was also one of the few female architects of the time). Maxwell was co-founder of the Modern Architectural Research Group which was charged with planning how London would be redeveloped after the war. Jane served on the Royal Institute of British Architects' reconstruction committee from 1941 and conceived and helped mount a Reconstruction Exhibition at the National Gallery in 1943. The Frys' book was published at the height of the reconstruction debates and offers an approach to rebuilding Britain along Socialist, communal lines.

Maxwell Fry was known for rethinking spaces normally associated with children, notably through his work with Walter Gropius in the 1930s on Impington Village College in Cambridgeshire (village colleges were specially designed buildings that served as schools by day and in term-time and as public amenities outside of school hours). He also designed high-quality apartment housing to replace run-down city tenements. These are the kinds of buildings that, alongside domestic housing, feature in *Architecture for Children*. That architects of the Frys' stature thought it important to inform children about their work is indicative of more than the hostility to innovation on the part of adults to which Clough Williams-Ellis refers. It is part and parcel of the radical determination to provide the next generation

**Figure 6.1.** 'New homes for the workers' from *An Outline for Boys and Girls and Their Parents*, 1932

with the knowledge, skills, and ideas necessary for joining in the rebuilding of Britain. In many ways the Frys' children's book can be seen as their professional manifesto, tellingly addressed to the next generation. It sets architecture at the centre of social renewal on the grounds that new kinds of buildings facilitate new kinds of behaviour. The couple's argument was that if, when the war was over, old patterns of life were not simply to be resumed and old mistakes repeated, Britons would have to learn to live differently. To be a force in the future, Britain had to build with the future in mind. If nationalism were to give way to internationalism, new aesthetic codes, sensibilities, and vocabularies needed to be developed and employed. This is the knowledge imparted and the challenge issued by two leading architects in *Architecture for Children*.

Oliver Hill was another British modernist architect who set out his ideas about architecture and the principles of design in the form of a book for young readers. The Frys chose to use black-and-white photographs to illustrate their book, but Hill's *Balbus: A Picture Book of Buildings* (1944) is illustrated in full colour by Hans Tisdall. *Balbus* is a sophisticated and idiosyncratic picturebook comprising a series of observations about good design. Hill, 'a playful, allusive architect, a man of sudden enthusiasms, a lover of silly jokes, sunbathing and nudity' (Harris, 2010 47), stresses that good design will always both be informed by nature and stand the test of time. As examples of good design he begins with a snail shell and moves on through ancient fortified cities and the palaces of Southern Arabia to the skyscrapers of New York.

Where many of the books that are discussed in this chapter articulate clear social agendas, *Balbus* is more concerned with radicalizing design aesthetics—it opens up the definition of 'architecture' to include all aspects of design (textiles, furnishings, sculpture, and the equipment of the modern home) and attempts to develop a modernist dimension to British taste. However, like many artists and architects of the period, Oliver Hill was inclusive as well as radical. As *Balbus* shows, he was interested in good design whenever, wherever, and however it occurred, and he enjoyed bringing successful examples from different periods and styles together. For some people the result was contradictory and incoherent, a criticism made against the British pavilion Hill designed for the Paris World's Fair of 1937. From the outside the building looked fully modernist: Kingsley Martin, Editor of the *New Statesman*, compared it to a 'white packing-case' (Harris, 2010 48). On the inside, however, it was decorated and furnished to make statements about Englishness and even Merrie Englandness (countryside, sheep, cathedrals, cottages). Hill's urge to create a fusion between ancient and modern was characteristic of Britain's response to modernism, as Alexandra Harris (2010) explains.

Harris regards Hill's pavilion as a 'barometer of the difficulties involved in the attempt to reconcile international modernism with the language of national tradition' (Harris, 2010 48). In *Balbus*, Hill explains how diverse elements from past and present can be used symbiotically; his attempt is echoed in radical books that urge young readers to make a place for modernist building in Britain.

Another book that sets out the case for incorporating modernist build-ings in Britain's villages, towns, and cities at a level basic enough even for very young readers is S.R. Badmin's *Village and Town* (1942). This was among the first Picture Puffins; several other early books in the imprint also focus on aspects of art and design, reflecting editor Noel Carrington's interest in the subject (he was at the time editor of the magazine *Design for Today*). Badmin was not a professional architect. He earned his living largely through producing traditional-to-twee images of the English land-scape for greeting cards. Nevertheless, he was a fully committed radical who supported the Republicans during the Spanish Civil War and was involved with a number of left-wing causes and projects. Like the Frys, Badmin wanted to involve children in discussions and plans for what Britain would look like in the future; he also wanted to be sure new building would make Britain fully able to function in a modern, global-izing, technologically advanced world. *Village and Town* is grounded in children's personal experience:

> Do you know we could have much better houses than we have, if they were well designed and better use was made of standardised doors, windows, cupboards and stoves? Do you know we could have towns which were clean and smokeless, which were easy to get about, which had plenty of playing grounds and no slums? And we could keep the country as real country for farming or holidays, instead of eating it up with bungalows. We could do all that and much more if we made plans in advance, instead of muddling along as we do now. . . . Look at your own home town. Surely something better must be built next time? (Badmin, 1942 31)

These, the closing lines of the book, ask readers to form an opinion; in doing so they enscript them as future planners and architects.

Badmin's own answer to the question of what 'better next time' might be is found on the back cover (Figure 6.2). This gives an example of what the text describes as the new 'English style of building' (30). At the centre of the image is the modernist structure of St John's Wood Underground station; to one side is the steel tracery of a multi-story car park, while a vast white block of flats rises vertically in the background. The message is clear: Britain must not ossify; good modern design must have a place in a modern Britain. The front cover makes the point in a different way. It depicts a

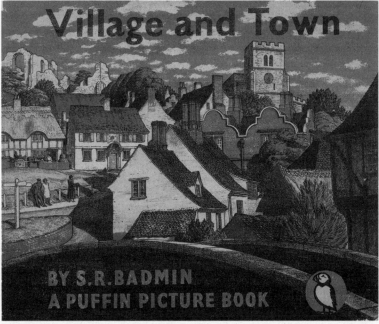

**Figure 6.2.** Continuity through change: back and front covers for *Village and Town*, 1942. Image courtesy of Penguin Books

generic, idealized English village complete with church and village green. Although it gives a harmonious impression, the effect has been achieved not by obstructing but by accommodating architectural change to suit the times. The village is a medley of houses and cottages from several periods, including some picturesque ruins in the background. Like all those who produced radical children's books on the subjects of architecture and design, in *Village and Town* S.R. Badmin advocates a creative rather than a reverential relationship with the past, with traditional aesthetic and design principles underpinning and informing but not holding back building in the present for the future.

Two other books that urge children to be receptive to architectural change are Agnes Allen's *The Story of the Village* (1947) and *The Story of Your Home* (1949). *The Story of Your Home* was awarded the Carnegie Medal for 1949, one of only a few information books to be so honoured; it appeared in multiple editions until 1972. Both books feature two children, Margaret and John, and their friend Mr Morrison, who has the ability to transport them back in time. *The Story of the Village* sees Margaret and John worrying about the impact of new building on their village. To help them decide whether their concerns are well founded, Mr Morrison takes them back to the time of the earliest settlement in their village. As they move forward through the centuries, they see the village change and grow. Though in each new period they happily greet surviving features from earlier periods such as buildings, bridges, and parts of the landscape, they also comment on how much more comfortable and healthy each age is. By the end of their journey the children have the facts and understanding they need to reach an informed and rational position on the changes to the village. They conclude that, as long as it is well planned and executed, change is often for the best. As Mr Morrison puts it: 'Be glad that the houses that will be built will be healthy and weather proof and warm, and that people won't have to live in the dreadful shacks that we saw in Idingford hundreds of years ago. Things weren't all perfect in the past, were they?' (212).

## RADICALIZING TASTE IN THE MACHINE AGE

As part of the message that modern designs and materials had an important role to play in rebuilding Britain, radical children's books had to take account of how buildings and objects were made. Unsurprisingly, radical publications value hand-crafted objects of the kind approved by Edward Carpenter and William Morris, but they also acknowledge the benefits of mechanically produced furniture, textiles, household objects—and even prefabricated houses—for those with limited means; especially in the years immediately after the Second World War when the nation needed to build and furnish homes rapidly. Radical children's books joined in campaigns to improve the quality, and so the perception, of machine-made items. A book that is specifically concerned with realizing the potential of mass production to provide objects that are well designed and well made using modern materials is Gordon Russell's and Jacques Groag's *The Story of Furniture* (1947), the fiftieth of Noel Carrington's popular Puffin Picture Books. Russell's and Groag's focus is on furniture, but the point holds across all areas of design: 'Surely you will not sit down and admit that this astonishing and complex industrial age is quite unable to give us beauty in everyday life, without which a high standard of living is impossible?' (1947 2). *The Story of Furniture* explores not only mass production but also the creation of interior design and furnishings based on modular systems made to standard sizes for maximum flexibility. These are the principles necessary for modern homes, and by extension, all places where people live, work, meet, and socialize.

If standards of design were to be improved, current and future con-sumers needed to be educated to distinguish good from bad.[4] Defining 'good' in an age of dynamic transition was not easy. Modernism reviled the décor of the Victorian age with its heavy drapes, ornate wall-papers, dark furniture, and penchant for filling rooms with ornaments and bric-a-brac, but many people found the minimalism of much modernist design impersonal and dehumanizing. As a rule, people wanted to decorate their living spaces with objects: bohemia opted for inexpensive rustic pottery and textiles from abroad; differently fashionable sets such as those associated with the photographer, designer, and artist Cecil Beaton opted for new takes on earlier periods. Experiments in taste and lifestyles abounded until, by the 1930s, as Alexandra Harris puts it, 'at least two opposing camps in the ornamentation debate had clearly established themselves: those arguing for the clarifying influence of minimal design and [those] . . . praising curlicues' (43). Both sides of the argument are set out and legitimized in *This or That?* (1947), a picture book commissioned by the Scottish Council of Industrial Design with illustrations by Barbara Jones (Figure 6.3).

*This or That?* offers information and guidance to help children under-stand why some artworks and objects are considered good and others inferior. The text, by Wyndham Goodden, Professor of Textiles at the Royal College of Art, bears some resemblance to Oliver Hill's *Balbus* in its

---

[4] Michael Saler (1999) points out that the dated nature of British design was also affecting exports, so this was a very practical exercise in shifting taste to something more modern.

**Figure 6.3.** Cover, Wyndham Goodden's *This or That?*, 1947. Image courtesy of the Design Council/University of Brighton Design Archives and The Bodleian Library, University of Oxford Opie BB 55

insistence that good design always mirrors nature, but instead of telling its readers what good design is, Goodden sets up a game that allows readers to decide what they like. Before they can play the game, however, they need to know on what to base their decisions since the point of the book is that readers should not choose instinctively but know why they like one style better than another. The book introduces different ideas about taste by following an argument between two children, Sheila and David, about the best way to decorate their home. David likes modern design (minimalist) while Sheila's taste is more traditional (curlicues). Each double-page shows the same room with Sheila's choices on one side and David's on the other. In the course of the children's argument, readers are shown how to look closely at the objects that surround them, seeking to find the forms that underpin good design. The forms are never mentioned, but at the bottom of page fifteen there is a series of drawings that shows a sphere, a cylinder, and a cube.[5] As long as it is based on such forms, readers are told, any

---

[5] The forms closely resemble the second set of 'gifts' designed by the progressive educationalist Friedrich Froebel to cultivate dexterity and creativity. Although Froebel

design can be good. At this point the verbal text ends, but turning the page reveals drawings of empty rooms and pages made up of pictures of items of furniture that can be cut out and used to decorate the empty rooms. One page includes traditional pieces and the other modern examples. At this point readers are ready to play the game of designing their own rooms, a game that allows them to practise for the time when they are householders (and consumers) in real life. More than that, having learned the principles of good design, they are charged with the task of demanding that the objects they buy when they are decorating their own homes are well designed and well made.

## THE PRAM IN THE GARDEN

*The Story of Furniture* and *This or That?* are optimistic texts that assume children who are taught the principles of design and taste will succeed in making good homes suited to modern life. Olive Dehn and Kathleen Gell's *Come In* (1946) offers a more ambivalent view of life in the kinds of garden cities and suburbs that were spreading across Britain and commended by many radical writers such as F.J. Gould. *Come In* is the only collaboration between two women who independently had long professional lives in the children's publishing industry, both producing otherwise competent but hardly radical material. If Kathleen Gell is remembered at all it is for her illustrations for some of Enid Blyton's books, including two picture books in the same series as *Come In* about the children who move to 'Happy House' in a country village.[6] It has not been possible to locate information about Gell's background or personal life. Although equally forgotten in her capacity as a children's writer, some of Olive Dehn's working materials and correspondence have been preserved, making it possible to put *Come In* into context in some telling ways.[7]

died in 1852, his teaching methods have frequently been credited with giving birth to modernism; Juliet Dusinberre (1987) and Marina Warner (2005) are among those who have pointed to affinities between Froebel's methods and modernist aesthetics.

[6] The series was published by Basil Blackwell and printed at the Shakespeare Head Press which he had recently acquired to rescue it from bankruptcy. The Press had a distinguished history of high-quality printing. Blackwell drew on this for his picturebooks which he hoped would make the imprint profitable. The fit was not congenial and the experiment did not last.

[7] The Olive Dehn papers are held at Seven Stories, the National Centre for Children's Books in Newcastle. They were deposited there by Dehn's daughters who have carried on their parents' interest in the arts and politics.

Olive Dehn's work appeared in a number of periodicals and annuals; in 1935 Basil Blackwell published four of her stories as illustrated children's books in a series based on material that first appeared in his influential *Joy Street* annuals. Dehn wrote radio scripts for the BBC as well as stories and poems for children's annuals, and tried her hand at most kinds of writing that might earn a fee. With the exception of *Come In* and *The Basement Bogle* (1935), a short piece about a happy and functional working-class family that pre-dates Eve Garnett's *The Family from One End Street*, her writing tends towards the conventional, but Olive Dehn's personal life was anything but conventional. It is the clash between her experience and the suburban world she imagines in this picturebook that give it radical power and originality. The clash is intensified because the story in *Come In* is a kind of distorted version of Dehn's life: the family who live at No. 23 Pine Tree Lane are called Markham, and the father is an actor; Olive Dehn was married to the actor David Markham. In 1946, when the book was published, Olive Dehn was the mother of three children, like the mother in her story. However, in real life, the Markhams were living, by choice, not in a garden city or suburb, but in the Ashdown Forest in Sussex, in a large, old cottage with no running water or electricity. Instead of the neat patchwork of gardens that spread out across Pine Tree Lane, the Sussex cottage had several acres of land which the couple farmed organically. The real Markham family moved between several of the interlocking circles that made up radical Britain during the years covered by this book; they regarded themselves as anarchists and bohemians and sent their daughters (there were eventually four) to Burgess Hill, a progressive school in Hampstead, London. David Markham was a Conscientious Objector during the Second World War and was sentenced to twelve months' hard labour.

Despite the fact that the father in *Come In* is an actor, there is nothing bohemian about life in Pine Tree Lane. Indeed bohemia, with its ramshackle furnishings, peasant pottery, unsupervised children, and casual attitude to hygiene, would seem to be the antithesis of this tale of everyday life in 1940s suburban Britain. In fact, through a combination of stylistic devices in the text and wry observations in the images, *Come In* offers a critique of suburbia and a protest against the effects of modern life on children and women. Its sympathies are implicitly with those who defy routine and convention as embodied by the artist who both illustrates the book and is a character in it.

The story begins when 'Mummy' complains to her husband that 'housekeeping and looking after children [are] the dullest work in the world'; while his life as an actor is full of variety, she 'has to be Mummy...all day long, and can never change at all—except into a clean dress' (Dehn, 1946 1). The father challenges her to write down everything that happens on a single day, establishing a metatextual frame for the story. Readers read what Mummy writes in the course of the day; the illustrations depict the same time frame (though not always from the same perspective), for the father has persuaded an artist from the theatre to come in and draw what happens, from the first thing in the morning to the last thing at night. For experienced adult readers, the fact that the events recorded in *Come In* take place on a single day which ends in bed may bring James Joyce's *Ulysses* (1922) to mind. Dehn's stylistic experiments, some of which are discussed below, suggest that she was deliberately setting the miniature world of Pine Tree Lane against Joyce's epic treatment of Dublin as part of her unflattering account of suburbia and its effects. Where Joyce's text is expansive and digressive and almost entirely concerned with what characters think, *Come In* is miniature in scale and Mummy is so busy that she claims thinking is impossible.

That the setting for *Come In* is a garden city or suburb is established by Kathleen Gell's endpapers, which feature garden-city-style houses set back from tree-lined streets that wind across the page to an open gate where the Markham family stands (Figure 6.4). Readers who respond to the invitation to 'come in' enter a 1940s house. The furniture is simply designed and functional—no Victorian frills, though also no highly stylized modernist pieces. The bathroom is spacious and fully tiled, in line with the latest ideas about hygiene. As was becoming usual for middle-class homes, the house in Pine Tree Lane has no rooms for servants. The mother manages the house with some daily help and such modern gadgets as a telephone, vacuum cleaner, and refrigerator. These are still so unfamiliar that the book gives space to each: the telephone always rings at just the most awkward time and is still supplemented by telegrams; the vacuum cleaner is cumbersome and noisy; while the family hasn't yet acquired the habit of using the refrigerator. Coming back from doing the shopping with some herrings, the grandmother speculates on the advisability of putting them in the refrigerator since 'Once Mummy put some Cod in her Refrigerator and forgot about it for nearly a week'; happily, 'when Daddy tried it he said it tasted as though it had just come from Iceland' (10–11).

Kathleen Gell often uses cut-away drawings that make the house resemble one of the show sets in the *Daily Mail*'s popular Ideal Home Exhibitions that had been running (bar a few interruptions caused by the wars) since 1910. As in the exhibitions, removing a wall allows readers to see into the house and get a sense of how the different rooms function within it and what happens at different times of day (Figure 6.5). The device implies this is an ideal family in an ideal home. However, where the display homes were pristine examples of modern living spaces, Gell's drawings capture the bustle and disorder of an inhabited family home; but this is not the kind of

**Figure 6.4.** Endpapers for Olive Dehn's *Come In*, 1947. Permission to reproduce the images from *Come In* courtesy of Jehane Markham

bustle and disorder that signals creativity or a disregard for routine. Rather, what is shown is the detritus of everyday life: laundry and dishes that need washing, beds that need making, floors that need to be cleaned.

The pictures in *Come In* underline the sense that suburban life is far from ideal for those who spend most time at home: women and children. What are meant to be spaces for passing through—halls and stairways— are shown as congestion points, as in the scene in the hall where Mummy is vacuuming the stairs, Granny is getting ready to go shopping, the cleaning lady's little girl is sitting patiently on a cushion while the grown-ups work—and the enormous, noisy vacuum cleaner is filling up most of the space and making it impossible to speak (Figure 6.6). As critics of modernist writing have observed, particularly in writing by women, liminal spaces such as corridors, doors, stairs, and thresholds tend to be used symbolically (see, for instance, Short, 2013). They may open up or block movement; bring people together; or separate them in ways that represent emotions, conditions, relationships, and destinies. Theoretically an 'ideal' home in modernist terms would prioritize movement, creativity, and relationships, symbolizing fulfilment in the present and readiness for the future, but the rhythms created by the modern house in Dehn and Gell's picture book are staccato, intense, and repetitive. They are also measured: the hands of the clock dictate what happens, ruling out

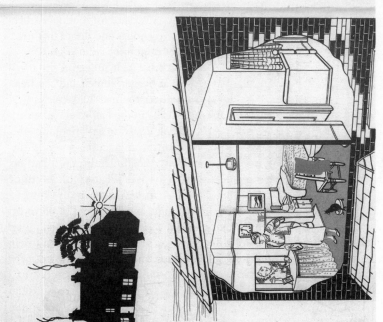

**Figure 6.5.** The ideal home? Cut-away images of the interior of 23 Pine Tree Lane

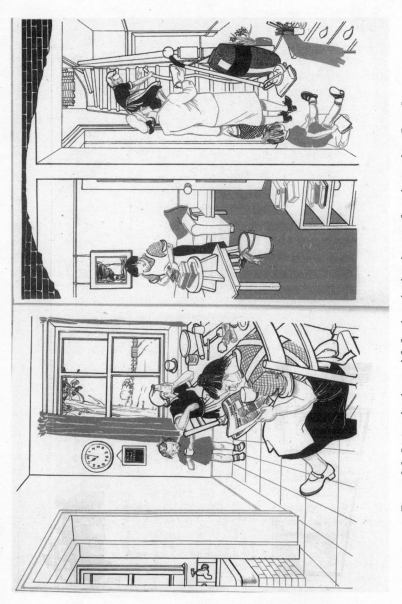

**Figure 6.6.** Living the dream; life for the suburban housewife as depicted in *Come In*

spontaneity, turning interruptions into additional sources of the incipient pressure that governs the day. In the cultural discourses of the time, an 'ideal' home was an efficient home where everything ran according to schedule. *Come In* highlights the fact that the most scheduled members of the family are the children, for whom regular meals, regular hours, and lives dictated by routine were believed to be health-promoting.[8] Presumably as a consequence of all the vigilance and routine, the children seem to lack an interior world. They come, go, dress, and play to order in a competent and cooperative but rather charmless way. This, the text implies, is the effect of growing up in suburbia.[9]

A discussion of how modern developments in housing were depicted in radical children's literature is not the place to dwell on the stylistic dimensions of *Come In* except insofar as they affect meaning. In addition to the metatextual and intertextual qualities already mentioned, Dehn employs limited focalization, shifts in the centre of conscious, alternating, and collective points of view, and free indirect speech. Simultaneity is achieved as much in the pictures as in the words: illustrations show different things happening in different rooms at the same time, sometimes in a sequence of juxtaposed panels. In suburbia as much as cities, it seems, the pace of modern life is hectic. Together these devices work to create a sense of the home as a place where identity dissolves, so it is a relief when, after the family has gone to bed, the narrator announces that it is time for 'us' to 'tiptoe out'. 'Us' clearly includes readers, since the announcement is followed by the questions, 'Ah, but how shall we get out? Who will show us the way? For now the whole house is in darkness, and all the doors are shut' (52). The artist comes to the rescue, letting 'us' and the cat out as she leaves the sleeping household and lights up a cigarette. She is an unencumbered, bohemian figure who does not belong to the orderly world of Pine Tree Lane. Readers are left to make up their own minds about whether busy days can also be dull, and the rewards—or lack of them— of life in suburbia for mothers. For children the message is clear: suburbia might offer comfortable, clean conditions in which to grow up, but it lacks the potential for exploration, risk-taking, and the 'spirit of place' that in Chapter 4 were shown to be essential for developing the creative, empowered young people who would run Britain in the future.

---

[8]  The doyen of regimented child-rearing in these years was Dr Truby King whose advice on raising infants according to schedule and with limited cuddling elevated experts over mother and was deeply bound up with eugenics and hygiene. The baby in *Come In* is evidently being reared according to Truby King's regimen as she is fed, bathed, and put at the bottom of the garden in her pram on a schedule (which like the baby gets forgotten as they day becomes more complicated).

[9]  The little boy manages to frighten himself by looking into a dark cupboard but the incident has no drama and is quickly forgotten.

Dehn and Gell's critique of suburban living flies in the face of much of the conventional wisdom circulating around women: the assumption was that a 'normal' woman would be happy and fulfilled by having a modern home with the latest gadgets, a nice garden, a working husband, and three healthy children. The fact that Mrs/mother Markham is dissatisfied can be seen as a feminist protest about the limited options available to woman and the way women who once would have expected to have servants were now required to service houses themselves. Alternatively, in Mrs Markham, Dehn may have sought to create a portrait of a woman suffering from what had recently been termed 'suburban neuroses'; a condition whose symptoms were associated with the atomized life of the suburbs and the ennui arising from the life of the modern housewife with her easy-to-clean home and convenient neighbourhood.[10]

For creators of children's books, ambivalence around the suburban home may owe as much to the need for atmosphere and plot as it does to how writers and illustrators believed children could, should, and did live. In this period—and indeed in any other as far as British children's literature goes—there is a conspicuous absence of fictional works set in modernist houses and flats: the clear glass, shiny metal, and minimalist environments associated with modernist architecture and design offer few nooks and wardrobes in which children can hide, objects can be discovered, or around which fantasies can be developed in the manner of some of the best-remembered children's books from this period. As Dehn and Gell show, suburbia lacks the obvious ingredients for works of imaginative fiction. This means that despite the efforts of architects and creators of information books to persuade children of the merits of modern materials and buildings, most radical children's books and stories set around houses feature the kind of large, old houses in city and country that had been a staple of traditional children's literature for more than a century. The paradoxical appeal of houses associated with privilege, Empire, colonization, and patriarchy for some radical writers may be linked to the fact that a good proportion of them grew up in and owned such houses, while those who were less well-off moved to houses in the country for economic reasons (most bohemians, for instance, could not afford to build new houses) or during the war.[11] By definition radical texts cannot set out

---

[10] The term was coined by Dr Stephen Taylor (1933) to describe women from new towns and suburbs who presented with particular sets of symptoms. Typically he advised having another baby.

[11] Harris offers a rather different (though perhaps not entirely unrelated) explanation of the attractions of the 'literary house' in the work of modernist writers such as Waugh, Bowen, Woolf, du Maurier, Henry Green, and Osbert Sitwell. Their appeal, she suggests, lay in their ability to supply 'what a chaotic present denied in the way of continuity, luxury and individualism' (271).

to reproduce patterns of living grounded in the networks of exploitation associated with capitalism, patriarchy, and class. In the hands of radical writers and illustrators, therefore, such houses become transitional and creative spaces where new kinds of relationships are made possible and where the competing claims of past, present, and future; town, city, and country; industry, domesticity, class, gender, and creativity are negotiated.

## HOUSES ANCIENT AS MODERN

When journalist and travel writer H.V. Morton went *In Search of England* (1927), he was left fulminating against the way the old order was being taxed out of existence, causing famous estates and old family farms to be broken up. When it came, the Second World War added to the decline of ancient homesteads and stately homes, turning some into hospitals and others into camps and hostels for evacuees from the cities. This is the scenario at the centre of Kitty Barne's *Visitors from London* (1940). Set during the summer of 1939, it features seventeen evacuees from London who are sent to Sussex to stay at Steadings, an ancient country house near where the four Farrar children, who appear in other of Barne's books, always spend their holidays with their aunt. In the middle of the holidays, their Uncle Roly sends word that he has leased Steadings and loaned it to the Women's Voluntary Services to use as a base for children being evacuated from London. (Although the story is fictional, it clearly draws on Kitty Barne's involvement in Operation Pied Piper, which managed the evacuation of children at the start of the Second World War.)

The Farrar children and their aunt take charge, with the children discovering competencies they did not know they had and rapidly acquiring skills such as persuading locals to help provide beds and cooking equipment since Steadings is largely empty. It also has no gas or electricity, which means all aspects of housekeeping are done in the traditional way: by hand with great effort. Eventually the Farrars are given some help by women from the Women's Voluntary Service, including 'a frightful expert' who 'ran something for the Basque children' (16), but for the most part they are in charge.[12] After a summer during which the city children and their families are introduced to the countryside—with varying degrees of success—everyone returns to home or school. The interlude stands for what came to be known as the 'Phoney War', but the way it brings different classes and constituencies together and has them learn how to 'pull together' anticipates the Blitz spirit.

---

[12] The reference is evidence that young readers were likely to be familiar with and interested in the young refugees from Spain as suggested in Chapter 1.

Although at one level this is a book about the upheavals of war and the way it throws people from different backgrounds together, at another it is very much the story of the house as a particular kind of space—a space that shapes the people who pass through it. With its fruit trees, slate roof, and sloping floor, the children judge it both a 'darling old house' and a house that 'makes you *think*' (15). The thinking is largely to do with the past, and it is stimulated by the sense that the house is a part of history, and particularly female history; the relationship between the house and its female occupants is cast as intimate and lasting. Reaching the kitchen Gerda, the eldest Farrar, is conscious that:

> This is where the wives, the farmers' wives, lived and worked. . . . She could almost see them whisking in and out of the doors, hanging up their bacon on those hooks, making their butter in that small dairy, turning their cheeses up on those shelves, boiling their washing in that copper, washing up at that sink, cooking at that old range with the bread-oven beside it. (23)

Such an account is problematic in terms of a radical agenda for the way it fails to confront the repressive nature of class and gender experiences that would have been the reality for many of the women who had previously occupied the Steadings kitchen. In other ways, though, it fits in with the exploration of Britain's folk and rural past in which many radical artists were involved, and with a newly heightened affection for a world that it was feared war would destroy. The treatment of Steadings has much in common with the depiction of Pointz Hall in Virginia Woolf's contemporaneous novella *Between the Acts* (1941). *Between the Acts* is set in the grounds of the Hall during the day of an annual village pageant which recapitulates the past by enacting it, rather as Mr Morrison transports Margaret and John through scenes from the past in Agnes Allen's books. Woolf makes Pointz Hall the serene centre in a world of change and transition; in the same way Steadings becomes a symbol of continuity and a guarantee of the future. As the book comes to a close, Sally Farrar is upset about leaving Steadings empty and shut up, but her aunt reassures her that 'Old houses like Steadings are used to waiting' and it will be there still when it is needed again (240). This confidence in the continuity and stability represented by old houses was not typical in experimental writing of the period. Because so many ancient country houses were being abandoned and left to moulder, more often writers of the 1930s and 1940s used them as metaphors for the decline, fragmentation, and vulnerability of Britain and the traditional British way of life in the modern world.[13]

---

[13] Alexandra Harris, for example, talks about this in relation to the work of Elizabeth Bowen and Evelyn Waugh (2010 252).

Barne's treatment of Steadings lays the foundation for a tendency in writing for children during the 1950s to use old houses that have witnessed much and 'are used to waiting' as conduits where past and present come together. In books such as Mary Norton's *The Borrowers* (1952), Lucy Boston's *The Children of Green Knowe* (1954), and Philippa Pearce's *Tom's Midnight Garden* (1958), the setting of an ancient house helps reconcile pre and postwar ideas about childhood, the family, and confidence in the future in a newly atomic world. But in 1939, *Visitors from London* was looking forward, and so Steadings is transformed into a democratic space. During the interlude at Steadings those who, like the Farrar children, have been accustomed to being served learn how to look after others, while for those whose lives have previously been stunted by the exigencies of urban poverty, their time at Steadings leads to new opportunities and ambitions. In the old house and its grounds, then, a new world and new kinds of social relationships are forged.

In its treatment of Steadings, *Visitors from London* promises that what is good from the past will endure and continue to enrich British life. This promise, as much as its optimistic and encouraging attitude to the challenges of a second global conflict, contributed to *Visitors from London*'s being awarded the Carnegie Medal in 1940. No doubt the warmth of its reception also reflected the fact that the book functioned like a fictional part of the Recording Britain project for children. The impetus to preserve risked fossilizing pre-war Britain, however. As other chapters have shown, how far and in what ways Britain embraced modernism and left-wing political regimes involved a series of compromises and re-workings. The same is true in the treatment of the country house. Ultimately radical children's writers agreed with Agnes Allen and S.R. Badmin: a new Britain needed new kinds of buildings, but it also needed to keep its connections with the past and find a creative way to fuse past and present to build the foundations for the future.

# Conclusion

## *Radical Visions, Compromises, and Legacies*

One day a boy of eight or nine appeared at the Child Art Centre carrying an enormous roll of paper under his arm. Set on end it would have stood half as high again as the youngster himself. He unrolled it.

> 'What's that you've got there?' he was asked.
> 'A Socialist City,' he replied briefly.

This anecdote opens the 1939 essay 'Children and Art in the Soviet Union' by Soviet champion of culture for children, Samuil Marshak. The image of a child who has been inspired to plan a city of the future and is capable of producing detailed technical drawings for building it encapsulates many of the themes of this final chapter—and of this book. In their different ways, each chapter has shown how radical writers and illustrators were attempting to give children and young people the kinds of skills and visions they would need to help plan and build a future based on interdependence, internationalism, and planned development assisted by the latest developments in science and technology. This final chapter begins by looking at how the future was imagined in radical children's literature and at books that introduce some of the intellectual tools writers believed readers would need to manage it. It ends by looking at what the future held for radical children's literature itself, considering both its legacies and its demise.

## IMAGINING A RADICAL FUTURE

Between 1910 and 1949 British children and young people had much less in the way of practical training and official support for taking up roles as planners and future citizens than Samuil Marshak's young city planner. The Russian boy belongs to the first generation of children raised under

Stalin's rule and so is what Marshak calls one of the 'future full-fledged masters'. Presumably he is also one of the urban élite who actually benefitted from the grand schemes to nurture Soviet children, meaning that he had access to facilities and mentoring unavailable in Britain and much of the Soviet Union as well as channels through which he could put forward his ideas (Marshak, n.p.). In Britain, images of the future were generally created for rather than by children. For the most part, mainstream children's books resisted looking to the future, focusing instead on the attractions of childhood and an idealized version of the nation's past. In such works, children are constructed as the inheritors rather than the makers of the future, and the future is always a diminished version of the past.

From its earliest manifestations, radical writing for children sought to overthrow idealized constructions of the past. Far from wanting to recover Britain's 'greatness', it sought to play down ideas of nationhood, empire, military might, and individual achievement, and to instil in readers a sense of connection between the peoples of the world and an awareness of the benefits of sharing resources and solving problems collaboratively. Throughout the decades covered by this study, radical writing for children and young people assumes that the work then being done by activist-adults will not be completed, and that children will be responsible for bringing a better future into being. Socialists in particular urged children to think of themselves as future-makers. To this end, those who attended Socialist Sunday Schools sang hymns especially written for them such as J. Bruce Glasier's 'The Children's International', with its rousing promise:

> We are children, but some day,
> We'll be big and strong and say,
> None shall slave and none shall slay,
> Comrades all together.

Another early example of how radical writers constructed children as builders of the future appears in the 'Cinderella Supplement'—the children's section of the *Labour Prophet*, a monthly penny newspaper published by the Labour Church from 1891.[1] Although it pre-dates the period of this book, the first in the series called 'Our Cinderella Letter from the Fairy', which appeared in the supplement between 1893 and 1897, shows British

---

[1] The Labour Church was a predominantly Northern movement founded in Manchester in 1891. It taught that Socialism was the political force that would bring about the just world God envisaged for humanity, one of its mottoes being 'Let labour be the basis of civil society'. The *Labour Prophet*, which continued until 1898, had a monthly circulation of between 5,000 and 6,000.

Socialists using enscripting strategies when writing for children to charge them with responsibility for the future. The letter begins:

> MY DEAR YOUNG PEOPLE,
> I am sure you will understand me when I say that a very great power lies in the hands of you children . . . you, boys and girls . . . have a great deal to do towards deciding what kind of country England shall be in the future. (in Sumpter, 2006 n.p.)

The use of direct address draws readers in; it assumes they want to be involved and that they have the power to shape the future. It also raises questions about what that future should be like and how change could be achieved. To answer these questions, readers needed writing and illustrations that fired their imaginations and gave them practical guidance about how to achieve the goals they set themselves. This was one of the central functions of radical children's literature.


## FUTURE VISIONS

Today, readers are accustomed to encountering visions of the future in speculative fiction such as science fiction and future fantasies. These tend to be dystopian works focusing on disasters brought about by human actions, usually involving science and technology. Between 1910 and 1949, the situation was rather different. Most writing about the future took the form of non-fiction, whether in the form of information books or features in magazines and annuals. For enscripting purposes drama was always important; in the case of future visions this is exemplified by Evelyn Pilkington's *The Dawn*. Written in 1909 for performance by children of the Co-operative Movement, Pilkington's play imagines a future when the struggle between the two goddesses, Co-operata and Commercia, has been brought to a happy conclusion by bringing industry and democracy together and thus 'moralizing' the economy (Gurney, 1996 70). During 1911, *The Dawn* was performed by children in at least eleven societies to an estimated audience of 4,500 adults and children (70). In its language and characterization, the play looks back to classical models; more commonly radical children's literature reflects the way rapid advances in science and technology were blurring the line between fact and fiction in how texts were being written and presented to young readers. New discoveries and inventions often seemed to promise that ideas from the worlds of fantasy, science fiction, and adventure would soon be part of daily life. Thinking about the possibilities of new discoveries and inventions could be as exciting as the plots and settings of the most elaborate future fictions.

This was not unique to radical children's literature. There were many areas where radical and mainstream juvenile publications agreed when it came to forecasting changes as to how people would soon be living. For instance, most writing for children about the future assumes a highly electrified world in which everything moves more quickly, works more cleanly, and requires less human effort than in the world readers knew. There were, however, some fundamental differences between books that imagined the future from a conservative perspective and those that offered radical visions.

Typical conservative images of the future regularly featured in the 'Wonder' section of Arthur Mees's *Children's Encyclopaedia* (originally published in fifty fortnightly instalments between 1908 and 1910). There, columnists and illustrators speculate about what the future holds in store, but the kind of changes they anticipate tend to be technological and scientific rather than political or social. For example, imagining future travel, a contributor suggests that trains will run on a single rail powered by a kind of gyroscope: 'Not only will enormous speeds be reached by trains of this kind, but the gyroscopes will keep the train so steady that we shall . . . even be able to play billiards' while travelling (in Tracy, 2008 40). In the accompanying illustration, well-dressed travellers are shown doing precisely that. The expectation that travellers will be privileged, and travelling for recreational purposes rather than for work, is far from a radical vision of the world. Equally significant is the fact that popular mainstream sources of images of the future such as Mee's make no use of enscripting strategies. They expect scientists and engineers to get on with the business of inventing and building new devices and infrastructure and assume that young readers will enjoy using them in due course rather than help bring them into being.

Radical writers, by contrast, both construct readers as makers of the future and emphasize the importance of planning, of having ethical foundations, and of learning from the mistakes and achievements of the past. Amabel Williams-Ellis's *Good Citizens* (1938), for instance, seeks to show that while mainstream history tends to remember military figures, the people who have and will 'make life worth living' are not warriors but 'scientists, inventors, artists and writers' (8–9). Through profiles of nine 'good citizens' including Thomas More, Robert Owen, Sarah Siddons, and Florence Nightingale, she encourages readers to identify with figures from the past whose efforts resulted in positive change for future generations. The need for future generations to improve access to education, training, and the facilities necessary for innovative work is another example of how radical writers worked to ensure that future visions took on board and addressed past mistakes. Past and future were powerfully connected in the sphere of radical publishing. So, for example,

O. Kuznetsova's *Enemy Under the Microscope* (1945) is more than just the story of how Louis Pasteur prevailed over the obstacles posed by poverty and succeeded in becoming a leading scientist. It also looks to a future when the obstacles in Pasteur's way have been overcome so that all those with ability have the opportunity to learn and the resources they need to contribute to society. Similar stories are found in Eleanor Doorly's *Microbe Man: A Life of Pasteur* (1936), *The Insect Man: A Tale of How the Yew Tree Children went to France* (1938), and *The Radium Woman: A Youth Edition of the Life of Marie Curie* (1939, awarded the Carnegie Medal for that year). The Curie biography also raises issues around the suppression of the Polish people and the oppression of women, two mistaken attitudes and areas of policy these books show need to be avoided in the world to come.

Radical visions of the future are not just concerned with learning from the past and celebrating technological innovation, however. They also point to the need for new kinds of social relationships, new attitudes to work, and the related needs for universal access to an education that provides the knowledge and skills that will be required in the future. A text that typifies the way radical writers were placing work at the centre of life in the future is J.H. Bingham's Socialist play *The World's May Day* (1924). Written to be performed by a large cast of children—nineteen girls and eight boys—it introduces a visitor from Mars to a future Earth. Although each child actor represents an individual country, the point of the story is that in the future, nationalism will have given way to inter-nationalism, and what people have in common will be more important than where they live or what they own. In Bingham's vision of the future, it is not just national barriers between people that have broken down: the class system too has become irrelevant so that each May Day, the Martian learns, the global population celebrates 'the world's real nobility', referring to the carpenters, builders, blacksmiths, millers, road menders, ploughmen, milkmaids, and all those who maintain society.

While workers are highly visible in Bingham's play, one sector of society is conspicuously absent: that made up of those who, when the play was written, enjoyed wealth and privilege. This is not an implicit threat, however. Radical fiction takes the view that being deprived of work is debilitating and leads to the kind of physical and mental feebleness that H.G. Wells had earlier given shape to in the form of the Eloi who his Traveller meets in *The Time Machine* (1895), and who are reared and consumed like cattle by the industrious Morlocks. The radical goal was to free humans from tedious, degrading, dirty jobs that machines can do but then to employ people in rewarding tasks that are of benefit to humankind. In R.A. Brandt and Stephen MacFarlane's *The Story of a Tree* (1946), for instance, work, whether it involves modern machines or traditional tools, is presented as exciting, creative, and equivalent to magic.

Young readers were taught to value the work—and workers—that underpin everyday life in the Anglo-American take on the production books published in the Soviet Union and discussed in Chapter 2. Both Basil Blackwell and Puffin published a range of books that explain the jobs people do and the processes involved in producing everyday objects. Blackwell launched American author Janet Smalley's *This is the Book that the Author Wrote* (1928) and *This is the Book that the Artist Drew* (1930), both of which use the nursery rhyme 'The House that Jack Built' to chart the stages in making a book. Smalley went on to write a number of books that use the same formula to tell how various items of food, clothing, and some household goods are made. The accumulative rhymes ('These are the suits of Dot and Dick, made in the building all of brick, where they weave the cotton the pickers pick, from the boll that blooms on the cotton tree that grows in the land of Dixie') emphasize how many steps there are from raw material to finished product and encourage readers to remember and respect each of them.[2] A more dramatic and detailed example of a British production book is Peggy Hart's *The Magic of Coal* (1945).

Although it is told in the present tense, *The Magic of Coal* is in many ways an idealized future vision of a time when the mining industry has become fully technologized, collectivized, and sanitized. Each job in the mining process is shown through a combination of images and factual text. There are no visible owners or bosses, suggesting that the miners are not working for the benefit of mine owners but for the nation (the industry was in fact nationalized two years later); significantly, the cover image of a miner bearing a tattoo of St. George fighting a dragon constructs miners as modern-day heroes and emblems of Britain (Figure C.1). The conditions in which miners are shown working reflect this elevated status: mining is depicted as an advanced industry, and miners are presented as valued citizens with good standards of living and an active interest in culture. Hart shows miners enjoying the facilities in the pit baths at the end of a shift before setting off to nice homes on a 'fine' housing estate or to participate in various activities including clubs and societies, higher education classes, and watching or putting on plays.

*The Magic of Coal* gives a futuristic spin to the realities of working in the mines in 1945, but otherwise it is a realistic account of how coal was

[2] Mickenberg discusses the vogue for production books in America (2006 61–4; 69–70; 196–7; 216–17).

**Figure C.1.** Cover, *The Magic of Coal*, 1945. Image courtesy of Penguin Books

produced. Other radical texts looked further ahead, asking what kind of work would be needed in the future and what kind of skills children would need to acquire to sustain and improve upon the better future once it had been achieved.

## PREPARING FOR THE FUTURE

Radical writers undertook to stir young readers' interest in a range of intellectual and professional spheres that would be useful as they began to play active roles as workers, decision and policy makers, and members of the public. Many books clearly seek to ensure that readers grasp at least the rudiments of how the economy is run to help them avoid being in thrall to future capitalists and politicians. 1930 saw the launch of the organization that called itself Political and Economic Planning (PEP) in which among others John Strachey, G.D.H. Cole, Julian Huxley, and Leonard and Dorothy Elmhirst (founders in 1926 of the progressive school, Dartington Hall) were involved in the early stages; all moved in some of the same circles as many of those producing radical children's literature and some of this group also wrote for children themselves. PEP's aim was to avoid economic catastrophe through a combination of planning and reorganizing 'on a national basis the country's economic, social and political organizations in ways consistent with its liberal traditions, the second asserting that the failure to adopt a National Plan would amount to a "major national danger"' (Overy, 2010 82).

Although PEP has not lingered in the public consciousness (its plans were rapidly superseded by the theories of John Maynard Keynes), throughout this period understanding of economics was increasingly seen as essential for a grasp of how modern societies work and even more so for planning—and changing—the future. E(lizabeth) F(lorence) Stucley's *Pollycon* (1933) was one of a number of books that sought to teach children and young people the principles of economics (Figure C.2). The importance afforded to learning about economics at this time is underlined by Stephen King-Hall in his 'candid' preface: candid because he takes issue with some of the author's claims and characterizations, notably of workmen as foolish for striking and factory owners as 'the kindest-hearted, most sensible chaps imaginable' (King-Hall in Stucley, 1933 7):

> I cannot tell you too often that *you* will be a stupid ass [which is how he describes some employers] if you do not make up your mind to learn about Economics, and Miss Stucley has got a way of writing about Economics which is most amusing, especially when she is helped by the pictures of Hugh Chesterman. (8)

*Pollycon* uses a series of stories, starting with Mr and Mrs Early Briton (cave people), to explain key economic principles such as exchange, distribution, wealth, money, capital, depreciation, borrowing, and lending. The stories and illustrations are entertaining, and the explanations well pitched for a young economist of about seven years of age, as the implied reader of the text is identified. These virtues were lost on the reviewer for *The Bookman*, who declared that 'a subject which is almost purely abstract and dependent on a wide knowledge of the other sciences connected with the organisation of the life of mankind can never be "popularised"' (Towers, 1934 415). The reviewer objected equally to all 'economics made easy books, whatever the age of the intended audience' (415). *The Bookman*'s reviewer had clearly not read Janusz Korczak's *Big Business Billy* (1939), which tells an engaging story at the same time as it teaches readers both some of the practical skills of running a business and some basic economic theory.

As well as writing for children, Korczak, nicknamed the 'King of Children', was a Polish paediatrician, campaigner for children's rights, and educator who worked closely with children, including in his work

**Figure C.2.** Making economics amusing: cover, E.F. Stucley's *Pollycon*, 1933. The Bodleian Library, University of Oxford 23211 e.487

with Polish orphanages. *Big Business Billy* was the first of his books to be translated into English, and it is true to his progressive educational views and his conviction that while children understand the world differently from adults, this does not mean that they *mis*understand it. Rather, as happens in *Big Business Billy*, adults often make the mistake of underestimating children's understanding and initiative.

Korczak's book tells the story of Billy Fulton, a boy growing up in a working-class part of an American city. His parents are hard-working and sensible, but his father finds Billy's desire to run a shop bemusing. In Mr Fulton's view, shopkeepers are suspect because they don't produce anything but live off the labour of others. He is the first of the adults who doesn't understand the world as well as Billy does. Billy is given a dollar by his grandfather and here begins Korczak's lesson in economics. With this capital Billy opens up a community shop at his school. Under the guidance of the local shopkeeper he learns how to identify a need, undertake market research, make a business plan, and record his profits and expenses. Readers learn alongside Billy, whose activities have moved him from the periphery of the class (he wasn't good at games or telling stories) to its centre.

Billy turns out to be an ethical capitalist: he sets up a committee of classmates to help manage the shop in the interests of the class. All goes so well that Billy has an even bigger idea: he imagines a bank for children where they could save money. The book sets out all the advantages of the scheme, but it is rejected by the Ministers of Finance and Education on the grounds that the business letter Billy wrote contains grammatical errors. The adults in the book are shown as foolishly missing an opportunity; by its end readers might be wiser. They have learned a great deal about how business works, including some carefully explained economic vocabulary, the financial benefits of collaborative, ethical practices over those that exploit workers and mislead customers, and the error of making decisions based on prejudices and power rather than informed vision.

The lessons they contain on collaboration and ethics as well as economics make *Pollycon* and *Big Business Billy* radical texts that are designed to equip young readers for a future free from exploitation and social divisions. If such a future were to be achieved, people had to learn to live differently, and radical children's books also spell out the consequences of failing to change existing patterns of consumption and traditional ways of dividing society between rich and poor. An episode in Erich Kästner's *The 35th of May, or Conrad's Ride to the South Seas* (1933), for instance, features a futuristic city known as Electropolis, the Automatic City, where people travel on moving walkways and use mobile telephones. The wonders of Electropolis are, however, doomed to be short-lived because its people consume indiscriminately and voraciously, with no idea of the labour and processes involved in supplying them. One elderly lady assumes that in the new age of mechanization, food is supplied effortlessly and inexhaustibly: 'Agriculture has been mechanized in every possible way', she tells Conrad and his Uncle, who have travelled there through a magic wardrobe on the 35th day of the month. 'Machines do most of the work.... Everybody can have all he wants. It's a well-known fact that the soil and machinery produce more than we need. Surely you know that!' (Kästner, 1933 124–5). Even quite a young reader will recognize the naïvety of her claims and the satirical note behind phrases such as 'a well-known fact' and 'Surely you know that!'

Kästner's story is humorous, but pointed in its depiction of the potential problems of over-production and too little work in an unplanned, unregulated, and unequal future (comparisons with the effects of Mrs Fox, Cox, and Box from Ilin's *Moscow has a Plan!* are unavoidable). Published in the UK in 1933, two years after it first appeared in Germany and at the height of the Depression, it is equally critical of myths about perpetual progress and plenty associated with both America and the collective farms of the Soviet Union. This did not exempt it from the Nazis' book purges: Kästner watched as copies of all his books, with the exception of the hugely popular *Emil and the Detectives*, were burned in 1933. The rise of Nazism and book burnings was evidence that there was no guarantee that a new, better future would be achieved. Radical writers found themselves caught between the need to explain how the future could be different and to warn against the forces that opposed positive social change. They also acknowledged the possibility that there might be no future.

## FEAR AND THE FUTURE

One of the lengthiest and most comprehensive sections of Victor Gollancz and Naomi Mitchison's *An Outline for Boys and Girls and Their Parents* is that written by Olaf Stapledon which deals with 'Problems and Solutions—The Future'. Stapledon is another of the figures who underlines the extent to which the different parts of British society who contributed to the creation of works of radical children's literature overlapped and interacted. He belonged to the first generation educated at Abbotsholme School (he was a pupil there from 1902–5), and he was a Conscientious Objector during the First World War, serving with the Friends' Ambulance Unit in France. When Naomi Mitchison commissioned him to write this section for the *Outline*, Stapledon was becoming known as a philosopher and what today would be called a futurologist. His first book, *Last and First Men: A Story of the Near and Far Future* (1930), had recently been published, and the ideas he sets out in it, especially his views on the cyclical nature of how human civilization progresses, inform 'Problems and Solutions'. Stapledon proposed a model in which primitive societies develop to advanced states before bringing about their own destruction, setting the process in motion again, though in a more extreme form, with both more spectacular advances and more devastating forms of destruction. The sense that humans had reached a particularly destructive cycle underpins both his vision of the future and his passionate opposition to war as he explains them in the *Outline*.

The radical agenda of the *Outline* is stated most directly in Stapledon's contribution, which creates a picture of a desired future for readers and then charges them to become disciples of that vision who will go out and teach others to see how things can and should be. There is a messianic quality to 'Problems and Solutions': the world, readers are told, must be changed, but 'It can only be changed by those who have the will to change it, to live for changing it' (Stapledon in Mitchison, 1932 711). It suggests that the process of transformative change—the only kind of change that might break the cycle of evolution and self-destruction—starts with reading the *Outline* and similar kinds of radical writing. The importance of these texts lies in their vision of the future and the work they set in motion for achieving it. For Stapledon, the vision is paramount since only by having a destination is it possible to move forward.

'Problems and Solutions' sets out a progressive vision of how governments and nations, economists and the military, health services and schools, peoples and families of all ages and backgrounds could come together to make a better human race and improve social organization in the future. As well as identifying the problems that need to be solved before the hoped-for future can be achieved, it contains many suggestions and vignettes about what that future could be like. These speculations anticipate ideas set out in a book that was to appear the following year: H.G. Wells's *The Shape of Things to Come* (1933). There are many connections between Wells's 'future history' and Stapledon's 'Problems and Solutions'. One of the working titles for Wells's work was 'An Outline of the Future'; the title identifies it as part of the genre that contained both Wells's own *Outline of History* (1920) and Victor Gollancz's series of Outlines in which Stapledon's piece appeared. Wells, Stapledon—and indeed his editor, Naomi Mitchison—characterize the current state of the nation and the world as 'muddled', and such commonalities of view and expression no doubt reflect the fact that they moved in the same social and intellectual circles and shared a publisher in Victor Gollancz.

Other obvious similarities arise around what Stapledon refers to as world-government and Wells calls, in *The Shape of Things to Come*, 'World-State'. In Wells's work it is the World-State that brings to an end 'The long, and often blind and misdirected, effort of our race for peace and security' (2005 393). That is also the aim of Stapledon's world-government. Both agree that the alternative is annihilation. Wells reports the effects of his World-State at the end of Book IV:

From pole to pole now there remains no single human being upon the planet without a fair prospect of self-fulfilment, of health, interest and freedom.

There are no slaves any longer; no poor; none doomed by birth to an inferior status; none sentenced to long unhelpful terms of imprisonment; none afflicted in mind or body who are not being helped with all the powers of science and the services of interested and able guardians.... The struggle for material existence is over. It has been won. The need for repressions and disciplines has passed.... No one now need live less nor be less than his utmost. (Wells, 2005 393)

This is the same vision that the *Outline* as a whole tries to impart to its readers, that Olaf's Stapledon's 'Solutions' delineates, and that underpins much radical children's literature. Similar, if less fully developed, future visions occur across a range of radical texts; for example, Geoffrey Trease's *Bows Against the Barons* (1934) includes a vision of a future in which 'the common people will have twice as much as they have now, and there will be no more hunger or poverty in the land' (Trease, 1934 102). This promise of a better future may have been set in the Middle Ages, but as comparison with the other radical works discussed here shows, its aspirations and expectations belong to the early decades of the twentieth century. In combination with an affirming domestic and social context, such visions could make a Socialist future seem immanent. Jennie Lee, who grew up in Scotland as a child of the Left and became an Independent Labour Party (ILP) MP in 1929 at the age of twenty-five, recalls:

It was an alive, bracing time. The Union was strong. The I.L.P. was growing rapidly in numbers and influence. In our part of the world it was a cordial fellowship proud of its anti-war record....Very soon now we would revolutionize the world. Our socialist hymns seemed to me to give a pretty good idea of what it was all about. (Lee, 1939 51)

Lee's confidence that the new Socialist future, which would also bring female suffrage, was on the horizon was so strong that she worried she and her peers would not have a chance to play their part in making it. Her grandfather reassured her that 'there will be plenty for you to do. It takes longer than you think' (54).

Wells's device of having a dreamer visit the future more or less guarantees readers that the future he reports will come to pass, though probably not in their lifetimes.[3] Writing for a juvenile audience for whom investment in the future is inevitably stronger, Stapledon holds out the prospect that his readers will live to see the future he describes, and enscripts them

---

[3] *The Shape of Things to Come* is framed as a dream in which the dreamer has actually visited the future in his dream and reports what he has seen in the present of his own day, thus making it a future that has already occurred or a history of the future.

**Figure C.3.** 'The next war' as pictured in *An Outline for Boys and Girls and Their Parents*, 1932

into the project of bringing it into being. The piece constantly refers to 'the world we are going to make' and 'the world we want to make' before explaining how and why changes need to be made. For example, 'In the world we are going to make, no one will be allowed to have a big house and three cars while elsewhere a whole family lives in a single room and cannot even share a push-bicycle' (1932 723). Stapledon does not point out that he, his editor, and many of the young readers they are addressing belong precisely to the 'fairly well off' group that he identifies as agreeing that there 'should not be rich and poor people' but who are 'seldom anxious to do anything much about it' (723). The paradoxes of this situation are discussed later; first it is necessary to look at the problems Stapledon identifies and the extent to which they threaten the radicals' vision of the future.

Olaf Stapledon was not alone in holding that the main—and very real—threat to the future was war, and thinking about what a future war would be like takes up a significant proportion of 'Problems and Solutions'. The section on 'War' begins: 'In the world that we want to make there must not be any national armies' (719), a statement that brings together both the desire to break down nationalism and the abiding goal of radical writers to achieve permanent peace. In his work as an ambulance driver during the First World War, Stapledon saw the consequences of fighting at first hand. Before giving his version of 'the-war-to-come' story for the 1930s, he writes about the costs and consequences of that war and how it was that people like him came to be caught up in it. Ultimately, he concludes, people 'suffered terrible things, and found the world merely grew worse and worse' (719). In a careful use of tense he shifts from the war that was to a war that *might* be, holding out the possibility that a second global conflict could be avoided if the information and changes set out in the *Outline* were acted upon. The alternative casts a shadow over the piece: 'If there is another war', Stapledon warns, 'it will be far worse than the last' (720). He goes on to explain that future wars will not be about defence and confined to battlefields but will use bombs, poison gases, and other weapons developed since the last war to damage enemy populations, including children: 'A few enemy planes over London could smash half the city and poison millions of people. The next war will be... like being run over by a motor or crushed under a falling house, or like dropping into a furnace' (720) (Figure C.3).

## RADICAL LEGACIES

Just as other chapters have shown the centrality in radical children's literature of developments in the Soviet Union, so the bulk of 'Problems and Solutions' assumes that the future world will be modelled along Soviet lines. Capitalism will be no more; money will not equate to power; industries, including agriculture, will be managed not for private profit but to meet world needs; education will be freely available to all as will culture and the time in which to enjoy it. In this future, Stapledon explains, governments will serve people rather than treating them as workers and cogs in a military machine; there will be less waste and more happiness. One of the greatest sources of happiness will come from breaking down the tradition of living in family groups with all the consequences of repression and oppression that psychology, child development, and psychoanalysis were associating with it:

> In Russia they are trying to make the child feel himself more a member of the State than a member of a family. He is taught to feel more interest and responsibility towards the children's group to which he belongs than towards his family . . . and parents understand that they don't own children but 'hold them on trust for the world's sake'. (743)

As set out in 'Problems and Solutions', reconfiguring relationships between parents and children in ways that make them friendly equals combined with universal state provision of education and health had made Soviet children 'healthy, vigorous, and very much alive' (being alive for Stapledon means to be fulfilled and fully engaged) (743). The same will be true for everyone in the future Stapledon imagines.

The energetic and broadly optimistic note on which 'Problems and Solutions' ends is closely linked to Olaf Stapledon's belief in 1931–2 when he was writing it that the Soviet experiment was working and that the kind of radical education provided in the *Outline* would finally break the cycle of progress and destruction. Just one year later, Adolf Hitler had seized power, Winston Churchill was issuing public warnings about German rearmament, civil war in Spain was brewing, the world learned about famine in Ukraine, and fears of a second, highly technologized global conflict likely to obliterate civilization seemed increasingly well founded. The effects of these developments on ideas about the future for those who had supported Socialism, extolled the virtues of the Soviet model, and who found themselves accepting that it was necessary to join the fight against fascism after years of opposing war were profound. The biographical note to the 1944 Puffin edition of the eminent scientist J.B.S. Haldane's collection of science-based fantasies for children, *My Friend Mr Leakey* (1937), sums up the mood:

> He [the author] hasn't felt like writing stories for children since 1933, when Hitler got power in Germany, and the world became a nastier place. But

he hopes the world will get nicer again after we have won the war; and then perhaps he will feel like writing more stories. (In Dudley-Edwards, 2009 279)

Haldane never did write any more children's stories, but this does not mean that he remained disillusioned. By the end of the 1930s the Left's dominance of the rhetoric and visions of transformation in children's literature receded as nationally focused projects and schemes for bettering life in Britain saw visions of the future featured in radical children's books move from the page into real life. William Beveridge's 1942 *Report of the Inter-Departmental Committee on Social Insurance and Allied Services*/The 'Beveridge Report' constituted an unofficial Six-Year Plan, the milestones of which became the 1944 Education Act, which made secondary education free for all; the 1946 National Insurance Act, to protect those in employment against illness and unemployment; the building of council housing, also from 1946; and the National Assistance Act of 1948, which provided for anyone in extreme poverty, culminating in the official launch of the National Health Service in 1948. In the knowledge of the abuses of Stalinism and in the context of the Cold War, the emergence of the Welfare State offered an achievable and sustainable compromise between the radical vision of a Soviet Britain and the conservative forces that had worked to maintain the status quo. As this book has shown, the gradualism, moderation, and pragmatism of this new strategy for building a better Britain for the future was very much in keeping with the British approach to modernity, even among some of those who fought most publicly and vociferously for change. Naomi Mitchison, for instance, acknowledged as much some decades later when thinking about how far she and her radical associates were committed to change:

> change was necessary, was admirable, but we went on planning for things to go on as they were going. So did a good many other people who realised that the economic system was not only unjust and internationally dangerous but very likely to break up through its own contradictions. Likely, perhaps, but the system was more flexible than it appeared to be and the old process of muddling through continued. (Mitchison, 1985 192)

This honest self-examination should not detract from the role played by radical children's literature in preparing the way for change in the generation that was responsible for managing Britain through the 1950s, 1960s, and 1970s. As Juliet Dusinberre has observed, 'in times of great change, some of the most radical ideas about what the future ought to be like will be located in the books for the next generation' (1987 34). Childhood reading is a potent force that works on intellects, imaginations, and tastes.

**Figure C.4.** 'Boys and Girls Bring in the New World!' from *An Outline for Boys and Girls and Their Parents*, 1932

In the years in question, when there was much less competition for children's time and interests than there is in our own media-rich epoch, this was even truer.[4]

The generation for whom these radical texts were written was responsible for seeing that the young Welfare State flourished, for making Britain part of Europe, and for placing it at the centre of popular youth culture and fashion. In 1934 Geoffrey Trease's *Bows Against the Barons* could only imagine a distant future when life would be better for ordinary people, but by 1949 Britain was a genuinely fairer place with cradle-to-grave care and world-class, child-centred primary education that saw children being educated in the spirit that gave rise to Samuil Marshak's young planner of future cities. While the hopes and ambitions for lasting peace and global government may not have materialized, the vision of a more socially just and progressive society that lies at the heart of radical children's writing continues to shape Britain today. The part played by radical children's literature in this social transformation deserves to be remembered. Repairing the hole in the cultural memory that was created when these books were left out of accounts of the first decades of the twentieth century not only changes how the history of children's literature is understood, but shows that for a significant group—those who created and were the first readers of the radical works discussed here—it was not a 'morbid age' but a time of optimism, engagement, effort, and achievement (Figure C.4).

---

[4] Mickenberg (2006) writes insightfully about radical writers in Cold-War America.

# APPENDIX

# Radical Children's Publications

The 249 publications listed below were either written and marketed for children and young people, or recommended to them in reviews, or featured on library and similar lists of recommended reading. Those that were originally intended for an adult audience appear in bold. The titles are separated by decades into books, plays, and pamphlets that are primarily concerned with social and political radicalism; books, plays, and pamphlets in which aesthetic radicalism predominates; and periodicals. Where books were originally published elsewhere, the dates given are for UK editions. The list is comprehensive but there are undoubtedly more works still to be identified.[1]

## CRITERIA: BOOKS LISTED BELOW WILL INCLUDE A HIGH PROPORTION OF THE FOLLOWING CHARACTERISTICS

*Social/political radicalism*: depict everyday lives of ordinary, working-class, refugee, and/or ethnic minority children—the children normally left out of children's books; construct child characters in the light of new sciences (psychology, child development, psychoanalysis, eugenics, genetics, anthropology); treat children as socially important and rational; shape readers as leaders of the future; utopian; internationalist; opposed to war; work to break down class stereotypes relating to class, gender, poverty, race, ethnicity, sexuality; democratic; progressive; anti-fascist; opposed to militarism; not technophobic; optimistic; future-orientated; seek to bring about a more equal, just, intellectually free society; provide information on a range of topics designed to encourage independent thought.

*Aesthetic radicalism*: aesthetically innovative, experiment with form, design, and medium, reference avant-garde arts and letters, promote new ways of seeing and thinking about the world, incorporate ideas from children's and primitive art.

### Social and Political Radicalism

1910s
Clarke, Allen. (1914). *The Men Who Fought for Us in the 'Hungry Forties': A Tale of Pioneers and Beginnings*. Manchester: Co-operative Newspaper Society.
Clarke, John S. (1919). *Satires, Lyrics and Poems*. Glasgow: Socialist Labour Press.

---

[1] Jane Rosen is currently working on an exhaustive bibliography of proletarian children's books. She has generously shared her work-in-progress with me.

Cradock, Mrs H.C. (1916). *Josephine and her Dolls*. Illus. Honor C. Appleton. London: Blackie and Sons.

Golding, Harry. (1915). *War in Dollyland (A Book and a Game)*. Photography Albert Friend. London: Ward, Lock & Co.

Gould, F.J. (1913). *Pages for Young Socialists*. London and Manchester: National Labour Press.

Malleson, Miles. (1915). *The Little White Thought. A Fantastic Scrap*. London: Hendersons.

Malleson, Miles. (1918). *Maurice's Own Ideas: A Little Dream Play*. London: Hendersons.

Milne, A.A. (1918). *The Boy Comes Home*. London and New York: Samuel French.

Wells, H.G. (1911). *Floor Games*. Illus. J.R. Sinclair. London: Frank Palmer.

Wells, H.G. (1913). *Little Wars: A Game for Boys of Twelve Years to One Hundred and Fifty and for that More Intelligent Sort of Girl Who Likes Games and Books*. Illus. J.R. Sinclair. London: Frank Palmer.

Wells, H.G. (1917). Master Anthony and the Zeppelin. Mary Josepha, Princess, Daughter of Alfred King of the Belgians. *Princess Marie-José's Children's Book*. London: Cassell and Co.

## 1920s

Anderson, Tom. (1920). *Across the Ages: Short Stories for Young Workers*. Glasgow: International Proletarian School.

Anderson, Tom. (1921). *The Round Table: A Short Sketch for Young Communists*. Glasgow: Communist Dramatic Society.

Badley, J.H. (1920). *School Talks in Peace and War*. Oxford: Basil Blackwell.

Baker, Percy, M. (1928). *The World of Machines*. London: Wells, Gardner, Darton & Co.

Bingham, J.H. (1927). *The World's May Day*. Manchester: The Co-operative Society.

Boumphrey, Esther. (1929). *The Hoojibahs*. London: Oxford University Press.

Carey, G.V. and Scott, H.S. (1928). *An Outline History of the Great War*. Cambridge: Cambridge University Press.

Dobson, Margaret. (1923). 'Sex Knowledge'. In *Proletcult*, 2, 1–3.

Fox, Ralph. (1922). *Captain Youth: A Romantic Comedy for all Socialist Children*. London: C.W. Daniel.

Frow, Marion. (1920). *Four Stowaways and Anna*. London: Hutchison.

Gould, F.J. (1920). *Youth's Noble Path: A Volume of Moral Instruction... Mainly Based on Eastern Tradition, Poetry and History*. London: Longman's Green.

Hayes, Nancy. M. (1928). *The Castle School*. London: Cassell.

Hill, A.V. (1927). *Living Machinery*. London: G. Bell and Sons.

Jesse, F. Tennyson (1927). *Moonraker, or, the Female Pirate and her Friends*. London: William Heinemann.

Le Pla, Lillie. (1922). *The Call of the Dawn*. London: C.W. Daniel.

Lenin, V.I. (1920). *The Tasks of the Youth Leagues*. Moscow: Co-operative Publishing Society of Foreign Workers in the USSR (speech delivered at the Third All-Russian Congress of the Russian Young Communist League, October 2).

Malleson, Miles. (1922). *Paddly Pools: A Little Fairy Play.* London: Hendersons.

Mitchison, Naomi. (1925). *Cloud Cuckoo Land.* London: Jonathan Cape.

Mitchison, Naomi. (1927). *The Conquered.* London: Jonathan Cape.

Ognyov, N [Mikhael Grigoryevitch Rozânov]. (1928). *The Diary of a Communist Schoolboy.* Trans. Alexander Werth. London: Victor Gollancz.

Ognyov, N [Mikhael Grigoryevitch Rozânov]. (1929). *The Diary of a Communist Undergraduate.* Trans. Alexander Werth. London: Victor Gollancz.

Smalley, Janet. (1929). *This is the Book that the Author Made.* Oxford: Basil Blackwell.

Vandercook, John Womack. (1928). *Black Majesty: The Life of Christophe, King of Haiti.* Illus. Mahlon Blaine. London: Harper and Brothers.

Williams-Ellis, Amabel. (1928). *How You Began. A Child's Introduction to Biology.* London: Gerald Howe.

Williams-Ellis, Amabel. (1929). *Men Who Found Out: Stories of Great Scientific Discoverers.* London: Gerald Howe.

Young, Winifred. (1922). *Clouds and Sunshine: A Fairy Play.* Music by B. Mansell Ramsey. Manchester: Co-operative Union Limited.


1930s

Anrade, E.N. da C. and Julian Huxley. (1934). *Simple Science.* Oxford: Basil Blackwell.

Anrade, E.N. da C. and Julian Huxley. (1935). *More Simple Science.* Oxford: Basil Blackwell.

Barbusse, Henri. (1933). *You Are the Pioneers, Being a Report of the World Youth Congress Against Fascism and War.* London: World Youth Congress Against Fascism and War.

Beales, Lance and R.S. Lambert. (1934). *Memoirs of the Unemployed.* London: Victor Gollancz.

Beauchamp, Joan (ed.). (1934). *Martin's Annual.* London: Martin Lawrence.

Binder, Pearl. (1936). *Misha and Masha.* London: Victor Gollancz.

Burke, Thomas. (1935). *Billy and Beryl in Chinatown.* Illus. Will Fyfe. London: George Harrap.

Burke, Thomas. (1936). *Billy and Beryl in Soho.* Illus. Will Fyfe. London: George Harrap.

Burke, Thomas. (1936). *Billy and Beryl in Old London.* Illus. Will Fyfe. London: George Harrap.

Clark, Frederick Le Gros and Ida Clark. (1936). 'Little Leopard Stories' Vol. I, *The Adventures of the Little Pig and Other Stories.* London: Lawrence and Wishart.

Clark, Frederick Le Gros and Ida Clark. (1936). Vol. II, *The Enchanted Fishes and other Stories.* London: Lawrence and Wishart.

Cloud, Yvonne with Richard Ellis. (1937). *The Basque Children in England. An Account of their Life at North Stoneham Camp.* Photographs by Edith Tudor-Hart and P.I.A. Photos. London: Victor Gollancz.

Cole, Margaret. (1938). *Women of Today.* London: Nelson.

Dehn, Olive. (1935). *The Basement Bogle.* Oxford: Basil Blackwell.

Doorly, Eleanor. (1936). *The Microbe Man: A Life of Pasteur.* Illus. Robert Gibbings. London and Toronto: William Heinemann.

Doorly, Eleanor. (1938). *The Insect Man: A Tale of How the Yew Tree Went to France.* Cambridge: Heffer and Sons.

Doorly, Eleanor. (1939). *The Radium Woman: A Youth Edition of the Life of Marie Curie.* London: Heinemann.

'Edith'. (1937). *Somersaults and Strange Company.* Illustrations also by 'Edith'. London: Lawrence and Wishart.

Elder, Josephine. (1938). *Exile for Annis.* London and Glasgow: The Children's Press.

Fischer, Marjorie. (1937). *Palaces on Monday.* Illus. Richard Floethe. Harmondsworth: Penguin Books.

Foreman, Elizabeth. (1935). *Ho-Ming.* London: Harrap.

Gallacher, William, M.P. (1936). *Revolt on the Clyde, an Autobiography.* London: Lawrence and Wishart.

Garnett, Eve. (1937). *The Family from One End Street.* London: Frederick Muller.

Gould, F.J. (1930). *This England and Other Things of Beauty.* London: Watts and Co.

Graham, Eleanor. (1938). *The Children Who Lived in a Barn.* London: Routledge.

Haldane, J.B.S. (1937). *My Friend Mr. Leakey.* London: Cresset Press.

Ilin, Mikhail. (1928/31). *Moscow has a Plan: A Soviet Primer.* Trans. G.S. Counts and N.P. Lodge. Illus. William Kermode. London: Jonathan Cape.

Ilin, Mikhail. (1932). *Black on White: The Story of Books.* Trans. Beatrice Kincead. Illus. N. Lapshin. London and Philadelphia: J.B. Lippincott.

Ilin, Mikhail. (1932). *What Time is it? The Story of Clocks.* Trans. Beatrice Kincead. Illus. N. Lapshin. London and Philadelphia: J.B. Lippincott.

Ilin, Mikhail. (1933). *100,000 Whys. A Trip Around the Room.* Trans. Beatrice Kincead. Illus. N. Lapshin. London and Philadelphia: J.B. Lipincott.

Ilin, Mikhail. (1936). *Men and Mountains. Man's Victory Over Nature.* Trans. Beatrice Kincead. Illus. N. Lapshin. London: Routledge.

Ilin, Mikhail. (1937). *Turning Night into Day.* Trans. Beatrice Kincead. Illus. N. Lapshin. London: Routledge and Sons.

'Ishmael'. (1934). *That's Sedition—That Was! London:* Sidney Parton.

Johns, Captain W.E. (1939). *Biggles in Spain.* London and New York: Oxford University Press.

Kassil, Lev. (1935). *The Story of Alesha Ryazan and Uncle White Sea.* London: Martin Lawrence.

Karazin, Nikolai Nikolaevich. ([1936] 1952). *Cranes Flying South.* Trans. M. Pokrovsky. Illus. Joan Kiddell-Monroe. London: Longmans, Green and Co.

Karrick [also spelled Carrick], Valerie. (1936). *Picture Tales from Many Lands.* Oxford: Basil Blackwell.

Kastner, Erich. (1933). *The 35th of May.* Illus. Walter Trier. Trans. Cyrus Brooks. London: Jonathan Cape.

Kastner, Erich. (1934). *Emil and the Detectives—A Children's Play in Three Acts.* London: Samuel French.

King-Hall, Commander Stephen. (1932). *Here and There Broadcasts for Children.* London: Sidgwick and Jackson.

King-Hall, Commander Stephen. (1934). *News for Children.* London: Ivor Nicholson and Watson Ltd.

Korczak, Janusz. (1939). *Big Business Billy*. Trans. Cyrus Brooks. London: Minerva Publishing Co.

Langdon-Davies, John. (1934). *Inside the Atom*. Illus. Betty Barr. London: George Routledge and Sons.

Leaf, Munro. (1937). *The Story of Ferdinand*. London: Hamish Hamilton.

Lindsay, Jack. (1935). *Runaway*. Illus. J. Morton Sale. London: Oxford University Press.

Lindsay, Jack. (1936). *Rebels of the Goldfields*. London: Lawrence and Wishart.

Lindsay, Jack. (1938). *To Arms: A Story of Ancient Gaul*. London: Oxford University Press.

Mitchison, Naomi. (1931). *Boys and Girls and Gods*. London: Watts and Co.

Mitchison, Naomi. (1932). *An Outline for Boys and Girls and Their Parents*. Illus. William Kermode and Ista Brouncker. London: Victor Gollancz.

Perkin, L.B. (1934). *Progressive Schools, their Principles and Practice*. London: L. & V. Woolf.

*Red Corner Book for Children*. (1931). London: Martin Lawrence.

*The Road to War*. (1937). London: Fabian Research Bureau.

Rowland, T.J.S. and Smith, L.G. (1937). *Vital Things for Lively Youngsters*. London: Cassell and Company.

Saxon, Lyle. (1937). *Children of Strangers*. London: John Lane.

Shannon, Monica. (1936). *Dobry: The Story of a Bulgarian Peasant Boy*. Illus. Atanis Katchamakoff. London: G.G. Harrap.

Shaw, Ruth and Harry Alan Potamkin. (1934). *Our Lenin*. Illus. William Siegel. London: Martin Lawrence.

Smith, Helen Zeena [Evadne Price]. (1930). *Not So Quiet: Stepdaughters of War*. London: A.E. Marriott.

Squire, Eileen. (1938). *Orphans of St. Petersburg*. Illus. Donia Nachsen. London: George Harrap & Co.

Strachey, John. (1933). *The Menace of Fascism*. London: Victor Gollancz.

Streatfeild, Noel. (1936). *Ballet Shoes*. London: J.M. Dent.

Streatfeild, Noel. (1939). *The Circus is Coming*. London: J.M. Dent.

Strong, L.A.G. (1933). *King Richard's Land: A Tale of the Peasant's Revolt*. Illus. C. Walter Hodges. London: J.M. Dent.

Strong, L.A.G. (1937). *The Fifth of November*. Illus. Jack Matthew. London: J.M. Dent.

Stucley, E.F. (1933). *Pollycon*. Preface, Stephen King-Hall. Illus. Hugh Chesterman. Oxford: Basil Blackwell.

Taylor, F. Sherwood. (1936). *The World of Science*. London: W. Heinemann.

'Ten Points Against Fascism'. (1934). London: Young Communist League.

Trease, Geoffrey. (1934). *Bows Against the Barons*. London: Martin Lawrence.

Trease, Geoffrey. (1934). *Comrades for the Charter*. London: Martin Lawrence.

Trease, Geoffrey. (1934). *Foiling the Death-Sellers*. London: Edinburgh House Press.

Trease, Geoffrey. (1935). *The Call to Arms*. London: Martin Lawrence.

Trease, Geoffrey. (1936/7). *Red Comet: A Tale of Travel in the U.S.S.R.* London: Lawrence and Wishart.

Trease, Geoffrey. (1937). *The Christmas Holiday Mystery.* London: A&C Black.

Trease, Geoffrey. (1937). *Missing from Home.* London: Lawrence and Wishart.

Trease, Geoffrey. (1937). *Mystery on the Moor.* London: A&C Black.

Trease, Geoffrey. (1938). *The Dragon who was Different and Other Plays for Children.* London: Frederick Muller.

Trease, Geoffrey. (1938). *In the Land of the Mogul: A Story of the East India Company's First Venture in India.* Oxford: Basil Blackwell.

*Twenty Years After!* (1934). London: Youth Council, British Anti-War Movement.

Van Til, W. (1938). *The Danube Flows Through Fascism.* New York and London: Charles Scribner's Sons.

Wedding, Alex. (1935). *Eddie and the Gipsy: A Story for Boys and Girls.* Trans. Charles Ashleigh, Photos John Heartfield. London: Martin Lawrence.

Williams-Ellis, Amabel. (1932). *How You are Made.* London: A.&C. Black.

Williams-Ellis, Amabel. (1938). *Good Citizens.* London: Bodley Head.

Williams-Ellis, Susan, Charlotte, Christopher, Amabel, and Clough. (1937). *In and Out of Doors.* London: G. Routledge.

Winter, Ella. (1933). *Red Virtue: Human Relationships in the New Russia.* London: Victor Gollancz.


1940s

Baker, Rachel. (1946). *The First Woman Doctor.* London: G.G. Harrap.

Banning, Nina Lloyd. (1949). *Pit Pony.* London: Routledge and Kegan Paul.

Barne, Kitty. (1940). *Visitors from London.* London: J.M. Dent and Sons.

Baum, Vicky. (1945). *The Weeping Wood.* London: Michael Joseph.

Binder, Pearl. (1942). *Misha Learns English.* Harmondsworth: Penguin Books.

Binder, Pearl. (1942). *Russian Families.* Illus. the author. London: Adam and Charles Black.

Blyton, Enid. (1940). *The Naughtiest Girl in the School.* London: Newnes.

Blyton, Enid. (1942). *The Naughtiest Girl is a Monitor.* London: Newnes.

Brandt, R.A. and Stephen MacFarlane. (1946). *The Story of a Tree.* London: Peter Lunn.

Cartmell, Esme. (1946). *Rescue in Ravensdale.* London: Thomas Nelson.

Curwen, Harold. (1948). *Printing.* Illus. Jack Brough. Harmondsworth: Penguin Books.

Dale, Norman [Norman George Denny]. (1947). *The Exciting Journey.* London: The Bodley Head.

Dale, Norman [Norman George Denny]. (1948). *Mystery Christmas.* Illus. Ley Kenyon. London: The Bodley Head.

Dale, Norman [Norman George Denny]. (1949). *Skeleton Island.* London: The Bodley Head.

Dehn, Olive. (1946). *Come In.* Oxford: Shakespeare Head Press.

De Sélincourt, Aubrey. (1948). *Micky.* Illus. Guy de Sélincourt. London: Routledge.

Dixon, Marjorie. (1941). *The King of the Fiddles.* Illus. G.N. Allan. London: Faber and Faber.

Ehrlich, Bettina. (1945). *Cocolo*. London: Chatto and Windus.

Elder, Josephine. (1940). *Strangers at the Farm School*. Glasgow: Collins.

Eyre, Katherine Wigmore. (1947). *Star in the Willows*. Illus. Gertrude Howe. London: Oxford University Press.

Gaidar, Arkadi. (1943). *Timur and his Squad*. Moscow: Novosti Press Agency Publishing House.

Hart, Peggy. (1945). *The Magic of Coal*. West Drayton: Penguin.

Ilin, Mikhail. (1942). *How Man became a Giant*. Trans. Beatrice Kincead. London: G. Routledge.

Ilin, Mikhail. (1945). *A Ring and a Riddle*. Trans. Beatrice Kincead. London: Hutchinson Books for Young People.

Kastner, Erich. (1940). *Emil and the Detectives*. London: Thomas Nelson.

Kuznetsova, O. (1945). *The Enemy Under the Microscope: A Story of the Life of Pasteur*. Trans. Edith Bone. London: Hutchinson.

Leacroft, Richard. (1949). *Building a House*. Harmondsworth: Penguin Books.

Lee, Jennie. (1948). *Tomorrow is a New Day: A Youth Edition of Jennie Lee's Autobiography*. Harmondsworth: Puffin.

Lenin, V.I. (1940). *Lenin and Stalin on Youth*. London: Lawrence and Wishart.

Linklater, Eric. (1944). *The Wind on the Moon*. London: Macmillan.

Naughton, Bill. (1946). *Pony Boy*. Illus. George Buday. London: The Pilot Press.

Nichols, Beverley. (1945). *The Tree that Sat Down*. Illus. Isobel and John Morton Sale. London: Jonathan Cape.

O'Casey, Sean. (1945). *Drums Under the Window*. London: Macmillan and Co.

Palencia, Isabel de. (1942 [1941 USA]). *Juan, Son of the Fisherman*. Illus. Ceferina Palencia Tubau. London: George Harrap.

Pollitt, Harry. (1940). *Serving My Time: An Apprenticeship to Politics*. London: Lawrence and Wishart.

Potter, Margaret and Alexander. (1944). *A History of the Countryside*. Harmondsworth: Penguin Books.

Potter, Margaret and Alexander. (1945). *The Building of London*. Harmondsworth: Penguin Books.

Prishvin, Mikhail. (1947). *The Black Arab and Other Stories*. Trans. David Magarshack. London: Hutchinson International Authors, Ltd.

Reyher, Becky. (1946). *My Mother is the Most Beautiful Woman in the World: A Russian Folk Tale*. London: Museum Press.

Roberts, C.E. (1942). *Bandy Loo*. Illus. Mabel R. Peacock. London: Edinburgh House Press.

Sancha, José. (1948). *Mitla and Lupe*. Harmondsworth: Penguin Books.

Serjeant, R.B.N. (1947). *The Arabs*. Illus. Edward Bawden. London: Puffin.

Shelley, Gerrard (ed and trans). (1945). *Folk Tales of the Peoples of the Soviet Union*. London: Herbert Jenkins.

Sigsgaard, Jens. (1947 [1942]). *Paul Alone in the World*. Illus. Arne Ungerman. London: Oxford University Press.

Steed, Wickham. (1942). *That Bad Man: A Tale for the Young of all Ages*. London: Macmillan.

Tabori, Paul. (1944). *The Lion and the Vulture*. London: Peter Lunn.

Todd, Barbara Euphan and Esther Boumphrey. (1943). *The House that Ran Behind*. London: Frederick Muller Ltd.

Trease, Geoffrey. (1941). *Running Deer*. Illus. W. Lindsay. London: G. G. Harrap.

Trease, Geoffrey. (1942). *The Grey Adventurer*. Illus. Beatrice Goldsmith. Oxford: Basil Blackwell.

Trease, Geoffrey. (1947). *Trumpets in the West*. Illus. Alan Blyth. Oxford: Basil Blackwell.

Trease, Geoffrey. (1949). *The Secret Fiord*. Illus. H.M. Brock. London: Macmillan.

Trease, Geoffrey. (1949). 'The Secret of Sharn' in *The Mystery of Moorside Farm*. Oxford: Basil Blackwell.

Trease, Geoffrey. (1948). *The Silver Guard*. Illus. Alan Blyth. Oxford: Basil Blackwell.

## Aesthetic Radicalism

### 1910s

Bosschère, Jean de. (1918). *Folk Tales of Beasts and Men*. London: William Heinemann.

### 1920s

Bosschère, Jean de. (1920). *The City Curious*. London: William Heinemann.

Bosschère, Jean de. (1921). *Weird Islands*. London: Chapman and Hall, Ltd.

Champneys, Adelaide M. (1924). *The House Made with Hands*. London: J.W. Arrowsmith.

Nicholson, William. (1926). *Clever Bill*. London: William Heinemann.

Nicholson, William. (1929). *The Pirate Twins*. London: Faber and Faber.

### 1930s

Bagnold, Enid. (1930). *Alice and Thomas and Jane*. London: William Heinemann.

Bone, Stephen. (1936). *The Little Boy and his House*. London: J.M. Dent.

Chukovsky, Kornei. (1932). *Crocodile*. Trans. Babette Deutsch. London: E. Matthews and Marrot.

Dunne, J(ohn) W(illiam). (1939). *An Experiment with St. George*. Illus. Rojankovsky. London: Faber and Faber.

King-Hall, Stephen. (1935). *Young Authors and Artists of 1935*. London: C. Arthur Pearson.

Lewitt-Him. (1939). *The Football's Revolt*. London: Country Life.

Mitchison, Naomi. (1931). *Boys and Girls and Gods*. London: Watts and Co. 'World of Youth Series no. 6'.

Peake, Mervyn. (1939). *Captain Slaughterboard Drops Anchor*. London: Country Life.

Saunders, Edith. (1932). *Fanny Penquite*. Oxford: Oxford University Press.

Tuwim, Julian. (1939). *Locomotive, The Turnip, The Bird's Broadcast*. Adapted from the Polish by Bernard Gutteridge and William J. Peace. London: Minerva.

1940s

Allen, Agnes. (1947). *The Story of the Village*. London: Faber and Faber.

Allen, Agnes. (1948). *The Story of Painting*. London: Faber and Faber.

Allen, Agnes. (1949). *The Story of Your Home*. London: Faber and Faber.

Badmin, S(tanley) R(oy). (1942). *Village and Town*. Illus. Jack Allen. Harmondsworth and New York: Penguin.

Brandt, R.A. and Stephen MacFarlane. (1946). *The Story of a Tree*. London: Peter Lunn (Publishers) Ltd.

Craigie, Dorothy. (1946). *The Little Train*. London: Eyre and Spottiswoode.

Fry, Jane and Maxwell Fry. (1946). *Architecture for Children*. London: Allen and Unwin.

Gabler, Grace. (1945). *A Child's Alphabet*. West Drayton: Penguin.

Garrett, Helen. (1948). *Jobie*. Illus. Kathleen Gell. Oxford: Shakespeare Head Press.

Goodden, Wyndham. (1947). *This or That?* Illus. Barbara Jones. Edinburgh: Scottish Council of Industrial Design.

Hill, Oliver and Hans Tisdall. (1944). *Balbus: A Picture Book of Building*. London: Pleiades Books Ltd.

'Klara'. (1941). *Paul and Mary*. London and Glasgow: Collins.

'Klara'. (1942). *7 Jolly Days*. London and Glasgow: Collins.

'Klara'. (1947). *A Baby Saved from the Enemy*. London and Glasgow: Collins.

Lewitt, Alina. (1944). *Five Silly Cats*. Illus. Lewitt-Him. London: Minerva Press.

Lewitt-Him. (1943). *Blue Peter*. Story and pictures by Lewitt-Him. Words by Alina Lewitt. London: Faber and Faber.

Marshak, Samuil. (1943). *The Ice-Cream Man, The Silly Little Mouse, The Circus*. Trans. Dora Lawson. Verse, Zabelle C. Boyajian. London and New York: Transatlantic Arts.

Marshak, Samuil. (1943 [UK]). *Play*. Trans. Herbert Marshall. London: Perry Colour Books.

Marx, Enid. (1941). *Bulgy the Barrage Balloon*. London: Oxford University Press.

Marx, Enid. (1942). *Nelson: The Kite of the King's Navy*. London: Chatto and Windus.

Marx, Enid. (1943). *Pigeon Ace, The*. London: Faber and Faber.

Newby, P.H. (1947). *The Spirit of Jem*. Illus. Keith Vaughan. London: John Lehmann.

Peake, Mervyn. (1948). *Letters from a Lost Uncle*. London: Eyre and Spottiswoode.

Ross, Diana. (1942). *The Little Red Engine Gets a Name*. Illus. Lewitt-Him. London: Faber and Faber.

Russell, Gordon and Jacques Groag. (1947). *The Story of Furniture*. West Drayton: Penguin.

Severn, David. (1942). *Rick Afire!* London: John Lane, The Bodley Head.

Severn, David. (1943). *A Cabin for Crusoe*. London: John Lane, The Bodley Head.

Severn, David. (1944). *Waggon for Five*. London: John Lane, The Bodley Head.

Severn, David. (1945). *Hermit in the Hills*. London: John Lane, The Bodley Head.

Severn, David. (1946). *Forest Holiday*. London: John Lane, The Bodley Head.

Stroud, John. (1949). *Airliners*. Harmondsworth: Penguin Books.

Thermerson, Franciszka. (1947). *My First Nursery Book*. London: George G. Harrap and Co.

Townsend, Jack. (1947). *The Clothes We Wear*. Harmondsworth: Penguin Books.

Trease, Geoffrey. (1944). *Black Night Red Morning*. Oxford: Basil Blackwell.

*Journals* (information about Young Communist League (YCL) and associated publications taken from the 2008 Communist Party of Great Britain bibliography compiled by David Cope, accessed at http://banmarchive.org.uk/cpgb_biblio/searchfrset.htm on 16 February 2016).

*Alive—Cultural Magazine* of the Young Communist League (YCL), three numbers in 1940.

*Challenge, the Fighting Fortnightly Newspaper for Youth* (YCL), 1935–85.

*Club News* (YCL), 1944–7.

*Communist Youth* (YCL), 1934.

*Communist Youth Information* (YCL), 1935.

*Correspondence of the Young International*—English edition (British Section of the Young Communist International (YCI)), 1920–1.

*The Drum*, Young Pioneers of Great Britain, 1932.

*League of Youth Organizations Bulletin* (YCI), 1921–34.

*MINE: A Magazine for all who are Young*, 1935–6.

*Monthly Bulletin for Girl Members* (YCL)—announced 1936 but no copies located.

*Our Circle* Co-operative Movement, 1907–60.

*Our Youth* (YCL), 1938–40.

*Out of Bounds: Action Against Reaction in the Public Schools*, 1934–5.

*Pioneer News* (Young Comrades' League), 1929.

*Proletcult: A Magazine for Boys and Girls*, 1922–4.

*Red Dawn*, 1919.

*The Revolution: A Magazine for Young Workers*, 1917–18.

*The University: A Review of the Life and Thought of British Universities*, 1924–39.

*The Worker's Child* (YCI), 1926–7.

*YCL News* (YCL), 1943.

*The Young Communist* (YCL), 1929.

*The Young Comrade* (Young Comrades' League), 1924–8.

*The Young Socialist*, 1907–60.

*The Young Striker*, 1926.

*The Young Worker*, 1923–34.

*Youth: An Expression of Progressive University Thought. (An International Quarterly of Youth Enterprise)*, 1920–4.

# Bibliography

## ARCHIVES AND SPECIAL COLLECTIONS CONSULTED

Abbotsholme School archives
Adam and Charles Black archive, Glasgow University
Basil Blackwell archive, Merton College, Oxford
Blackie and Sons archives, Glasgow University
Bootham School archives
Butler Collection, Newcastle University
Olive Dehn papers, Seven Stories, the National Centre for Children's Books
HarperCollins archive, London
King Alfred School archives
Lawrence and Wishart archive, Beinecke Library, Yale University
Left Book Club Collection, Special Collections, University of Sheffield
London School of Economics, Archive Collection
Marx Memorial Library
People's History Museum
Puffin Picture Book Collection, Seven Stories, the National Centre for Children's Books
Victor Gollancz archive, Modern Records Centre, University of Warwick
Geoffrey Trease Collection, Seven Stories, the National Centre for Children's Books
Working Class Movement Library

## INTERVIEWS AND PERSONAL CORRESPONDENCE

Laurian Jones, Comtesse d'Harcourt. Private correspondence, 25 November 2013
Martin Kettle. 14 February 2012
Robert Leeson. Interview, 1 March 2012
Kika Markham. Interview, 22 April 2012
Rosen, Jane. Private correspondence, 6 June 2012; 5 November 2012; 30 May 2013; 24 November 2013; 16 July 2014; 9 August 2014
Rosen, Michael. Private correspondence, 24 April 2012

## ARCHIVAL MATERIAL CITED

**Blackwell archive**
BLK/3/50 announcements, circulars, directors' minutes
Blackwell publishing ledgers 1923–49

**Victor Gollancz archive**
MSS. 151/4/LB/2/1–26 Left Book Club leaflets
MSS. 154/3/2b/238 letter to Naomi Mitchison dated 3 May 1935 about *We have been warned*
MSS. 157/4/LB/1/1 *Left Book News*
MSS. 318/2/1/5 production book, 1932
MSS. 318/2/1/7 production book, 1932–3
MSS. 318/2/2/1–3 contract ledgers
MSS. 318/4/4 catalogues and lists starting 1930
MSS. 318/4/7a prepublication pamphlet for *An Outline for Boys and Girls and Their Parents*
MSS. 946/39/ii minutes and items relating to Spanish conflict and peace activities


**Geoffrey Trease archive**
GT/05/01 MS of *A Whiff of Burnt Boats*
GT/07/01/15 Nottingham Festival lecture, 1938, 'Fifty Years Hard Labour: An Author Looks Back'
GT/07/01/43 lecture notes 'Historical Fact—and Historical Fiction', c. 1947–8
GT/07/04 Press cuttings
GT/07/07/01/16 'A Children's Library in the Ukraine' for *The Library Association Record*
GT/07/07/04/01/50 'And What Can You Children Do?' for the *Daily Worker*
GT/07/07/04/01/51 'What Shall Our Children Read?' for *The Worker's Monthly*, March 1937
GT/10/02/03 Accounts

## CHILDREN'S BOOKS CITED

Allen, Agnes. *The Story of the Village*. London: Faber and Faber, 1947.
Allen, Agnes. *The Story of Painting*. London: Faber and Faber, 1948.
Allen, Agnes. *The Story of Your Home*. London: Faber and Faber, 1949.
Badmin, S(tanley) R(oy). *Village and Town*. Illustrated by Jack Allen. Harmonds-worth and New York: Penguin, 1942.
Bagnold, Enid. *Alice and Thomas and Jane*. Illustrated by Enid Bagnold and Laurian Jones. London: William Heinemann, 1930.
Barbusse, Henri. *You Are the Pioneers, being a report of the World Youth Congress Against Fascism and War*. London: World Youth Congress Against Fascism and War, 1933.
Barne, Kitty. *Visitors from London*. Illustrated by Ruth Gervais. London: J.M. Dent, 1940.
Beauchamp, Joan (ed.). *Martin's Annual*. London: Martin Lawrence, 1934.
Binder, Pearl. *Misha and Masha*. London: Victor Gollancz, 1936.

Binder, Pearl. *Russian Families*. London: Adam and Charles Black, 1942.

Bingham, J.H. *The World's May Day*. Manchester: The Co-operative Society, 1927.

Blyton, Enid. *The Naughtiest Girl in the School*. London: Newnes, 1940.

Blyton, Enid. *The Naughtiest Girl is a Monitor*. London: Newnes, 1942.

Blyton, Enid. *The Happy House Children*. Illustrated by Kathleen Gell. Oxford: Shakespeare Head Press, 1946.

Blyton, Enid. *The Happy House Children Again*. Illustrated by Kathleen Gell. Oxford: Shakespeare Head Press, 1947.

Boston, Lucy, M. *The Children of Green Knowe*. Illustrated by Peter Boston. London: Faber and Faber, 1954.

Brandt, R.A. and Stephen MacFarlane. *The Story of a Tree*. London: Peter Lunn, 1946.

Brereton, F.S. *With Our Russian Allies*. London: Blackie and Son, 1916.

Burke, Thomas. *Billy and Beryl in Chinatown*. Illustrated by Will Fyfe. London: George Harrap & Co., 1935.

Burke, Thomas. *Billy and Beryl in Old London*. Illustrated by Will Fyfe. London: George Harrap & Co., 1936.

Burke, Thomas. *Billy and Beryl in Soho*. Illustrated by Will Fyfe. London: George Harrap & Co., 1936.

Carey, G.V. and Scott, H.S. *An Outline History of the Great War*. Cambridge: Cambridge University Press, 1928.

Carpenter, Edward. *St. George and the Dragon. A Play in Three Acts for Children and Young Folks*. London: Independent Labour Party, 1905.

*Children's Treasury of Peace, The*. Wisbech: Wisbech Local Peace Association (c. 1890).

Clark, Frederick Le Gros and Ida Clark. 'Little Leopard Stories' Vol. I, *The Adventures of the Little Pig and Other Stories* and Vol. II, *The Enchanted Fishes and Other Stories*. London: Lawrence and Wishart, 1936.

Cloud, Yvonne with Richard Ellis. *The Basque Children in England. An Account of their Life at North Stoneham Camp*. Photographs by Edith Tudor-Hart and P.I. A. Photos. London: Victor Gollancz, 1937.

Crane, Walter. *The Child's Socialist Reader*. London: The Twentieth Century Press, 1907.

Dale, Norman. *The Exciting Journey*. London: The Bodley Head, 1947.

Dale, Norman. *Mystery Christmas*. Illustrated by Ley Kenyon. London: The Bodley Head, 1948.

Dale, Norman. *Skeleton Island*. Illustrated by Ley Kenyon. London: The Bodley Head, 1949.

De Bosschère, Jean. *The City Curious*. London: William Heinemann, 1920.

De Bosschère, Jean. *Weird Islands*. London: Chapman and Hall, Ltd., 1921.

De Selincourt, Aubrey. *Micky*. Illustrated by Guy de Selincourt. London: Routledge, 1948 (erroneously dated 1947).

Dehn, Olive. *The Basement Bogle*. Oxford: Basil Blackwell, 1935.

Dehn, Olive. *Come In*. Oxford: Shakespeare Head Press, 1946.

Doorly, Eleanor. *The Microbe Man: A Life of Pasteur*. Illustrated by Robert Gibbings. London and Toronto: William Heinemann, 1936.

Doorly, Eleanor. *The Insect Man: A Tale of How the Yew Tree Went to France.* Cambridge: Heffer and Sons, 1938.

Doorly, Eleanor. *The Radium Woman: A Youth Edition of the Life of Marie Curie.* London: Heinemann, 1939.

Dunne, J(ohn) W(illiam). *An Experiment with St. George.* Illustrated by Rojankovsky. London: Faber and Faber, 1939.

El Lissitzky. *About Two Squares, a Suprematist Tale.* Forest Row: Artists Bookworks, 1990 (first published 1922; first English translation 1990).

Elder, Josephine. *Exile for Annis.* London and Glasgow: The Children's Press, 1938.

Elder, Josephine. *Strangers at the Farm School.* Glasgow: Collins, 1940.

Everett, Russell. 'The Bugle Call. How the German lad answered it'. *The Young Socialist*, 1916, 52.

Fischer, Majorie. *Palaces on Monday.* Illustrated by Richard Floethe. Harmondsworth: Penguin Books, 1937; reprinted Harmondsworth: Puffin, 1944.

Fox, Ralph. *Captain Youth: A Romantic Comedy for all Socialist Children.* London: C.W. Daniel, 1922.

Frow, Marion. *Four Stowaways and Anna.* London: Hutchison, 1920.

Fry, Jane and Maxwell Fry. *Architecture for Children.* London: Allen and Unwin, 1946.

Gaidar, Arkadi. *Timur and his Squad.* 'Retold' (reteller not credited). Moscow: Novosti Press Agency, 1982.

Gaider, Arkadi. *Timur and his Comrades.* Translated by Musia Renbourn. Illustrated by Donia Nachshen. London: Pilot Press and Moscow: Novosti Press Agency Publishing House, 1943.

Garnett, Eve. *The Family from One End Street.* London: Frederick Muller, 1936.

Gilson, Charles. *In Arms for Russia.* London; Humphries Milford, 1918.

Golding, Harry. (ed.) *Our Darlings.* London; Ward, Lock and Co., 1905.

Golding, Harry. (ed.) *Day Dreams.* London: Ward. Lock and Co., 1910.

Golding, Harry. *War in Dollyland (A Book and a Game).* Photography Albert Friend. London: Ward, Lock & Co., 1915.

Goodden, Wyndham. *This or That?* Illustrated by Barbara Jones. Edinburgh: Scottish Council of Industrial Design, 1947.

Gould, F.J. *On the Threshold of Sex: A Book for Readers aged 14 to 21.* London: C.W. Daniel, 1909.

Gould, F.J. *Pages for Young Socialists.* London and Manchester: National Labour Press, 1913.

Gould, F.J. *This England and Other Things of Beauty.* London: Watts & Co., 1930.

Graham, Eleanor. *The Children who Lived in a Barn.* London: Routledge, 1938.

Haldane, J.B.S. *Science in Peace and War.* London: Lawrence and Wishart, 1940.

Hart, Peggy. *The Magic of Coal.* West Drayton: Penguin, 1945.

Hawley, E.J. *The Toy Soldier: A Children's Peace Story.* Leicester: Leicester Peace Society, c. 1902.

Hazell, A.P. *The Red Catechism for Socialist Children*. London: Twentieth Century Press, 1907.

Hennell, Thomas. *Lady Filmy Fern or The Voyage of the Window Box*. Illustrated by Edward Bawden. London: Hamish Hamilton, 1980.

Henty, G.A. *With Clive in India*. London: Blackie and Son, 1884.

Henty, G.A. *Under Wellington's Command*. London: Blackie and Son, 1898.

Hill, Oliver. *Balbus: a Picture Book of Building*. Illustrated by Hans Tisdall. London: Pleiades Books Ltd., 1944.

Hughes, Richard. *The Innocent Voyage*. London: Harper and Bros., 1929.

Hughes, Richard. *The Spider's Palace and Other Stories*. London: Chatto and Windus, 1931.

Ilin, Mikhail. *Moscow has a Plan: a Soviet Primer*. Trans. G.S. Counts and N.P. Lodge. Illustrated by William Kermode. London: Jonathan Cape, 1931.

Ilin, Mikhail. *Black on White: The Story of Books*. Trans. Beatrice Kincead. Illustrated by N. Lapshin. London and Philadelphia: J.B. Lippincott, 1932.

Jesse, F. Tennyson. *Moonraker, or, the Female Pirate and Her Friends*. London: William Heinemann, 1927.

Johns, Captain W.E. *Biggles in Spain*. London and New York: Oxford University Press, 1939.

Karazin, N. *Cranes Flying South*. Translated by M. Pokrovsky. Illustrated by Vera Block. London: G. Routledge and Sons, 1936.

Kassil, Lev. *The Story of Alesha Ryazan and Uncle White Sea*. London: Martin Lawrence, 1935.

Kastner, Erich. *The 35th of May*. Translated by Cyrus Brooks. Illustrated by Walter Trier. London: Jonathan Cape, 1933.

*King Alfred School Magazine*. London: King Alfred School, 1910–49.

King-Hall, Stephen. *Young Authors and Artists of 1935*. London: C. Arthur Pearson, 1935.

King-Hall, Stephen (ed.). *MINE: A Magazine for all who are Young*. London: C. Arthur Pearson, 1935–6.

'Klara'. *Paul and Mary*. London and Glasgow: Collins, 1941.

'Klara'. *7 Jolly Days*. London and Glasgow: Collins, 1942.

Korczak, Jaunsz. *Big Business Billy*. Translated by Cyrus Brooks. London: Minerva Publishing, 1939.

Kuznetsova, O. *The Enemy Under the Microscope: A Story of the Life of Pasteur*. Translated by Edith Bone. London: Hutchinson, 1945.

Leaf, Munro. *The Story of Ferdinand*. London: Hamish Hamilton, 1937.

Lee, Jennie. *Tomorrow is a New Day*. London: The Cresset Press, 1939.

Lee, Jennie. *Tomorrow is a New Day: A Youth Edition of Jennie Lee's Autobiography*. Harmondsworth: Puffin, 1948.

Lewitt-Him. *Blue Peter*. Story and pictures by Lewitt-Him. Words by Alina Lewitt. London: Faber and Faber, 1943.

Lewitt-Him. *The Football's Revolt*. London: Country Life, 1939.

Malleson, Miles. *Paddly Pools: A Little Fairy Play*. London: Hendersons, 1922.

Marchant, Bessie. *Hope's Tryst: A Story of the Siberian Frontier.* London: Blackie and Son, 1905.

Marchant, Bessie. *A Girl and a Caravan: The Story of Irma's Quest in Persia.* London: Blackie and Son, 1915.

Marchant, Bessie. *A Dangerous Mission: A Tale of Russia in Revolution.* London: Blackie and Son, 1918.

Mary Josepha, Princess, Daughter of Alfred King of the Belgians. *Princess Marie José's Children's Book.* London: Cassell and Co., 1917.

Mee, Arthur (ed.). *The Children's Encyclopedia.* London: Amalgamated Press, 1908–10.

Mee, Arthur (ed.). *The New Children's Encyclopedia.* London: Amalgamated Press, 1910.

Mee, Arthur (ed.). *The Children's Encyclopedia.* London: Educational Book Co., 1939.

Milne, A.A. *The Boy Comes Home.* A comedy in one act. Accessed at http://www.readbookonline.net/readOnLine/37786/,1918.

Mitchison, Naomi. *Cloud Cuckoo Land.* London: Jonathan Cape, 1925.

Mitchison, Naomi. *The Conquered.* London: Jonathan Cape, 1927.

Mitchison, Naomi. *Boys and Girls and Gods.* London: Watts and Co, 1931.

Mitchison, Naomi. *An Outline for Boys and Girls and Their Parents.* Illustrated by William Kermode and Ista Brouncker. London: Victor Gollancz, 1932.

Newby, P.H. *The Spirit of Jem.* Illustrated by Keith Vaughan. London: John Lehmann, 1947.

Niven, Barbara. *Little Tusker's Own Paper.* Illustrated by Ern Brook. London: Daily Worker League, 1945.

Norton, Mary. *The Borrowers.* Illustrated by Diana Stanley. London: J.M. Dent & Sons, 1952.

Ognyov, N [Mikhael Grigoryevitch Rozânov]. *The Diary of a Communist Schoolboy.* Translated by Alexander Werth. London: Victor Gollancz, 1928.

Ognyov, N [Mikhael Grigoryevitch Rozânov]. *The Diary of a Communist Undergraduate.* Trans. Alexander Werth. London: Victor Gollancz, 1929.

Peake, Mervyn. *Captain Slaughterboard Drops Anchor.* London: Country Life, 1939.

Pearce, Philippa. *Tom's Midnight Garden.* Illustrated by Susan Einzig. Oxford: Oxford University Press, 1968.

Perkin, L.B. *Progressive Schools, their Principles and Practice.* London: L.&V. Woolf, 1934.

Pilkington, Evelyn. *The Dawn.* Manchester: Co-operative Union, 1909.

*The Red Corner Book for Children.* London: Martin Lawrence, 1931.

*The Revolution: A Magazine for Young Workers.* Glasgow: Socialist School. Vol 1, 1917–18.

Reyher, Becky. *My Mother is the Most Beautiful Woman in the World: A Russian Folk Tale.* London: Museum Press, 1946.

Russell, Gordon and Jacques Groag. *The Story of Furniture.* West Drayton: Penguin, 1947.

Saunders, Edith. *Fanny Penquite.* London: Oxford University Press, 1932.

Schwitters, Kurt. *The Scarecrow*. In Jack Zipes, trans., *Lucky Hans and Other Merz Fairy Tales*. Princeton: Princeton University Press, 2009 (first published 1925).

Severn, David. *Rick Afire!* London: John Lane, The Bodley Head, 1942.

Severn, David. *A Cabin for Crusoe*. London: John Lane, The Bodley Head, 1943.

Severn, David. *Waggon for Five*. London: John Lane, The Bodley Head, 1944.

Severn, David. *Hermit in the Hills*. London: John Lane, The Bodley Head, 1945.

Severn, David. *Forest Holiday*. London: John Lane, The Bodley Head, 1946.

Shannon, Monica. *Dobry: The Story of a Bulgarian Peasant Boy*. Illustrated by Atanis Katchamakoff. London: G.G. Harrap, 1936.

Shaw, Ruth and Harry Alan Potamkin. *Our Lenin*. Illustrated by William Siegel. London: Martin Lawrence, 1934.

Smith, Helen Zeena [Evadne Price]. *Not So Quiet: Stepdaughters of War*. London: A.E. Marriott, 1930.

Squire, Eileen. *Orphans of St. Petersburg*. Illustrated by Donia Nachsen. London: George Harrap & Co., 1938.

Starr, Mark. 'Books and the Young Socialist'. *The Revolution: A Magazine for Young Workers*. 1.10, 1918, 161–4.

Stevens, F.L. *Through Merrie England: The Pageantry and Pastimes of the Village and the Town*. London; Frederick Warne and Co., 1928.

Stucley, E.F. *Pollycon*. With a candid preface by Stephen King-Hall. Illustrated by Hugh Chesterman. Oxford: Basil Blackwell, 1933.

'Ten Points Against Fascism'. London: Young Communist League, 1934.

Thermerson, Franciszka. *My First Nursery Book*. London: George G. Harrap and Co., 1947.

Todd, Barbara Euphan and Esther Boumphrey. *The House that Ran Behind*. London: Frederick Muller Ltd., 1943.

Tolstoy, Leo. *Ivan the Fool and Three Other Parables*. London: W. Scott, 1896.

Trease, Geoffrey. *Bows Against the Barons*. London: Martin Lawrence, 1934.

Trease, Geoffrey. *Comrades for the Charter*. London: Martin Lawrence, 1934.

Trease, Geoffrey. *Foiling the Death-Sellers*. London: Edinburgh House Press, 1934.

Trease, Geoffrey. *The Call to Arms*. London: Martin Lawrence, 1935.

Trease, Geoffrey. *Red Comet: A Tale of Travel in the U.S.S.R.* London: Lawrence and Wishart, 1936–7.

Trease, Geoffrey. *Missing from Home*. London: Lawrence and Wishart, 1937.

Trease, Geoffrey. *Mystery on the Moors*. London: A.&C. Black, 1937.

*Twenty Years After!*. London: Youth Council, British Anti-War movement, 1934.

Tuwim, Julian. *Locomotive, The Turnip, The Birds' Broadcast*. Illustrated by Lewitt and Him. London: Minerva Publishing Co., 1939.

Vandercook, John Womack. *Black Majesty. The Life of Christophe, King of Haiti*. Illustrated by Mahlon Blaine. London: Harper and Brothers, 1928.

Wedding, Alex. *Eddie and the Gipsy. A Story for Boys and Girls*. Translated by Charles Ashleigh. Photographs by John Heartfield. London: Martin Lawrence, 1935.

Wells, H.G. *Floor Games*. Illustrated by J.R. Sinclair. London: Frank Palmer, 1911.

Wells, H.G. *Little Wars: A Game for Boys of Twelve Years to One Hundred and Fifty and for that More Intelligent Sort of Girl Who Likes Games and Books*. Illustrated by J.R. Sinclair. London: Frank Palmer, 1913.

Wells, H.G. 'Master Anthony and the Zeppelin'. In Mary Josepha, Princess, Daughter of Alfred King of the Belgians. *Princess Marie-José's Children's Book*. London: Cassell and Co., 1917.

Westerman, Percy. *The Dreadnought of the Air*. London: S.W. Partridge, 1914.

Westerman, Percy. *Under Fire in Spain*. London and Glasgow: Blackie and Son, 1937.

Williams-Ellis, Amabel. *How You Began. A Child's Introduction to Biology*. London: Gerald Howe, 1928.

Williams-Ellis, Susan, Charlotte, Christopher, Amabel, and Clough. *In and Out of Doors*. London: G. Routledge, 1937.

Woolf, Virginia. *Nurse Lugton's Golden Thimble*. Illustrated by Duncan Grant. London: Hogarth Press, 1966.

Woolf, Virginia. *The Widow and the Parrot*. Illustrated by Julian Bell. London: Hogarth Press, 1988.

*Young Socialist, The*. Bound volumes for 1907–15.

## SECONDARY WORKS

*Abbotsholmian, The*. Uttoxeter: Abbotsholme School, 1900–50.

*Abbotsholme School Magazine*. Uttoxeter: Abbotsholme School, 1900–50.

*Adventures in the Soviet Imaginary: Children's Books and Graphic Arts*, exhibition organized by the Special Collections Research Centre, University of Chicago Library, August–December 2011. Accessed at http://www.lib.uchicago.edu/e/scrc/ on 18 November 2012.

Allinson, Francesca. *A Childhood*. Illustrated by Enid Marx. London: Leonard and Virginia Woolf, 1937.

Angell, Norman. *The Unseen Assassins*. London: Hamish Hamilton, 1932.

Ariès, Philippe. *Centuries of Childhood*. Translated by Robert Baldick. London: Pimlioc, 1996 (first published 1962).

Armstrong, Tim. 'Micromodernism: the places of modernist dissidence'. *Moving Modernisms* conference, University of Oxford, 22–4 March 2012.

Badley, J.H. *School Talks in Peace and War*. Oxford: Basil Blackwell, 1920.

Badley, J.H. (ed.). *Experiments in Sex Education*. London: Federation of Progressive Societies and Individuals, 1935.

Baines, Phil. *Puffin by Design: 70 Years of Imagination 1940–2010*. London: Allen Lane, 2010.

Balina, Marina and Larissa Rudova (eds). *Russian Children's Literature and Culture*. New York and Abingdon: Routledge, 2008.

Barai, Aneesh. *Names, Places and Spaces in British Modernist Children's Literature and its Translation into French*. PhD thesis, Queen Mary, University of London, 2014.

Basque Children of '37 Association. Official website: http://www.basquechildren. org/. Accessed on 18 October 2012.

Battle of the Books. London: Ministry of Information, 1941. Accessed at http:// www.iwm.org.uk/collections/item/object/1060016336 on 20 October 2012.

Bavidge, Jenny. 'Exhibiting Childhood: E. Nesbit and the Children's Welfare Exhibitions'. In Adrienne E. Gavin and Andrew F. Humphries (eds), *Childhood in Edwardian Fiction: Worlds Enough and Time*. Basingstoke: Palgrave Macmillan, 2009.

Beard, Mary. 'Do come to me funeral'. Review of Peter Sussman (ed.). *Decca: The Letters of Jessica Mitford*, 2006. *London Review of Books*, 5 July 2007, 31–2.

Beauvais, Clémentine. *The Mighty Child: Time and Power in Children's Literature*. Amsterdam and Philadelphia: John Benjamins, 2015.

Beetles, Chris. *S.R. Badmin and the English Landscape*. London: Collins, 1985.

Benton, Jill. *Naomi Mitchison: A Biography*. London: Pandora, 1990.

Bernstein, Robin. *Racial Innocence: Performing American Childhood from Slavery to Civil Rights*. New York: New York University Press, 2011.

Binder, Pearl. 'Children's Books in Russia'. *Design for Today* 11.9, 1934, 23–6.

Black, Alistair, Pepper, Simon and Kaye Bagshaw. *Books, Buildings and Social Engineering: Early Public Libraries in Britain from Past to Present*. Farnham: Ashgate, 2006. Accessed at http://radicalmanchester.wordpress.com/2010/08/ 11/the-clarion-movement/ on 13 July 2013.

Blishen, Edward (ed.). *The Thorny Paradise: Writers on Writing for Children*. Harmondsworth: Kestrel, 1975.

Bolton, Paul. *Education: Historical Statistics*. House of Commons Library: SN/ SG/4252, 2012. Accessed at www.parliament.uk/briefing-papers/sn04252.pdf on 8 August 2014.

Bonnett, Alistair. *Left in the Past: Radicalism and the Politics of Nostalgia*. New York: Continuum, 2010.

*Bootham*. York: Bootham School, 1909–49.

Breton, André. *First Manifesto of Surrealism*. Accessed at http://www.tcf.ua.edu/ Classes/Jbutler/T340/SurManifesto/ManifestoOfSurrealism.htm on 16 February 2016.

Bridge, Mrs Charles. Compiler. *Catalogue of the Circulating Library of the Children's Book Club*. London: The Children's Book Club, 1934.

Briggs, Julia. *A Woman of Passion: The Life of E. Nesbit, 1858–1924*. London: Hutchinson, 1987.

Britton, Sarah. '"Come and See the Empire by the All Red Route!": Anti-Imperialism and Exhibitions in Interwar Britain'. *History Workshop Journal* 69, 2010, 68–89.

Brock, Peter. *Pacifism in Europe to 1914*. Princeton: Princeton University Press, 1971.

Burnett, Frances Hodgson. *The Secret Garden*. London: Walker, 2007 (first published 1911).

Butts, Dennis. *Children's Literature and Social Change: Some Case Studies from Barbara Hofland to Philip Pullman*. Cambridge: Lutterworth Press, 2010.

Byron, Robert. *First Russia, then Tibet: Travels in a Changing World*. London: Taurus Parke, 2011 (first published 1933).

Calder, Jenni. *The Nine Lives of Naomi Mitchison*. London: Virago, 1997.

Carpenter, Edward. *My Days and Dreams*, 1916. Accessed at http://www.edwardcarpenter.net/ecdd9.htm on 24 July 2014.

Carrington, Noel. 'A Century of Puffins'. *Penrose Annual* 51, 1957, 62–5.

Carrington, Noel. 'The Birth of Puffin Picture Books'. Penguin Collectors Society *Newsletter*, 13, 1979, 62–4.

Catalogue of Copyright Entries, Part I. Washington: Library of Congress, 1934.

Chambers, Roland. *The Last Englishman: The Double Life of Arthur Ransome*. London: Faber and Faber, 2009.

Chilvers, Ian. 'Stanley Spencer'. *A Dictionary of Twentieth-Century Art*. Oxford: Oxford University Press, 1999, 596–7.

Christiansen, Nina. 'Ideological, aesthetic, and educational transformations in Danish picture books around 1933'. *Children's Literature and European Avant-Garde* conference, University of Norrköping, Sweden, 26–30 September 2012.

Clarke, I.F. *Great War with Germany, 1890–1940: Fictions and Fantasies of the War-to-Come*. Chicago: University of Chicago Press, 1997.

Corbett, David Peters, Holt, Ysanne, and Fiona Russell (eds). *Geographies of Englishness: Landscapes and the National Past 1880–1940*. New Haven and London: Yale University Press, 2002.

Croft, Andy. *Red Letter Days: British Fiction in the 1930s*. London: Lawrence and Wishart, 1990.

Cross, Gary. 'Vacations for All: The Leisure Question in the Era of the Popular Front'. *Journal of Contemporary History*, 24.4, October, 1989, 599–621.

Crouch, Marcus. *Treasure Seekers and Borrowers: Children's Books in Britain 1900–1960*. London: The Library Association, 1962.

Crouch, Marcus. *The Nesbit Tradition: The Children's Novel 1945–1970*. London: Ernest Benn Ltd., 1972.

Cunningham, Hugh. *Children and Childhood in Western Society since 1500*. London and New York: Longman, 1995.

*Daily Worker*. London: Communist Party of Great Britain/People's Printing Society, 1930–50.

Davin, Anna. *Growing Up Poor: Home, School and Street in London 1870–1914*. London: Rivers Oram Press, 1996.

Dibattista, Maria and Lucy McDiarmid. *High and Low Moderns: Literature and Culture 1889–1939*. New York and Oxford: Oxford University Press, 1996.

Dimitrov, Georg. *Youth Against Fascism*. Speech delivered at the opening of the sixth congress of the Young Communist International, 1935. Accessed at http://www.marxists.org/reference/archive/dimitrov/works/1935/09_25.htm on 11 November 2012.

Druker, Elina and Bettina Kümmerling-Meibauer (eds). *Children's Literature and European Avant-Garde*. Amsterdam and Philadelphia: John Benjamins, 2015.

Duckworth, Jeannie Shorey. 'The Open-Air Schools of Bristol and Gloucester'. Transcript of Bristol and Archaeological Society 123, 2005, 133–41. Accessed at http://www2.glos.ac.uk/bgas/tbgas/v123/bg123133.pdf on 24 July 2014.

Dudley Edwards, Owen. *British Children's Literature in the Second World War.* Edinburgh: Edinburgh University Press, 2009.

Dusinberre, Juliet. *Alice to the Lighthouse: Children's Books and Radical Experiments in Art.* Basingstoke: Macmillan, 1987.

Eby, Cecil Degrotte. *The Road to Armageddon: The Martial Spirit in English Popular Literature, 1870–1914.* Durham and London: Duke University Press, 1987.

Elezar, Daniel. *American Federalism: A View from the States.* New York: Thomas Y. Crowell, 1966.

Ellis, Havelock. *Studies in the Psychology of Sex. Vol. 1: Sexual Inversion.* London: London University Press, 1897.

Ellis, Havelock. *Studies in the Psychology of Sex. Vol. VI: Sex in Relation to Society,* 1927. Accessed at http://www.aolib.com/reader_13615_31.htm on 16 August 2014.

Elstob, Ivy. 'Children's Stories Must "Play the Game"'. *Daily Worker,* 2 December 1936.

Esty, Jed. *Unseasonable Youth: Modernism, Colonialism, and the Fiction of Development.* Oxford: Oxford University Press, 2012.

Eve, Matthew. *A History of Illustrated Children's Books and Book Production in Britain During the Second World War.* Unpublished doctoral thesis, Oxford University, 2003.

*Experimental Art of Russian Children's Books, The.* Catalogue for the Read Russia 2012 Exhibition at 172 Duane Street, New York, 2012. Accessed at http://www.experimentalbookart.org/on 18 November 2012.

*Eye, The: The Martin Lawrence Gazette.* London: Martin Lawrence, 1935.

Eyre, Frank. *Twentieth-Century Children's Books.* London: British Council in conjunction with Longmans, Green, 1952.

Faraday, J.G. *Twelve Years of Children's Books: A Selection of the Best Books for Children Published During the Years 1926 to 1937.* Birmingham: C. Combridge, 1939.

Feinstein, Stephen C. 'Zbigniew Libera's Lego Concentration Camp: Iconoclasm in Conceptual Art about the Shoah', 2000. Accessed at http://www.othervoices.org/2.1/feinstein/auschwitz.php on 19 November 2013.

Fitzpatrick, Sheila. *The Commissariat of Enlightenment: Soviet Organization of Education and the Arts under Lunacharsky.* Cambridge: Cambridge University Press, 1970.

Fitzpatrick, Sheila. *The Cultural Front: Power and Culture in Revolutionary Russia.* New York: Cornell University Press, 1992.

Fitzpatrick, Sheila. *Everyday Stalinism: Ordinary Life in Extraordinary Times: Soviet Russia in the 1930s.* New York: Oxford University Press, 1999.

Fitzpatrick, Sheila. *My Father's Daughter: Memories of an Australian Childhood.* Melbourne: Melbourne University Press, 2010.

Foster, Hal, Krauss, Rosalind, Bois, Yve-Alain, and Benjamin H.D. Buchloh. *Art since 1900: Modernism, Antimodernism, Postmodernism.* London: Thames and Hudson, 2007.

Fussell, Paul. *The Great War and Modern Memory.* Oxford: Oxford University Press, 1975.

Fussell, Paul. *Abroad: British Literary Traveling between the Wars.* Oxford: Oxford University Press, 1980.

Fry, Roger. 'Children's Drawings'. *The Burlington Magazine* 30.171, June, 1917, 225–31.

Fry, Roger. 'Art of the Bushman'. *Vision and Design*. London: Chatto and Windus, 1928 (first published 1910), 56–64.

Fry, Roger. 'Essay in Aesthetics'. *Vision and Design*. London: Chatto and Windus, 1928 (first published 1909), 16–38.

Fry, Roger. 'Negro Sculpture'. *Vision and Design*. London: Chatto and Windus, 1928, 65–8.

Gardiner, Juliet. *The Thirties: An Intimate History*. London: Harper Collins, 2011.

Gerrard, Jessica. *Emancipation, Education and the Working Class: Genealogies of Resistance in Socialist Sunday Schools and Black Saturday Schools*. PhD thesis, Jesus College, Cambridge, 2011.

Giesbers, J.H.G.I. *Cecil Reddie and Abbotsholme: A Forgotten Pioneer and his Creation*. Druk: Nijmegen, 1970.

Goldman, Emma. '*Spring Awakening*: a synopsis and analysis of the play by Frank Wedekind'. *The Social Significance of the Modern Drama*. Boston: Richard G. Badger, 1914, 118–28.

Gollancz, Victor (ed.). *The Betrayal of the Left: An Examination and Refutation of Communist Policy from October 1939 to January 1941: With Suggestions for an Alternative and an Epilogue on Political Morality*. London: Victor Gollancz, 1941.

Green, Jonathan and Nicholas J. Karolides. *Encyclopedia of Censorship*. New York: Facts on File, 2009.

Grenby, M.O. '"A Conservative Woman Doing Radical Things": Sarah Trimmer and *The Guardian of Education*'. Donelle Ruwe (ed.). *Culturing the Child, 1690–1914*. Lanham, Maryland and Oxford: The Scarecrow Press, 2005, 137–61.

Grierson, Philip. *Books on Soviet Russia 1917–1942. A Bibliography and a Guide to Reading*. London: Methuen and Co., 1943.

Gritten, Sally. *The Story of Puffin Books*. Harmondsworth: Puffin, 1991.

Gurney, Peter. *Co-operative Culture and the Politics of Consumption in England, 1870–1930*. Manchester: Manchester University Press, 1996.

HANSARD. *The Seditious and Blasphemous Teaching to Children Bill*, vol. 58, 3 July, 1924. Accessed at http://hansard.millbanksystems.com/lords/1924/jul/03/seditious-and-blasphemous-teaching-to on 16 August 2014.

Harding, Jeremy. 'A Kind of Greek'. Review of Peter Conradi's *A Very English Hero: The Making of Frank Thompson* (2012). *London Review of Books*. 35.5, 2013 11–14.

Hare, Steve (ed.). *Allen Lane and the Penguin Editors 1935–1970*. London: Penguin, 1995.

Harris, Alexandra. *Romantic Moderns: English Writers, Artists and the Imagination from Virginia Woolf to John Piper*. London: Thames and Hudson, 2010.

Halbwachs, Maurice. *On Collective Memory*. Chicago: University of Chicago Press, 1992 (first published in French, 1950).

Hardy, Barbara. 'Introduction'. *Not So Quiet: Stepdaughters of War*. Helen Zenna Smith. London: Virago, 1988.

Hauser, K. *Stanley Spencer*. London: Tate, 2001.

Hellman, Ben. 'Samuil Marshak: Yesterday and Today'. Marina Balina and Larissa Rudova (eds). *Russian Children's Literature and Culture*. New York and Abingdon: Routledge, 2008, 217–40.

Hettinga, Donald and Gary D. Schmidt (eds). *British Children's Writers, 1914–1960*. Detroit and Washington, DC, Gale Research Inc: 1996.

Higonnet, Margaret. 'Modernism and childhood: violence and renovation'. *The Comparatist*. 33, May 2009, 86–108.

Hogben, Lancelot. 'Brighter Babies: *An Outline for Boys and Girls and their Parents*'. *Nature* 130.3287, 1932, 643–5.

Hodge, Marion. 'The Sane, the Mad, the Good, the Bad: T.S. Eliot's *Old Possum's Book of Practical Cats*'. *Children's Literature* 7, 1978, 129–46.

Hodgkins, Hope Howell. 'High Modernism for the Lowest: Children's Books by Woolf, Joyce, and Greene'. *Children's Literature Association Quarterly* 32.4, 2007, 354–67.

Hollowell, Clare. 'Enforcing Performance: Disciplining Girls in British Co-educational Boarding School Stories, 1928–1958'. *International Research in Children's Literature* 1.2, 2008, 125–38.

Holt, Ysanne. 'An Ideal Modernity: Spencer Gore at Letchworth'. David Peters, Ysanne Holt and Fiona Russell (eds). *The Geographies of Englishness: Landscape and the National Past 1880–1940*. New Haven and London: Yale University Press, 2002, 91–113.

Howard, Ebenezer. *Garden Cities of Tomorrow*. London: Swan Sonnenschein & Co., 1902. Accessed at http://archive.org/stream/gardencitiestom00howagoog#page/n148/mode/1up on 1 May 2013.

Howkins, Alun. 'The discovery of rural England' in *Englishness: Politics and Culture 1880–1920*. Robert Colls and Philip Dodd (eds). London: Croom Helm, 1986, 62–88.

Hubler, Angela E. (ed.). *Little Red Readings: Historical Materialist Perspectives on Children's Literature*. Jackson: University Press of Mississippi, 2014.

Humphries, Stephen. *Hooligans or Rebels? An Oral History of Working-Class Childhood 1889–1939*. Oxford: Blackwell, 1981.

Hunt, Peter. *An Introduction to Children's Literature*. Oxford and New York: Oxford University Press, 1994.

Hunt, Peter. 'Retreatism and Advance (1914–1945)'. Peter Hunt (ed.). *Children's Literature: An Illustrated History*. Oxford and New York: Oxford University Press, 1995, 192–224.

Hürlimann, Bettina. *Three Centuries of Children's Books in Europe*. Translated and edited by Brian Alderson. London: Oxford University Press, 1967.

Ingram, Kevin. *Rebel: The Short Life of Esmond Romilly*. London: Weidenfeld and Nicolson, 1985.

Jacobus, Mary. 'Magical Arts: From Play Techniques to Transitional Objects' in Marina Warner (ed.). *Only Make Believe: Ways of Playing*. Catalogue of the exhibition at Compton Verney, Warwickshire 25 March–5 June, 2005, 20–32.

Jagusch, Sybille, A. *Stepping Away from Tradition: Children's Books of the Twenties and Thirties*. Washington: Library of Congress, 1988.

James, Emily. 'Virginia Woolf and the Child Poet'. *Modernist Culture* 7.2, 2012, 279–305.

James, Simon, J. *Maps of Utopia: H.G. Wells, Modernity and the End of Culture*. Oxford: Oxford University Press, 2012.

James, William. 'The Moral Equivalent of War'. Address given at Stamford University, 1906. Accessed at http://www.constitution.org/wj/meow.htm on 17 May 2012.

Joannou, Maroula (ed.). *Women Writers of the 1930s: Gender, Politics and History*. Edinburgh: Edinburgh University Press, 1999.

Jones, Greta. *Social Hygiene in Twentieth Century Britain*. Beckenham, Kent and Wolfeboro, New Hampshire: Croom Helm, 1986.

Jones, Julia. *Fifty Years in the Fiction Factory: The Working Life of Herbert Allingham*. Pleshey: Golden Duck, 2012.

Kelly, Catriona. *Children's World: Growing up in Russia, 1890–1991*. New Haven and London: Yale University Press, 2007.

Kettle, Arnold. 'My Very Best Half-Dozen Novels'. *Daily Worker*, 22 January 1951.

Key, Ellen. *The Century of the Child*. London: Putnam, 1909.

Kinchin, Juliet and Aidan O'Connor (eds). *Century of the Child: Growing by Design 1900–2000*. New York: Museum of Modern Art, 2010.

*King Alfred School Magazine*. King Alfred School Archive, December 1917, 9820/ R4/1917.

Kirschenbaum, Lisa, A. *Small Comrades: Revolutionizing Childhood in Soviet Russia 1917–1932*. London and New York: Routledge, 2001.

Kirschner, Paul. 'The Dual Purpose of *Animal Farm*'. *Review of English Studies*, 55.222, 2004, 759–86.

Klaus, Gustav H. 'Socialist Fiction in the 1930s'. John Lucas (ed.). *The 1930s: A Challenge to Orthodoxy*. Hassocks: Harvester, 1978, 13–41.

Kravitz, Samantha. *The Business of Selling the Soviet Union: Intourist and the Wooing of the American Traveller, 1929–1939*. Montreal: Concordia University, 2006.

Kümmerling-Meibauer, Bettina. 'Childhood and Modernist Art'. *Libri & Liberi* 2.1, 2013, 11–28.

Kunitz, Stanley J. and Howard Haycroft. *The Junior Book of Authors*. New York: H.W. Wilson Co., 1934.

*The Labour Woman*. London: Transport House. May and June 1918.

Langdon-Davies, John. *Militarism in Education: A Contribution to Educational Reconstruction*. London: Headley Bros., 1919.

Leavis, F.R. and Denys Thompson. *Culture and Environment*. London: Chatto and Windus, 1964 (first published 1933).

Leeson, Robert. *Reading and Righting: The Past, Present and Future of Fiction for the Young*. London: Collins, 1985.

Leith, Sam. 'Writing in terms of pleasure'. Interview with A.S. Byatt. *The Guardian*, Saturday 25 April 2009. Accessed at http://www.theguardian.com/ books/2009/apr/25/as-byatt-interview on 5 June 2012.

Lenin, V.I. 'For Bread and Peace'. 1917. Accessed at http://www.marxists.org/archive/lenin/works/1917/dec/14a.htm accessed 27/11/2013 on 17 August 2014.

Lethbridge, Lucy. *Servants: A Downstairs View of Twentieth-Century Britain.* London: Bloomsbury, 2013.

Leyland, Eric. *The Public Library and the Adolescent.* London: Grafton & Co., 1937.

Lieberman, William S. *Art of the Twenties.* New York: Museum of Modern Art, 1979.

Light, Alison. *Forever England: Femininity, Literature and Conservatism Between the Wars.* London: Routledge, 1991.

Lunn, Arnold. 'The Scandal of the *Outline*'. *English Review* 55. November 1932, 471–84.

Lutman, Stephen. 'Orwell's Patriotism'. *Journal of Contemporary History* 2.2., April 1967, 149–58.

Lynd, Sigle. '*An Outline for Boys and Girls and Their Parents*'. *Left Book News*, 1, May 1936, 11–12.

Main, Peter. *Peter Lunn: Children's Publisher. The Books, Authors and Illustrators.* Stirling: Lomax Press, 2012.

Main, Peter. *John Westhouse and Peter Lunn: Two Wartime Publishing Houses and their Founders.* Stirling: Lomax Press, 2013.

Marshak, Samuel. *Children and Art in the USSR.* Moscow: Foreign Languages Publishing House, 1939. Accessed at http://www.marxists.org/subject/art/literature/children/texts/marshak/art.html on 18 November 2012.

Martin, Jane. *Making Socialists: Mary Bridges Adams and the Fight for Knowledge and Power, 1855–1939.* Manchester: Manchester University Press, 2010.

Marwick, Arthur. 'Youth in Britain, 1920–1960: Detachment and Commitment'. *Journal of Contemporary History* 5.1, 1970, 37–51.

Maslen, Elizabeth. 'Naomi Mitchison's Historical Fiction'. Maroula Joannou (ed.). *Women Writers of the 1930s: Gender, Politics and History.* Edinburgh: Edinburgh University Press, 1999, 138–51.

Matlass, David. *Landscape and Englishness.* London: Reaktion Books, 1998.

Mayall, Berry and Virginia Morrow. *English Children's Work in the Second World War.* London: Institute of Education, 2011.

Mayer, Peter (ed.). *The Pacifist Conscience.* London: Rupert Hart-Davis, 1966.

McAleer, Joseph. *Popular Reading and Culture in Britain 1914–1950.* Oxford: Clarendon, 1992.

Mendlesohn, Farah. 'The man who told the people's stories'. *The Morning Star*, 26 February 2010. Accessed at http://www.morningstaronline.co.uk/index.php/news/content/view/full/87313 on 8 November 2012.

Mendlesohn, Farah. *The Trease Project* website. http://treaseproject.livejournal.com/.

Mickenberg, Julia, L. *Learning from the Left: Children's Literature, the Cold War, and Radical Politics in the United States.* New York and Oxford: Oxford University Press, 2006.

Mickenberg, Julia, L. and Philip Nel (eds). *Tales for Little Rebels: A Collection of Radical Children's Literature.* New York: New York University Press, 2010.

Mishler, Paul C. 'Communism for Kids: Class, race and gender in communist children's books in the United States'. In Anne Lundin and Wayne E. Wiegand (eds). *Defining Print Culture for Youth: The Cultural Work of Children's Literature*. Westport, CT: Libraries Unlimited, 2003, 27–39.

Mitchison, Naomi. *Home and a Changing Civilization*. London: John Lane the Bodley Head, 1934.

Mitchison, Naomi. *We have been Warned*. London: Constable and Co., 1938.

Mitchison, Naomi. *You May as well Ask: A Memoir 1920–1940*. London: Victor Gollancz, 1979.

Mitchison, Naomi. *Mucking Around: Five Continents Over Fifty Years*. London: Victor Gollancz, 1981.

Mitchison, Naomi. *The Wartime Diary of Naomi Mitchison 1939–45*, ed. Dorothy Sheridan. London: Victor Gollancz, 1985.

Mitford, Jessica. *A Fine Old Conflict*. London: Quartet Books, 1977.

Mitford, Jessica. *Faces of Philip: A Memoir of Philip Toynbee*. London: Heinemann, 1984.

Myers, Mitzi. 'Impeccable Governesses, Rational Dames, and Moral Mothers: Mary Wollstonecraft and the Female Tradition in Georgian Children's Books'. *Children's Literature 14*, 1986, 31–58.

Myers, Mitzi. 'Socializing Rosamond: Education Ideology and Fictional Form'. *Children's Literature Association Quarterly*, 14.2, 1989, 52–8.

National Fitness Council: Minutes, Papers and Reports. Accessed at http://discovery.nationalarchives.gov.uk/SearchUI/details?Uri=C6912 on 15 May 2013.

Natov, Roni. *The Poetics of Childhood*. London: Routledge, 2003.

Nelson, Claudia and Ann Sumner Holmes (eds). *Maternal Instincts: Visions of Sexuality and Motherhood in Britain, 1875–1925*. London: Macmillan, 1997.

Neill, A.S. *A Dominie's Log*. London: Herbert Jenkins Ltd, 1915.

Nora, Pierre. 'Between Memory and History: Les Lieux de Mémoire' in *Representations* 26, Spring 1989, 7–25.

Nicholson, Heather Norris. 'Journeys into Seeing: Amateur Film-making and Tourist Encounters in Soviet Russia, c. 1932'. In *New Readings* 10, 2009, 57–71.

Nicholson, Virginia. *Among the Bohemians: Experiments in Living 1900–1939*. London: Penguin 2003 (first published 2002).

Norrington, A.L.P. *Blackwells 1879–1979. The History of a Family Firm*. Oxford: Blackwell, 1983.

Oakes, John. *Kitchener's Lost Boys: From the Playing Fields to the Killing Fields*. Stroud: The History Press, 2009.

*Observer*. York: Bootham School. Bound volumes 1889–1949.

O'Neill, Morna and Michael Hart (eds). *The Edwardian Sense: Art, Design, and Performance in Britain, 1900–1910*. New Haven and London: Yale University Press, 2010.

O'Sullivan, Emer. *Friend and Foe: The Image of Germany and the German People in British Children's Fiction from 1870 to the Present*. Tübingen: Narr, 1990.

Olson, Marilynn Strasser. 'Children's Culture and the Avant-Gardes: Higgledy-Piggledy Modernism'. *Children's Literature and European Avant-Garde* conference, University of Norrköping, Sweden, 26–30 September 2012.

Olson, Marilynn Strasser. *Children's Culture and the Avant-Garde: Painting in Paris, 1890–1915*. London and New York: Routledge, 2013.

Op de Beeck, Nathalie. *Suspended Animation: Children's Literature and the Fairy Tale of Modernity*. London and Minneapolis, 2010.

Orwell, George. 'Boys' Weeklies', 1940. *Fifty Orwell Essays*. Accessed at http://gutenberg.net.au/ebooks03/0300011h.html#part9 on 5 November 2012.

Orwell, George. 'My Country Right or Left', 1940. *Orwell's England: The Road to Wigan Pier in the Context of Essays, Reviews, Letters and Poems*. London: Penguin, 2001, 242–8.

Orwell, George. *Orwell's England: The Road to Wigan Pier in the Context of Essays, Reviews, Letters and Poems Selected from the Complete Works of George Orwell*. Peter Davison (ed.). London: Penguin, 2001.

*Our Circle. A Magazine for Young People*. Manchester: Cooperative Society, 1907–60.

Overy, Richard. *The Morbid Age: Britain and the Crisis of Civilization, 1919–1939*. London: Penguin, 2010 (first published 2009).

'Oxford Union Decides Spain Concerns Us'. *Oxford Mail*, Friday 11 June 1937, 3.

Pankenier Weld, Sara. *Voiceless Vanguard: The Infantilist Aesthetic of the Russian Avant-Garde*. Evanston, IL: Northwestern University Press, 2014.

Parsons, L. Dorothy. See Reid-Heyman, Stephen.

'Pearl Binder, artist & writer', May 2011 blog entry. Accessed at Spitalfield Life, http://spitalfieldslife.com/2010/05/01/pearl-binder-artist-writer/ on 10 November 2012.

Pearson, Joe. *Drawn Direct to the Plate: Noel Carrington and the Puffin Picture Books*. London: Penguin Collectors' Society, 2010.

Pearson, Lucy. *The Making of Modern Children's Literature in Britain: Publishing and Criticism in the 1960s and 1970s*. Farnham: Ashgate, 2013.

Pemberton, John, Pemberton, Gwen and Jerry White. 'The Boyd Orr Survey of the Nutrition of Children in Great Britain 1937–9'. *History Workshop Journal* 50 (Autumn 2000), 205–7.

Pollitt, Harry. 'Stories We Can Gladly Give Our Children'. *Daily Worker*, 16 December 1936.

Pomfret, David, M. 'Lionized and Toothless': Young People and Urban Politics in Britain and France. 1918–1940'. Axel Schildt and Detlef Siegfried (eds). Aldershot: Ashgate, 2005.

Powers, Alan and Alison Smithson. *Houses in Children's Books*. London: The Prince of Wales's Institute of Architecture, 1999.

Priestley, J.B. '*English Journey*. Being a rambling but truthful account of what one man saw and heard and felt and thought during a journey through England during the autumn of the year 1933'. London: Heinemann with Victor Gollancz, 1934.

*Prospectus*. London: King Alfred School, 1907.

Protopopova, Darya. 'Primitivism in British Modernism: Roger Fry and Virginia Woolf on French Post-Impressionists, African Sculpture and the Ballet Russes'. *Movable Type: Journal of the Graduate Society, Department of English, University College London*. 4.2008, 85–104.

Putnam, Samuel. *The World of Jean de Bosschère*. London: The Future Press, 1932.

Ransome, Arthur. 'Famine on the Volga'. *Guardian*, 11 October 1921. Accessed at http://century.guardian.co.uk/1920-1929/Story/0,6051,126591,00.html on 18 November 2012.

Rationalist Peace Society. Accessed at http://www.bishopsgate.org.uk/content/1037/Rationalist%20Peace-Society on 4 May 2012.

Reid-Heyman, Stephen [pen-name of Dorothy Parsons]. *Life How it Comes: A Child's Book of Elementary Biology*. Oxford: Basil Blackwell, 1921.

Remarque, Erich. *All Quiet on the Western Front*. Translated by A.W. Wheen. London: G. Putnam's Sons, 1929.

Reynolds, Kimberley. *Radical Children's Literature: Future Visions and Aesthetic Transformations*. Basingstoke: Palgrave Macmillan, 2007.

Reynolds, Kimberley. 'Words about War for Boys: Representations of Soldiers and Conflict in Writing for Children before World War I', *Children's Literature Association Quarterly* 34.5, 2009, 255–71.

Reynolds, Kimberley. 'Modernism'. In Philip Nel and Lissa Paul (eds). *Keywords for Children's Literature*. New York and London: New York University Press, 2011.

Reynolds, Kimberley. 'Recoupling Text and Image: Graham Greene's *The Little Train*'. *The Lion and the Unicorn* 37.1, 1–19, 2013.

Reynolds, Kimberley. 'Firing the Canon! Geoffrey Trease's Campaign for an Alternative Children's Canon in 1930s Britain'. In Bettina Kümmerling-Meibauer and Anja Muller (eds). *Canon Constitution and Change*. London: Routledge, forthcoming 2016.

Robb, George. 'Race Motherhood: Moral Eugenics vs Progressive Eugenics, 1880–1920'. In Claudia Nelson and Ann Sumner Holmes (eds). *Maternal Instincts: Visions of Sexuality and Motherhood in Britain, 1875–1925*. London: Macmillan, 1997, 58–73.

Rodker, John. '*The City Curious*'. *The Little Review: A Magazine of the Arts*. 7.3, 1920, 67–8. Accessed at http://modjourn.org/render.php?id=1299776632203127&view=mjp_object on 12 August 2014.

Rogerson, Ian. *Books Printed at the Shakespeare Head Press*. Manchester: Manchester Polytechnic Library, 1988.

Rogerson, Ian. *Noel Carrington and his Puffin Picture Books* (exhibition catalogue). Manchester: Manchester Polytechnic Library, 1992.

Romilly, Esmond. *Boadilla*. London: Hamish Hamilton, 1937.

Romilly, Giles and Esmond. *Out of Bounds: The Education of Giles and Esmond Romilly*. London: Hamish Hamilton, 1935.

Rose, Jacqueline. *The Case of Peter Pan, or, the Impossibility of Children's Fiction*. Basingstoke and London: Macmillan, 1984.

Rose, Jonathan. *The Intellectual Life of the British Working Classes*. New Haven and London: Yale University Press, 2001.

Rosen, Jane. 'Thou Shalt Teach Revolution—Tom Anderson and his Contribution to the Education of the Children in Glasgow'. In Ruth Ewan (ed.). *The Glasgow Schools*. Glasgow: The Common Guild for Glasgow International Festival, 2012, 20–7.

Rosen, Jane. 'In Darkest Russia'. *Diverging Diversities* conference, University of South Carolina, 18–21 June 2014.

Rosen, Jane. '*The Young Socialist:* A Magazine of Justice and Love (1901–1926)'. In Angela E. Hubler (ed.). *Little Red Readings: Historical Materialist Perspectives on Children's Literature*. Jackson: University Press of Mississippi, 2014, 133–50.

Rosenfeld, Alla. 'Does the Proletarian Child Need a Fairy Tale?' *Childhood*, 9, Winter 2003, n.p. Accessed at http://cabinetmagazine.org/issues/9/rosenfeld.php on 5 November 2012.

Rosenquist, Rod. *Modernism, the Market and the Institution of the Market*. Cambridge: Cambridge University Press, 2009.

Rothenstein, Julian and Olga Budashevskaya (eds). *Inside the Rainbow. Russian Children's Literature 1920–35. Beautiful Books, Terrible Times*. London: Redstone, 2013.

Russell, John. *On Alfredianism: Some Published and Unpublished Writings of John Russell, Headteacher 1901–1920 at King Alfred School, North End Road, London NW11*. Compiled by Brian Rance. London: King Alfred School, 2010.

Russell, John. *The School of War*. London: King Alfred School, 1914.

Russell, John. 'Headmaster's Report'. (November 1916). London: King Alfred School Society.

'Russian Children's Books'. *Manchester Guardian*, 19 February 1931.

'Saki'. *The Toys of Peace, and Other Papers with a Portrait and Memoir by Rothay Reynolds*. London and New York: John Lane, 1919.

Saler, Michael. *The Avant-garde in Interwar England: Medieval Modernism and the London Underground*. New York and Oxford: Oxford University Press, 1999.

Samuel, Raphael. 'Country Visiting: A memoir'. *Island Stories: Unravelling Britain*. London: Verso, 1998, 132–52.

Saunders, Gill. *Recording Britain*. London: Victoria and Albert Museum, 2012.

Sayle, Alexei. *Stalin Ate My Homework*. New York: Scepter, 2010.

*Socialist Sunday Schools: A Manual*. Gateshead: National Council of British Socialist Sunday Schools, 1923.

Shavit, Zohar. *The Poetics of Children's Literature*. Athens, GA and London: University of Georgia Press, 1986.

Sheeky, Hazel. *Camping and Tramping, Swallows and Amazons: Interwar Children's Fiction and the Search for England*. PhD thesis, Newcastle University, 2012.

Sheeky, Hazel. *Class, Leisure and National Identity in British Children's Fiction, 1918–1950*. Basingstoke: Palgrave, 2014.

Shiff, Richard. 'From Primitivist Phylogeny to Formalist Ontogeny: Roger Fry and Children's Drawings'. Jonathan Fineberg (ed.). *Discovering Primitivism and Modernism*. Princeton: Princeton University Press, 1998, 157–200.

Short, Emma. '"Always coming and going": The In-Between Spaces of Elizabeth Bowen's Early Novels'. Teresa Gómez Reus and Terry Gifford (eds). *Women in Transit through Literary Liminal Spaces*. Basingstoke: Palgrave Macmillan, 2013.

'Socialist and Revolutionary Schools'. Memorandum by the Home Secretary. National Archives CAB/24/136, 25 April 1922.

Somper, Justin. *The Story of Puffin*. Harmondsworth: Puffin, 2001.

Steedman, Carolyn. *Childhood, Culture and Class in Britain: Margaret Macmillan 1860–1931*. London: Virago, 1990.

Stephenson, Andrew. 'Edwardian Cosmopolitanism, ca. 1901–1912' in Morna O'Neill and Michael Hart (eds). *The Edwardian Sense: Art, Design, and Performance in Britain, 1900–1910*. New Haven and London: Yale University Press, 2010, 251–84.

Steiner, Marion. 'Tracing the Invisible—Electropolis Berlin'. A paper delivered at the fifteenth international congress of the International Committee for the Preservation of the Industrial Heritage, Taiwan, 4–11 November 2012. Accessed at http://www.industrie-kultur-berlin.de/web/medien/pdfs/TICCIH2012_STEINER_TracingtheInvisible_1363178175.pdf on 13 August 2013.

Stevenson, Lillian. *A Child's Bookshelf*. 5th edn. London: Student Christian Movement, 1922.

Stewart, Susan. *On Longing: Narratives of the Miniature, the Gigantic, the Souvenir, the Collection*. Baltimore: Johns Hopkins University Press, 1984.

Subramanian, Aishwarya. '(Anti-con)Quest: Anticolonial Struggle and Colonial Gaze in the Chronicles of Narnia'. Paper delivered at Wonderlands: Reading/Writing/Telling Fairy Tales and Fantasy, a symposium at the Sussex Centre for Folklore, Fairy Tales and Fantasy, May 2015.

Sumpter, C.R. 'Joining the Crusade Against the Giants: Keir Hardie's Fairy Tales and the Socialist Child Reader'. *Literature and History*, 1.2, 2006, 34–49.

Taylor, Dr Stephen. 'The Suburban Neurosis'. *The Lancet*, 26 March 1933, 759–61.

'Things in General'. *British Medical Journal*, 29 October 1932, 799.

Timms, Edward. *Visions and Blueprints: Avant-Garde Culture and Radical Politics in Early Twentieth-Century Europe*. Manchester: Manchester University Press, 1988.

Towers, F.L. '*Pollycon*. By E.F. Stucley' in *The Bookman*. January 1934, 414–15.

Townsend, John Rowe. *Written for Children. An Outline of English-language Children's Literature*. Harmondsworth: Penguin, 1974 (first published 1965).

Toynbee, Philip. *Friends Apart: A Memoir of Esmond Romilly and Jasper Ridley in the Thirties*. London: Sidgwick and Jackson, 1980.

Tracy, Michael. *The World of the Edwardian Child as seen in Arthur Mee's Children's Encyclopedia, 1908–1910*. Belgium: Hermitage, 2008.

Trease, Geoffrey. 'Revolutionary Literature for the Young'. Letters from writers section of *International Literature: Organ of the International Union of Revolutionary Writers*. 7, 1935, 100–2.

Trease, Geoffrey. *Tales Out of School*. 2nd edn. London: Heinemann Educational, 1964.

Trease, Geoffrey. *A Whiff of Burnt Boats*. London: Macmillan, 1971.

Trease, Geoffrey. 'The Revolution in Children's Literature'. Edward Blishen (ed.). *The Thorny Paradise: Writers on Writing for Children*. Harmondsworth: Kestrel, 1975.

Trites, Roberta Seelinger. *Disturbing the Universe: Power and Repression in Adolescent Literature*. Iowa City: University of Iowa Press, 2000.

Trotter, David. 'Transit Writing'. *Moving Modernisms* conference, University of Oxford, 22–4 March 2012.

Trumpener, Katie. 'Picture-book worlds and ways of seeing'. In M.O. Grenby and Andrea Immel (eds). *The Cambridge Companion to Children's Literature*. Cambridge: Cambridge University Press, 2009, 55–75.

Turner, Christopher. *Adventures in the Orgasmatron: Wilhelm Reich and the Invention of Sex*. London: Fourth Estate, 2011.

Ulanowicz, Anastasia. *Second Generation Memory and Contemporary Children's Literature: Ghost Images*. New York and London: Routledge, 2013.

Unwin, David. *Fifty Years with Father: A Relationship*. London: George Allen and Unwin, 1982.

Unwin, Stanley. *Publishing in Peace and War with Some Notes on the 'Future of English Books on the Continent after the War' and 'The Status of Books'*. London: George Allen and Unwin, 1944.

Van Emden, Richard. *Boy Soldiers of the Great War*. London: Headline, 2004.

Vansittart, Peter. *Voices: 1870–1914*. London: Jonathan Cape, 1984.

Vincent, Timothy. '"Subjective Deformation": Expressionism and the Modernist Child'. *Red Feather: An International Journal of Children's Visual Culture*. 2.1, Spring 2011, 16–29.

Ward, Paul. *Red Flag and Union Jack: Englishness, Patriotism and the British Left, 1881–1924*. London: Royal Historical Society, 1998.

Warner, Marina (ed.). *Only Make Believe: Ways of Playing*. Catalogue of the exhibition at Compton Verney, Warwickshire 25 March–5 June 2005.

Waters, Chris. 'William Morris and the Socialism of Robert Blatchford'. In *Journal of William Morris Studies*, 5.2, 1982, 20–31.

Webster, Charles. 'Healthy or Hungry Thirties?' *History Workshop Journal* 13, Spring 1982, 110–29.

Wedekind, Frank. *Spring Awakening*. Translated and introduced by Julian and Margaret Forsyth. London: Nick Hern, 2010 (first UK translation 1969).

Wells, H.G. *The Time Machine*. London: William Heinemann, 1895.

Wells, H.G. *The War that will End War*. London: F.&C. Palmer, 1914. Accessed at http://archive.org/details/warthatwillendwa00welluoft on 17 April 2012.

Wells, H.G. *The Shape of Things to Come*. London: Penguin, 2005 (first published 1933).

West, Geoffrey. 'Towards To-Morrow! *An Outline for Boys and Girls and Their Parents*'. *The Bookman*, October 1932, 60–1.

Westman, Karin E. 'Children's Literature and Modernism: The Space Between'. *Children's Literature Association Quarterly* 32.4, 2007, 283–6.

Williams, Raymond. *Problems in Materialism and Culture*. London: Verso, 1960.

Williams, Raymond. *The Country and the City*. St Albans: Paladin, 1975.

Woolf, Virginia. *Between the Acts*. London: The Hogarth Press, 1941.

Wootten, William and George Donaldson (eds). *Reading Penguin: A Critical Anthology*. Newcastle-upon-Tyne: Cambridge Scholars, 2013.

Wright, Anne. *Literature of Crisis, 1910–22*. London: Macmillan, 1984.

Yorke, Malcolm. *Edward Bawden and his Circle: The Inward Laugh*. Woodbridge: Antique Collectors' Club, 2007.

Zweiniger-Bargielowska, Ina. 'Building a British Superman: Physical culture in Interwar Britain'. *Journal of Contemporary History* 41.4, October 2006, 595–610.

# Index